THE
HEROIC
IDEAL
IN
AMERICAN
LITERATURE

THEODORE L. GROSS

The Heroic Ideal in American Literature

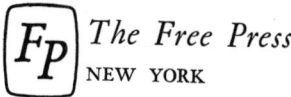 The Free Press
NEW YORK

Collier-Macmillan Limited
LONDON

For
Selma

The Free Press
A Division of The Macmillan Company
866 Third Avenue, New York, New York 10022

Collier-Macmillan Canada Ltd., Toronto, Ontario

Library of Congress Catalog Card Number: 72-142366

printing number
1   2   3   4   5   6   7   8   9   10

INTRODUCTION

Literary heroes dramatize the moral texture of a country. Creations of the imagination, they embody the unspoken ideals, the undesired terrors, the dream life and the mundane existence of their readers. Heroes represent a people, and by discovering the meaning of their character, by returning to the roots of their behavior, we discern the moral figure in the tapestry of a nation. This book considers some of the representative heroes of American literature and their struggle with a conflict central to the moral life of our country—the conflict between idealism and authority.

Critics have recognized the importance of the hero in American literature, although they have called him by different names: the American Adam, Prometheus, the Rebel-Victim, Faust. Indeed, the concept of the hero has provoked some of the most exciting criticism within the past generation, as authors have sought to discover a mythology for America. I write in the spirit of this criticism, although I hope that I am aware of its many dangers. As William Gilman has suggested, in an important essay concerning "The Hero and the Heroic in American Literature," it is too facile to fashion "American heroes by making them gods and eliminating through reductive generalization the very things which make them distinctive." Gilman censures D. H. Lawrence, Richard Chase, Henry A. Murray, and R. W. B. Lewis for treating the hero as symbolic, for obscuring the literal character of a man "by the light of the myth into which he is assimilated." He offers an alternative definition of the hero in American literature, one that derives from the formulations of Kenneth Burke and Francis Fergusson in which tragic rhythm depends upon "the constant interplay of purpose, passion, and perception"; and he argues that "the capacity for perception, the nature and the quality of the perception, and the effects of the perception upon the perceiver would seem to be of at least as much importance as a norm for the hero as anything else. . . . A male character in American literature may be a hero in almost any circumstance; all he must do is struggle, see things as they really are, and benefit from his knowledge." *

Gilman's empirical view of heroism is sensible, for those critics who appropriate the American hero to suit their own mythologies are as guilty as V. L. Parrington, who represents a literalness against which many of them react. They use the language of the Age of Names, to borrow Proust's metaphor, and often forget the discrete humanity of the individual hero. Their books—I am thinking of *Studies in Classic American Literature, Herman Melville* (by Richard Chase), *The American Adam,* and *Love and Death in the American Novel*— are brilliant distortions, as their singular vision forces them to be, and at times they are more faithful to the critics' vision than to that of the particular authors they consider. But this imaginative criticism, with all of its obvious limitations, is essentially close to the spirit of American literature, to the ways in which our finest writers have conceived of their most memorable characters; it affirms and explores the heroic vision as well as the skepticism of significant American authors.

William Gilman seems justified in chastising R. W. B. Lewis for talking about "one and only one kind of hero in American literature" and in asking, "Who talks about *the* English hero, or *the* French hero, or *the* Italian hero?" We are indeed a pluralistic

* William Gilman, "The Hero and the Heroic in American Literature: An Essay in Definition," *Patterns of Commitment,* Edited by Marston La France (Toronto, 1966), pp. 3-17.

society in which many kinds of heroes have emerged bearing many different styles; but heroes we insist upon, as the English or the French or the Italians do not. A central paradox of our culture has been its political commitment to the common man and its literary obsession—on the part of our greatest writers—with the exceptional man, with the hero. Our important nineteenth-century authors were romantic—far more so than, say, Thackeray or Flaubert whose work is not concerned with the extraordinary individual. Our early twentieth-century authors (one remembers Hemingway and Fitzgerald) reject the possibilities of heroism as they create heroes more romantic than those of their predecessors. Our contemporaries (one thinks of Salinger, Bellow, Mailer, and Ellison) describe comic and Gothic heroes who resist those leveling forces in modern society that frustrate and inhibit the heroic gesture. Between "The American Scholar" and *The American Dream* fall the shadows of our heroes—The American Adam, The False Prometheus, the Faustian Hero, the Radical Innocent—all of them *partially* true, all of them critical refractions of a literary mosaic. We are, after all, the only nation that insists upon speaking of a Dream as though it is an endemic characteristic. Who speaks of the English dream, or the French dream, or the Italian dream?

Yet it is not an idle phrase, the American Dream, whether in the voice of Emerson and Whitman or Norman Mailer and Edward Albee. It reflects our romanticism and our sentimentality; our energetic chauvinism and our parochialism; our idealism and our authority; our hungry need for heroism. For still another paradox of the American sensibility is that we are the most powerful nation in the world, commanding greater authority than any other nation in the history of the world, and yet we are founded upon Christian principles that speak of humility and *pietas,* of abnegation and *caritas.* This paradox troubled nineteenth-century authors who sensed we would be powerful; it is the subject of contemporary American writers who seek to measure the nightmarish aspects of our power. Idealism and authority tangle in American literature and produce distinctive patterns of heroism that lie beneath the shadow of our swords: our actual power in the world has conditioned the heroic posture of the characters in our literature.

It is precisely this tension between idealism and authority that I wish to trace in five heroic figures of American literature: the Emersonian hero; the Southern hero; the Black hero; the Disenchanted hero; the Quixotic hero. Although these five types constitute the major sections of my study and suggest its direction and scope, they serve as a flexible framework for individual "heroes" who often have the exciting habit of violating any categories. I have sought to obey the organic movement of American heroes rather than impose a pattern upon them, to remember always that being an American is indeed a complex fate in which the individual may finally be larger or more interesting than the type that he personifies. My singular and common point of view, however, has been the conflict between idealism and authority in the various heroes of American literature.

I am not interested in offering a new definition of the hero. Although I am aware that different emphases have been placed upon the concept of the hero at different times in European literature and that the scholarship on this subject is vast, I have been content to use the term as American authors themselves have used it. The hero of American literature is the exceptional man who seeks to realize an ideal. He may be Emerson's American Scholar—an intellectual hero; he may be Arthur Dimmesdale—an ethical hero; he may be Ahab—a religious hero; he may be the Southern Gentleman, who functions as a kind of social hero. Whatever his distinctive features and however idiosyncratic he may be, the hero pursues an ideal and in the process demonstrates certain common characteristics. Like heroes in the writing of other countries and of other times, the hero of American literature is a courageous, active, social man whose passions are more intense than those of the people whom he usually represents. I agree with William Gilman that the American hero follows a rhythm, even though not always "tragic," which depends upon "the constant interplay of purpose, passion, and perception"; but I do not believe as Gilman asserts, that "a male character in American literature may be a hero in almost any circumstance," that "all he must do is struggle, see things as they really are, and benefit from his knowledge." The hero of American literature must certainly struggle and view his experience with perception; but he must, in some sense, be extraordinary, and he must pursue an ideal—in protest or in accommodation to some form of authority.

Although I have examined many works closely and critically, my central concern has been to evaluate our literature in terms of the conflict between the ideal of America and the authority of America, between the conception and the reality, between—in certain instances—the dream and the nightmare. This tension has most dramatically centered upon literary heroes, and as authors have adopted an attitude toward heroism, as they have sought to realize their idealistic faith in their country, they have written their moral criticism of America.

Moral. That word, so vague to the modern ear, takes on particular relevance as we seek to measure heroism in American literature. When Emerson speaks of "The American Scholar" and James describes The American, we know that the individual serves a moral ideal which openly opposes a cultural or social authority. Authority may take the form of institutionalized religion or antiquated traditions or repressive European as well as American customs; the enemy is clear, the conflict is open, and the belief in heroism is absolute. But when the concept is rendered suspect, as in the work of Hawthorne and Melville, and authority is not only an institution or a tradition or a custom but also a quality within the individual himself, then we know that heroism falls beneath the shadow of our swords; we know that the honorific moral connotations attributed to heroism by Emerson, Whitman, and James can easily become perverted. I realize that these distinctions are too broad, that there is a great imaginative distance between "The American Scholar" and The Conduct of Life, between "Song of Myself" and "Out of the Cradle Endlessly Rocking," between The American and The Ambassadors; and in the chapters on Emerson, Whitman, and James, I trust that I have been faithful to the subtleties of these complex authors and that I have taken into account the many modulations of their thought. But the point I wish to make here is that the tension between an evolving moral idealism and a fixed social authority led to a particular kind of American hero. Call him Emersonian. He is anticipated by the writers of the Revolution; he is the self-reliant man of the Transcendental movement; he is Walt Whitman, with inevitable variations; he is the central figure of all those Jamesian novels in which ideals are in no sense vague. He is, in short, the first significant hero to appear in American literature.

The moral tension between the heroic ideal and authority is largely absent from nineteenth-century Southern writing. It is no accident that, except for the expatriates Poe and Twain, the South produced authors of little significance before the time of Faulkner. Personal idealism and sectional authority fuse in the minds of typ-

ical writers like William Gilmore Simms and Thomas Nelson Page;
the heroic ideal merges with the authority of Southern civilization
—particularly as the authors defend slavery or Southern culture—
and the lack of tension between the ideal of self-realization and
social or religious authority prevents the hero from becoming a
distinct individual or an impassioned man who challenges the gods.
I am not speaking of slavery in moral terms; I am simply suggesting—and exploring rather extensively in the section on Southern
literature—that the imagination of the Southern author was frustrated and even atrophied by the authority of the Southern conception of heroism. Emerson could protest the cultural authority of
Europe; Hawthorne the theological parochialism of the Puritan
community; James the restraints of tradition. The Southern author
created little distance between the ideal of the individual and the
ideal of the South—he saw his hero almost exclusively in social
terms; and because he wrote within a more "realistic" form than
Gothic novelists like Hawthorne and Melville, because he wrote
novels without developing the cultural tensions necessary to the
novels, he created sentimental figures whose actions the reader could
anticipate rather than heroes whose moral ideals were frustrated by
some kind of social, cultural, or theological authority. Consider, by
way of contrast, the moral conflicts of *Huckleberry Finn* and *The
Bear.* The terror of Huck's decision, the degree to which it partakes
of the heroic, lies in his commitment to a human ideal as opposed
to a cultural authority. The revelation that comes to Ike McCaslin
creates a conflict between his personal ideals and an historical authority imposed upon him that dictates his extreme moral solution.
Both these works by Southerners ask questions that few nineteenth-
or early twentieth-century Southern writers permitted themselves to
ask.

The absence of moral tension also characterizes the early writing of Negroes in America. Although Frederick Douglass and
W. E. B. DuBois challenged the authority of white America, most
Negroes of the nineteenth and early twentieth century accepted the
basic myths of their country. DuBois' most impressive work deals
with the *souls* of black folk, with the immorality of the social
existence of Negroes, with the conflict between idealism and authority; but the spirit of his work is not recaptured until the Negro
Awakening of the 1920's. Between 1880 and 1919, Negroes wrote
latter-day slave narratives that do not quarrel with fundamental

American myths. The titles of some of these books suggest their contents: *Up From Slavery* (1901), *Out of the House of Bondage* (1914), *In Spite of Handicap* (1916), *Finding a Way Out* (1920). One can understand the social necessity of these works—as one can understand the social necessity of fiction by William Gilmore Simms and Thomas Nelson Page—but the absence of real moral conflict makes them homiletics rather than works of art. Consider, by way of contrast, the point of view of James Baldwin's personal essays, his adoption of the white man's angle of vision for the purposes of implicitly indicting the American power structure; one recognizes that Baldwin's idealism is inextricable from the authority he deplores, that love and power are the moral polarities of his best work. The flowering of Negro literature in our time stems largely from the authors' ability to believe in an heroic ideal as it clashes with the authority of America—and this is still another paradox of our literature. The black author, who has greater historical justification for bitterness than his white contemporary, is genuinely idealistic, bearing many similarities—as I shall point out in my essay on Negro literature—to Emerson and other transcendental writers.

My last two sections trace the concept of heroism in modern literature. In the fiction of Hemingway and Fitzgerald, heroism is denied as an abstraction because the authority of the external world has grown too great. For these authors and for the twentieth-century Americans who have read them, the great dividing line is the First World War. Just as the Civil War served as a nodal point in the sensibility and prose style of nineteenth-century writers, the First World War marks a profound ideological shift for Americans of this century. One remembers the famous lines from *A Farewell to Arms:* "I was always embarrassed by the words sacred, glorious, and sacrifice and the expression in vain. . . . Abstract words such as glory, honor, courage, or hallow were obscene beside the concrete names of villages, the numbers of roads, the names of rivers, the numbers of regiments and the dates." Concepts are dead for Frederick Henry and other Hemingway heroes; they have said a farewell to heroism—although not to the hero. Hemingway writes with great confidence when he denies the validity of heroism and asserts his belief in only personal courage. His private code serves as protection against the absurdity of a world whose people speak in platitudes. As that code grows more rigid and artificial, as Hemingway finds it increasingly difficult to maintain a distinction between the ideals of the hero and the objective authority he criticizes, his work suffers: the hero of *For Whom the Bell Tolls* speaks in abstract pieties the hero of *The Sun Also Rises* would only mock. One senses the insecurity that lies just behind the formal posturing of *Across the River and Into the Trees,* the author's unwillingness to reflect the ambiguities of a later period. Ultimately Hemingway's loss of confidence results in silence or in the creation of a sentimental memoir that lacks the toughness of his early fiction.

Fitzgerald shares Hemingway's disillusionment with abstract heroism, although he reflects, to a greater extent, a despair that succeeds in destroying the individual himself. The loss of belief in the concept is integrally related to self-disillusionment—one can never divorce heroism and the hero as one can in Hemingway's work. Idealism and authority, linked in the most intimate fashion, are personified through lovers in *The Great Gatsby,* through husband and wife in *Tender is the Night,* through a man and his work in *The Last Tycoon.* As Fitzgerald grew to understand the social implications of what was at first a limited personal theme, his work became less narcissistic, less sentimental, and took on a tragic quality that is artistically compelling even though it now seems historically distant—like the end of a dream.

However absolute and compelling the denial of idealism may be in the art of Hemingway and Fitzgerald, contemporary authors have not pursued a literature of despair. There is an ambiguity, an irony, a humor, at times a prolixity in the work of Bellow, Salinger, and Mailer that suggest a lack of certainty and a lack of confidence which one does not feel in the best work of Hemingway and Fitzgerald. Current writers refuse to sacrifice their idealism before the overwhelming authority of the world in which they live; they refuse, as Bellow says of himself, "to speak 'the last word.'" The attempt of the contemporary author to justify his abstract belief in idealism by an actual life that he can respect is his special burden. It is a burden that produces curious literary results. Moses Herzog, Seymour Glass, and Norman Mailer are uncomfortable heroes, figures who aspire to heroism rather than realize it in any traditional manner; they must laugh at themselves in order to believe in themselves. But whatever the inward convolutions of their characters and however unlikely they appear as candidates for heroism, they believe —or rather they need to believe—in an heroic ideal; they cannot afford anything less. The terms of idealism and authority may be translated into J. D. Salinger's "Fat Lady" and her audience or into Norman Mailer's "Christians and Cannibals"; but the hero still emerges, struggling to discover, in Bellow's words once more, truths which are "on the side of life . . . truths which are, after all, our friends in the universe."

These then are the heroes I discuss: the Emersonian hero as he appears in Emerson's essays, Whitman's poetry, and the fiction of Hawthorne, Melville, and James; the Gentleman of nineteenth- and early twentieth-century Southern literature; the Black hero of Negro literature; the Disenchanted hero in the fiction of Hemingway and Fitzgerald; the Quixotic hero who figures in the work of Bellow, Salinger, Mailer, and other contemporary writers. I have not chosen to speak of the hero in the work of other important authors—Cooper, Thoreau, Twain, and Faulkner, for example—because in certain instances critics have anticipated me and in other cases I have indicated so clear a direction that close examination of an author's particular work has seemed unnecessary. My gallery is not complete: other portraits will surely follow, drawn by other critics, as indeed they have been in the past. But these five heroes, when given definition, may suggest something of the conflict between idealism and authority that has so concerned American authors.

This book has seemed to me most natural to write at this moment in the history of America and at this stage in my own professional career. In one form or other, America rules much of the world with an authority that is clearly dangerous—to Americans even more than to the people of other nations. All that can save us from ourselves, it would seem, is an irrepressible idealism that forever challenges our own authority. Now idealism flourishes most obviously among Negroes and young people, who use the terms Black Power and Student Power to express their desire to convert abstract idealism into concrete action and who compel every man not black and not a student to reconsider the forms of authority he has always assumed. This idealism is by no means simple or pure, as recent events in our universities have shown, and reminds us of the dangers that attend the idealistic spirit whenever it grows rigid and implacable; lurking within the heroic ideal is the very totalitarianism it denounces. Hawthorne's Puritans; Melville's Ahab; James' Gilbert Osmond; Simms' and Page's Southern Gentlemen; Baldwin's black heroes; and Mailer's Cummings and Croft—these various figures have succumbed to a totalitarian idealism that mocks freedom, diversity, and human complexity among all Americans, young or old, black or white. The delicate line between the heroic ideal and the authority it challenges has never been more precarious than in our generation; and the fine edge of this sword has cast its shadow everywhere on my work.

"Make it new," a generation once demanded. "Make it relevant," this generation insists. Every man whose profession is the love of learning knows that the practical relevance of all the old, honored, unassailable books has been called into question by the students who face him every day. The assumptions which I made about American culture twenty years ago are no longer made by my most sensitive students. I find myself attempting to persuade young people of the relevance of Emerson, Hawthorne, and Melville in a way that I never thought would be necessary; and this is a task for which no professional school has trained me. I can deplore this fact or I can be stimulated by it into a new awareness of my students, myself, and the literature of my country.

As the following book suggests, I have chosen the latter alternative.

Whatever scholarly discipline controls my many judgments in this study, I owe to the early guidance of Lewis Leary, Jay B. Hubbell, and Richard Chase. I would like to thank my colleagues at the City College of New York for reading individual chapters and suggesting a variety of improvements. Louis D. Rubin read an earlier version of the chapter on Southern literature and offered helpful criticism. I owe a particular debt of gratitude to my colleague and friend Arthur Waldhorn, who helped me to clarify conceptual problems that always seem to appear when a book is only three-fourths finished. To Edmond Volpe special thanks: he is the sort of sympathetic chairman every scholar deserves.

During the writing of this book I received generous financial assistance from The City College of New York and from the City University of New York. Portions of chapters have appeared in *Bucknell Review, Yale Review, The Colorado Quarterly, Phylon, Critique, Georgia Review, The Mississippi Quarterly,* and *South Atlantic Quarterly* and are reprinted with permission of those journals.

New York, September, 1965
Paris, June 1969

T. L. G.

CONTENTS

ONE

The Emersonian Hero

1

UNDER	*Emerson*
THE	*and*
SHADOW	*the*
OF	*Heroic*
OUR	*Ideal*
SWORDS	

"I wish
you would take an American hero," Carlyle urged Emerson in 1845, "one whom you really love; and give us a History of him,—make an artistic bronze statue (in good *words*) of his Life and him!" This advice seems strange indeed, for in the previous decade Emerson had published essays whose specific intention was to characterize and define the distinctive hero in America—to create him, as it were, for the imagination of the people in the new world; and Carlyle himself was largely instrumental in the reprinting and circulation of Emerson's works in England. The Scotsman did add, in this same letter, that "No other voice in this wide waste world seems to my sad ear to be *speaking* at all at present"; but there remains Carlyle's dissatisfaction with Emerson's conception of the hero, his feeling that Emerson was somehow not forceful enough, not "concrete" enough. 3

Carlyle, of course, was never completely reconciled to Emerson's mystical tendencies, as Emerson remained discontent with Carlyle's "defense of mere force," his attempt "to find a hero, and let [people] be his slave."

The two writers clearly perceived each other's strengths and limitations, but as we consider Emerson's achievement, his special contribution to the idealistic strain in American culture, we begin to sense that Carlyle did not fully recognize that the author of "The American Scholar" (1837) and the "Divinity School Address" (1838) was significantly different from the aristocrat who created *Representative Men* (1850), *English Traits* (1856), and *The Conduct of Life* (1860), that the representative American hero projected in Emerson's early essays yields to the extraordinary, powerful man of the later work, that the youthful egalitarianism or freedom, to borrow Stephen Whicher's term, succumbs to a measured recognition of fate. There is a change in Emerson's concept of the hero, from that of an emerging idealist who challenges the "courtly muses of Europe" and the religious authority of his Puritan heritage to that of an exceptional man for whom power in the public world is paramount. This shift from a moral idealism to a social authority should be emphasized, not only because of its significance to the development of Emerson's own writing but because it suggests a similar tension in the work of his contemporaries—the transcendentalists, Thoreau, Hawthorne, and Melville—and it anticipates many of the problems that confronted Whitman and James, even though many of these other authors wrote in different forms. The clear conflict between Emerson's initial idealism and the authority of other cultures or past theologies became a conflict within Emerson himself. The Emersonian hero who spoke for all Americans ultimately speaks for only himself.

Emerson's decreasing faith in the potential heroism of the common American, his growing interest in the accomplished, fully finished man of all nations, suggests some of the reasons why the heroic ideal could not survive in nineteenth-century American thought. For it is one thing to speak of the democratic hero in the 1830's when one is thinking specifically in religious terms and only generally in social terms, when one is not challenged by the social fact. It is another matter to write, in 1850, of representative men who do not represent democratic Americans; to turn to the traits of Englishmen, in 1856, in search of an exemplary use of practical power; to speak, in 1861, of the conduct of life as though it has nothing to do with the power of God and everything to do with the power of man—in short, to write these later books, which concentrate on force and authority, precisely at the time (the period of abolitionism and the Civil War) when moral idealism is being tested in the actual world. The concept of idealism, so forcefully expressed in *Nature,* "The American Scholar," and "The Divinity School Address," surrenders to a social authority that encroaches upon the Emersonian hero; the balance is gone; and heroism, which is no longer evolving but is fully grown, becomes what we fear it has become in America today—success, power, and authority in the external world itself.

In concentrating upon Emerson's altered view of the hero—the ideal hero—we admit its central significance to his thought. We recognize that his theory of correspondences, his ideas about Nature and language and the Reason subserve his overriding concern with the perfectible man. From this point of view, Emerson's early essays form not only the history of the hero that Carlyle requested but a philosophical epic in which he defines the characteristics necessary for heroism in America. The Emersonian hero assumes the preternatural qualities of an epic figure; he emerges rather than appears, becomes rather than is; and he stands as an ideal in the mind of the American, representing the most complete embodiment of the American dream in our literature. "Our day of dependence, our long apprenticeship to the learning of other lands draws to a close," he announces in "The American Scholar," seeking to define a form of heroism that is peculiarly organic to America. And when he reminds his audience, in the same address, that they are different from the ancient Greeks, the Troubadours, and their contemporaries in Europe, that in fact they are unique in the history of man, he is attempting to specify the peculiar attributes of the hero in America. Indeed the famous early essays—*Nature,* "The American Scholar," and the "Divinity School Address"—define the essence of the American hero from the historical point of view: the secular man who ideally can establish a harmony between himself and Nature; the scholar who can be more than "a farmer, or a professor, or an engineer," who can become a transcendental egoist and include the Universe within himself; and lastly the servant of God who must discover personally the "one mind that is everywhere active" and thus be free of tradition, of society—of the constricting and crippling forces that reach out from the past. Each of these addresses is historically oriented and does battle with a past that inhibits the American from establishing his own originality; each is an affirmation of self-trust; each focuses upon one dominant philosophical aspect of Emerson's thought—Nature, the mind, the spirit—although each, inevitably, includes the concerns of the other two addresses. Taken together, the three statements constitute prolegomena to the essays in the first and second series.

In the conclusion to *Nature,* Emerson reminds the reader that "At present, man applies to nature but half his force. He works on the world with his understanding alone." Impatient with man's acceptance of himself as limited, Emerson exhorts him to the full use of his Reason and concludes by celebrating the need for self-reliance. "All that Adam had, all that Caesar could, you have and can do," he reminds his contemporary American. "Adam called his house, heaven and earth; Caesar called his house, home; you perhaps call yours, a cobbler's trade; a hundred acres of ploughed land; or a scholar's garret. Yet line for line and point for point your dominion is as great as theirs, though without fine names. Build therefore your own world." Self-trust also informs the final paragraphs of "The American Scholar" and the "Divinity School Address"; indeed, as we turn to the *Essays: First Series,* we discover that all of Emerson's statements—charged with confidence and affirmation, free of doubt and hesitation, fixed like individual maxims on the page—lead to the climactic assertion that "there are resources in us on which we have not drawn." He defies the past in his desire to champion the insurgent American hero. In "History," which begins *Essays: First Series,* Emerson conditions his argument with the proclamation that "there is properly no history, only biography"—history is "incarnate in every just and wise man"—and his expression of admiration for "the Heroic or Homeric age down to the domestic life of the Athenians and Spartans" leads inevitably, as he considers the great ages in which the great heroes have lived, to the present emergence of the American hero—an epic rather than a tragic hero.*

* American authors before Emerson's time—particularly those who wrote immediately after the Revolutionary War—also thought of the epic as a literary genre especially well-suited to Americans. Crévecoeur defined the characteristics that might inform the American hero in his *Letters from an American Farmer* (1782), and other writers, who saw themselves as newborn bards, tried to create epics worthy of the rising republic. See, for example, John Trumbull's ode on "The Genius

Emerson seems to provide the conditions for tragedy in "Self-Reliance," the essay that follows "History," for he sees the confident hero in confrontation with "the unintelligible brute force that lies at the bottom of society"; he recognizes that "to be great is to be misunderstood." But his hero has no essential weakness because he is always in a state of possibility, of becoming. Society is rigid, in conspiracy against the manhood of the hero; the past intimidates the hero and makes him "timid and apologetic," a little man afraid to act instinctually in response to the moral idealism that is his most natural attribute. "Greatness appeals to the future," Emerson concludes, suggesting that whatever limitations man may presently suffer from will eventually lose their force in the process of evolutionary melioration. "Life only avails, not the having lived. . . . This one fact the world hates; that the soul *becomes.*"

Because he sees man evolving into greatness, Emerson does not seriously consider, in his first two books of essays, the ways in which man is limited; he knows very well, as he observes in "Compensation," that "there is a crack in everything God has made," but he refuses to define that crack, to take a complete account of tragedy. As Newton Arvin points out, in a persuasive consideration of Emerson's treatment of tragedy, Emerson is a thinker who is unwilling to offer "a steady confrontation of Tragedy, or a sustained and unswerving gaze at the face of Evil"; he is a writer who develops his ideas beyond tragedy and offers "perhaps the fullest and most authentic expression in modern literature of the more than tragic emotion of thankfulness."

Of all our significant nineteenth-century American authors, Emerson is most obsessed with greatness, with the heroic ideal; and if he does not see his hero in tragic terms—"there is no writer in the world," Mr. Arvin reminds us, "in whose work we are not conscious

---

of America," his Yale commencement oration entitled "Prospect of the Future Glory of America" (1770), *The Progress of Dulness* (1773), and especially *M'Fingal, an Epic Poem* (1776, 1782); Philip Freneau's and Hugh Henry Brackenridge's commencement piece at Princeton, "A Poem on the Rising Glory of America" (1771), and Freneau's later *Pictures of Columbus* (1774); Joseph Barlow's *Vision of Columbus* (1787) and his even more elaborate epic, *Columbiad* (1807); and Timothy Dwight's *Greenfield Hill* (1794). These poems are little more than extrapolations of a patriotic notion, but they anticipate Emerson's desire for a native literature (even though the poems themselves are highly derivative and imitative), his conception of the American as a man of heroic proportions.

of missing *something* that belongs to experience"—he does see him as someone defending and representing the new world. In his essays of the 1840's he defines those characteristics necessary for the full development of the epic hero—spirituality, love, friendship, prudence, intellect, art, character, manners, and heroism—as if he is offering the kind of moral instruction that religious mentors gave young knights in the Middle Ages as an essential part of their education into life. And, in "Heroism," he defines explicitly the type of hero that he envisages for America: "The hero is a mind of such balance that no disturbances can shake his will, . . . There is somewhat not philosophical in heroism; there is somewhat not holy in it; it seems not to know that other souls are of one texture with it; it has pride; it is the extreme of individual nature. Nevertheless we must profoundly revere it. There is somewhat in great actions which does not allow us to go behind them. Heroism feels and never reasons, and therefore is always right."

In the hero the Reason finds its fullest expression as the intuition asserts itself and dominates human action. Emerson ascribes to the extraordinary man innumerable positive attributes—self-trust, virtue, naturalness, nobility, persistence, courage—until we realize that this man, in transcending the common person, in embodying ideal traits that are beyond the capacity of the common man, is in part mystically conceived, the idea of man rather than any actual man. We do not know the sources of the hero's greatness—"heroism is an obedience to a secret impulse of an individual's character"—and we follow Emerson's enumeration of the hero's characteristics in "Heroism" and the other early essays, always conscious that the author is suggesting what man ought to be rather than what he is.

Our present impatience with Emerson stems from Emerson's own impatience with man as he existed in his time. He is unwilling to view the human being as completely human, as he actually is; and the record of the intervening century, it would seem, has undermined and mocked many of his fundamental ideas. But if he has not proven to be historically or practically accurate, he does express an idealistic strain that is central to American life and culture, one that has recurred regardless of the bleak moment of history in which we have been living. When Emerson wrote his early essays the historical moment in America was, of course, not bleak, and much of his strength and self-confidence arise from a felicitious convergence of literary, religious, and economic revolutions that helped to liberate Americans. "The circumstances of man," he acknowledges in "Heroism," "are historically somewhat better in this country at this hour than perhaps ever before. More freedom exists for culture." The truth of the observation suggests why Emerson felt so free to demand ideal behavior from the people of his time. His attraction to scientific advancement; his awareness of the physical growth and industrial progress of the country; his nationalistic fervor; his success in promulgating transcendentalism—all of these factors buttressed his central desire to see an epic hero, absolutely unique in the history of the world, emerge in America.

After Emerson had written his early addresses and the essays of the first and second series, he focused less on the hero as representative of the common man than on the hero whom the common man should emulate. In championing the ordinary person—"I embrace the common," he had announced in "The American Scholar," "I explore and sit at the feet of the familiar, the low"—he found himself unable to use the language of the ordinary person; and as he came to analyze the hero in his essays he discovered, as early as 1842, that "the heroic cannot be the common, nor the common the heroic." The idealism that informs his vision of the average American, who is in the process of seeking heroic powers, yields to an altered vision in which the historical hero—Plato, Goethe, Shakespeare, Napoleon, the Englishman—has realized his ideals. The American is asked to watch this hero—to watch and to learn. Emerson's repeated conviction that "the only sin is limitation" leads to his rather aristocratic view of the hero in *Representative Men* and *The Conduct of Life;* his view that "we are born believers in great men," as expressed in "Character," leads directly to the opening statement in *Representative Men:* "It is natural to believe in great men. If the companions of our childhood should turn out to be heroes, and their condition regal, it would not surprise us. . . . The search after the great is the dream of youth, and the most serious occupation of manhood." Although Emerson was at odds with Carlyle's notion of the hero, although he emphasized the particular qualities represented by his heroes rather than the militant attributes of extraordinary men, he nevertheless grew more particular, more rigid, and more distant to the common man in the decade before the Civil War. In the thirties and forties, Emerson's works reflected the theological tensions then paramount in New England life; but the cultural break that he suggests in "The American Scholar" had not yet occurred, and when it developed in the 1850's and 1860's, Emerson was not prepared to adjust his thought or his style to the consequences—to the actualities of democracy that one sees reflected, for example, in the poetry of Whitman or in the political essays of Thoreau.*

Representative Men is Emerson's attempt to define those ideal aspects of human character in individual heroes. These men—Plato, Swedenborg, Montaigne, Shakespeare, Napoleon, and Goethe—represent us only in so far as they have achieved what we desire to achieve; it seems clear that Emerson is more interested in the heroes than in those common people whom they represent. In "The American Scholar," Emerson was a man speaking to men and his impatient attitude stems from his deep feelings about the individual's possibilities. In *Representative Men* he speaks of how the "imbecility of men is always inviting impudence of power"; and though he claims that "true genius will not impoverish, but will liberate, and add new senses," clearly he has greater faith in the representative man, the hero, than in "the victim" who gropes at minds of powerful method. "Mankind have, in all ages, attached themselves to a few persons, who, either by the quality of that idea they embodied, or by the largeness of their reception, were entitled to the position of leaders and law-givers."

In the opening chapter of Representative Men—"The Uses of Great Men"—Emerson approaches heriosm from a utilitarian point of view. The basic use to which great men can be put, he believes,

---

* My intention is not to praise Whitman and Thoreau at the expense of Emerson, certainly not in this cursory a manner, but to point toward the differing forms that their work assumed as they lost a firm and idealistic faith in the common man. One may say—with all the excess that generalizations invite—that Emerson looked outwards, away from America, either in time (as in *Representative Men*) or in space (as in *English Traits*). Whitman and Thoreau faced the political facts of mid-nineteenth-century America more directly.

The response of these authors to the emerging Republic of mid-century presents many problems which it is not within my scope to discuss—F. O. Matthiessen and other critics have already written perceptively about the subject. Whitman's changing conception of the hero as the common American I discuss in a later chapter. Thoreau came to grips with actual social problems like slavery and, curiously, the literary development of his attitudes is analogous to Emerson's: from the general to the particular, from the ideal to the specific example. Compare, for example, the theoretical, idealistic quality of "Civil Disobedience" (1849) with the militancy of an essay like "A Plea for Captain John Brown" (1859).

is their salutary influence on the common person. "We love to associate with heroic persons, since our receptivity is unlimited; and with the great, our thoughts and manners easily become great." But as he attempted to define those characteristics that render Plato or Swedenborg or Montaigne superior, he confronts them personally, pitting them against himself in almost an exclusive way—and the average person is largely forgotten. In the early essays great men were genuine models, and Emerson stood between them and his audience—*he* represented his readers; but now the audience is absent, and the writer, fully developed and certain of his own artistic power, measures his chosen heroes in terms of himself alone—the dominant characteristics that each representative man exemplifies are characteristics which Emerson considers essential to himself. If he can sympathize with the "broad humanity" and "the patrician polish" of Plato, he can also find the strong will and democratic heroism of Napoleon attractive; if he finds the mysticism of Swedenborg significant, although excessively classified, he also values personally the skepticism of Montaigne. Philosophy, mysticism, skepticism, poetry, democratic heroism, and writing: these are aspects of Emerson, refractions of his total character, that he seeks to measure in a privative manner. In his conclusion to the introductory chapter he reminds us that "within the limits of human education and agency, we may say, great men exist that there be greater men. The destiny of organized nature is amelioration, and who can tell its limits?" Who can tell, that is, the limitations of Emerson as he measures himself in his full maturity against his chosen heroes of the past.

Of the six representative men only one is in fact a man exclusively involved in the democratic actualities of everyday life, and he, Napoleon, whom Emerson characterizes as "the man of the world," is a military hero. In an age of industrial growth, no hero of commerce is included; in an era of scientific development, no great scientist is represented; in a time of political tensions no political figure appears. These various heroes, again with the exception of Napoleon, are representative of the poetic or philosophic disposition —passive men, ultimately, who invoke the muse or the oversoul to inspire them. The entire volume is retrospective, general, impressionistic—safe, even tame, in a way that the early addresses and essays are not. The descriptions of Swedenborg and Montaigne are diffuse; the treatment of Plato, Shakespeare, and Goethe are effusive, hyperbolic—almost the tributes of an undiscriminating mind. Although F. O. Matthiessen is justified in stressing Emerson's achievement as part of a "literature for our democracy," *Representative Men* is not the text most illustrative of that achievement.

Emerson himself was aware that his representative men did not suggest the types of all mankind, to say nothing of the democratic America in which he lived. He introduces the essay on "Swedenborg; or, the Mystic" by asserting that "Among eminent persons, those who are most dear to men are not of the class which the economist calls producers"; they are the poets, the inspirational leaders, and not those who tend to govern or lead or live in any practical sense. This may be the reason that no chapter in *Representative Men* is devoted to an American, for then Emerson surely would have had to draw upon a political or a military leader—or, as he wrote shortly after having finished the book, "the unexpressed greatness of the common farmer and laborer." The farmer or laborer would surely have been an adequate representative of America, but his presence would have jarred with the tone of the other chapters. Furthermore, it is difficult to conceive of Emerson approaching the common American as he treats Plato or Shakespeare or Goethe; these are particular heroes who are representative in only the most conceptual sense—they are heroes rather than representative men. The common man does not occupy the center of Emerson's thought at this stage of his career—he is, to use the term that Emerson employed when he regretted his omission of "the common farmer and laborer" in *Representative Men,* an afterthought. It remained for Whitman to develop an heroic myth of the common American.

The absence of a contemporary American hero reflects, more precisely, Emerson's belief that the representative man who exhibited one dominant trait could not function in his time. In "Goethe; or, the Writer," Emerson acknowledges that Goethe

> appears at a time when a general culture has spread itself, and has smoothed down all sharp individual traits; when, in the absence of heroic characters, a social comfort and cooperation have come in. There is no poet, but scores of poetic writers; no Columbus, but hundreds of post-captains, with transit-telescope, barometer, and concentrated soup and pemmican, no Demosthenes, no Chatham, but any number of clever parliamentary and forensic debators; no prophet or saint, but colleges of divinity; no learned man, but learned societies, a cheap press, read-

ing-rooms, and book-clubs, without number. There was never such a miscellany of facts. The world extends itself like American trade. We conceive Greek or Roman life,—life in the middle ages,—to be a simple and comprehensible affair; but modern life to respect a multitude of things, which is distracting.

Just a decade or so after Tocqueville, in his *Democracy in America,* had written of the American's concern with the future and with the multiplicity of democratic life, it is curious that the American who was most eloquent in urging a cultural as well as a theological revolution should be looking backwards, or, as in his next book, *English Traits,* looking away from his own country. But sensing that America would not yield the kind of hero whom Carlyle had called for in 1845 and whom he himself foresaw in his early work, Emerson turned to England, "the best of actual nations," and offered the "History" of the Englishman that Carlyle had wanted him to write of the American.

Still *English Traits* is a history of heroism and the great names fill the pages. The traits of the English people are really the traits of their heroes and when Emerson considers the people themselves he does so because he feels that they should become like their representatives. Furthermore, his eulogy of English culture—"the culture of the day, the thoughts and aims of men, are English thoughts and aims"—is meant to remind Americans whom they should emulate, for "the American is only the continuation of the English genius into new conditions." * The aristocracy of talent that he emphasized in *Representative Men* is now attributed to English heroes and leads to the social aristocracy that one finds in *The Conduct of Life,* which is, as Stephen Whicher has suggested, a "gospel for patricians."

What impressed Emerson most about the English was their power. As he discusses race and character, wealth and aristocracy, he reminds us that the English "assimilate other races to themselves, and are not assimilated," that "the stability of England is the security of the modern world." He recognizes that the American system is more democratic, more humane; yet the American people "do not yield better or more able men or more inventions or books or benefits than the English." The English dominate the world, the most accomplished nation in modern European history, and Emer-

* Compare these observations with the famous declaration of intellectual independence in "The American Scholar": "We have listened too long to the courtly muses of Europe."

son's admiration is almost wholly devoted to those aspects of character that "have helped to make the English the leaders that they are." He does conclude, in a kind of afterthought, that the quality "which lures a solitary American in the woods with the wish to see England, is the moral peculiarity of the Saxon race—its commanding sense of right and wrong, the love and devotion to that—this is the imperial trait, which arms them with the sceptre of the globe"; but, in fact, as he notes early in the book, the English "are with difficulty ideal." His emphasis throughout *English Traits* is on the practical and not the ideal traits of the people, on their authority in the world and not their idealism. He is less concerned with what the English will become than with what they were and are. "The power of performance has not been exceeded," he reminds us finally, and the power of that performance is "the creation of value. The English have given importance to individuals, a principal end and fruit of every society. Every man is allowed and encouraged to be what he is, and is guarded in the indulgence of his whim."

Emerson's fascination with power and success becomes most manifest in *The Conduct of Life,* in which he asserts that life is, in effect, a search after power. The first two chapters, "Fate" and "Power," are in a mutual tension—"the antagonist of Fate is Power," Emerson states at the outset—and the reader recognizes the antipodal forces that Emerson conceives of as governing human nature. Although he admits that we are at the mercy of natural forces and that we are fated in many ways, Emerson insists that fate "can teach us a fatal courage," so long as we realize that the strongest power comes from Nature and that "There are sources on which we have not drawn. . . . For though Fate is immense, so is Power, which is the other fact in the dual world, immense. If Fate follows and limits Power, Power attends and antagonizes Fate."

The tone of these essays is patronizing, the attitude toward the common person condescending. Whereas the early work concentrated upon the moral virtues that stem from self-reliance, the later essays in *The Conduct of Life* are guides to practical success—and though they often use the same terminology, it now has a more secular, different purpose. Whereas self-reliance meant God-reliance in the early essays, now it means literally reliance on the individual self. Thought and the moral sentiment make us free so that we can transcend our fate and achieve a "sovereignty of power"; manners, whose basis is self-reliance, are a force and "impress us as they indicate real power"; power is what "men of esteem" want—"power to

exec
to tl
pow
The
of o
that
men
hum
corr
achi
]
"The
natic
man
Eme
wors
life,
comr
the c
demc
powe
has t
a cen
to th
"well
view,
Engl
of ou
whon
becon
kind
politi
E
again
effect
the e

ing-rooms, and book-clubs, without number. There was never such a miscellany of facts. The world extends itself like American trade. We conceive Greek or Roman life,—life in the middle ages,—to be a simple and comprehensible affair; but modern life to respect a multitude of things, which is distracting.

Just a decade or so after Tocqueville, in his *Democracy in America,* had written of the American's concern with the future and with the multiplicity of democratic life, it is curious that the American who was most eloquent in urging a cultural as well as a theological revolution should be looking backwards, or, as in his next book, *English Traits,* looking away from his own country. But sensing that America would not yield the kind of hero whom Carlyle had called for in 1845 and whom he himself foresaw in his early work, Emerson turned to England, "the best of actual nations," and offered the "History" of the Englishman that Carlyle had wanted him to write of the American.

Still *English Traits* is a history of heroism and the great names fill the pages. The traits of the English people are really the traits of their heroes and when Emerson considers the people themselves he does so because he feels that they should become like their representatives. Furthermore, his eulogy of English culture—"the culture of the day, the thoughts and aims of men, are English thoughts and aims"—is meant to remind Americans whom they should emulate, for "the American is only the continuation of the English genius into new conditions." * The aristocracy of talent that he emphasized in *Representative Men* is now attributed to English heroes and leads to the social aristocracy that one finds in *The Conduct of Life,* which is, as Stephen Whicher has suggested, a "gospel for patricians."

What impressed Emerson most about the English was their power. As he discusses race and character, wealth and aristocracy, he reminds us that the English "assimilate other races to themselves, and are not assimiliated," that "the stability of England is the security of the modern world." He recognizes that the American system is more democratic, more humane; yet the American people "do not yield better or more able men or more inventions or books or benefits than the English." The English dominate the world, the most accomplished nation in modern European history, and Emer-

* Compare these observations with the famous declaration of intellectual independence in "The American Scholar": "We have listened too long to the courtly muses of Europe."

for example, possesses a crafty smile of a rather elementary kind: he has not even seen the evil that Robin Molineux and Goodman Brown acknowledge. He senses the absurdity of the world but only begins to sense the absurdity and inhumanity of his own actions. The Reverend Hooper, in "The Minister's Black Veil," smiles at his congregation because they do not understand the meaning of the veil; in their vulgar voyeurism they yearn to see under the veil, but they cannot comprehend its symbolic significance. No one—not even the Reverend's fiancée—asks him the meaning of the black veil, and Hooper dies with the knowledge that the people have only a partial glimpse into the reality of their lives; the people are absurd and limited, but Hooper, in his self-imposed isolation and ultimate madness, is absurd too. These tales, suggestive of Hawthorne's thematic approach throughout his fiction, inevitably interpose a symbolic device or humor or paradox or the reality of the social world itself between Hawthorne and the tragic conception he is developing. His description of the mother in "The Snow-Image" defines his attitude: "all through life she had kept her heart full of childlike simplicity and faith, which was pure and clear as crystal. And looking at all matters through this transparent medium, she sometimes saw truths so profound that other people laughed at them as nonsense and absurdity." Her husband, "with a most benevolent smile on his sagacious visage," represents the social, sensible reality that prevents her from articulating the truths she sees; he evokes Hawthorne's admiration, but it is clear that his "healthy" skepticism permits him to apprehend reality in only a partial manner—certain truths are beyond his capacity.

Hester Prynne has only a limited vision, also. Of all Hawthorne's important work, *The Scarlet Letter* would seem to satisfy the requirements of a romantic narrative in which heroism triumphs; for surely Hester converts the community from hatred to respect, from hostility to acceptance. But her conversion manifests

---

Hooper in modern dress, but there is a tragic finality to their lives that one does not find in modern fiction. Idealism is crushed in a way it never is in the work of Salinger, Bellow, Mailer, and other writers. Hawthorne's themes of isolation, manipulation, sin, and guilt are taken up by these authors; they too are fond of paradox, ambiguity, and irony. But they see the hero as someone who is unwilling to succumb to authority of any kind. One of the incidental paradoxes of our day is that in a world of greater authority, our writers are increasingly idealistic.

ing-rooms, and book-clubs, without number. There was never such a miscellany of facts. The world extends itself like American trade. We conceive Greek or Roman life,—life in the middle ages,—to be a simple and comprehensible affair; but modern life to respect a multitude of things, which is distracting.

Just a decade or so after Tocqueville, in his *Democracy in America,* had written of the American's concern with the future and with the multiplicity of democratic life, it is curious that the American who was most eloquent in urging a cultural as well as a theological revolution should be looking backwards, or, as in his next book, *English Traits,* looking away from his own country. But sensing that America would not yield the kind of hero whom Carlyle had called for in 1845 and whom he himself foresaw in his early work, Emerson turned to England, "the best of actual nations," and offered the "History" of the Englishman that Carlyle had wanted him to write of the American.

Still *English Traits* is a history of heroism and the great names fill the pages. The traits of the English people are really the traits of their heroes and when Emerson considers the people themselves he does so because he feels that they should become like their representatives. Furthermore, his eulogy of English culture—"the culture of the day, the thoughts and aims of men, are English thoughts and aims"—is meant to remind Americans whom they should emulate, for "the American is only the continuation of the English genius into new conditions." * The aristocracy of talent that he emphasized in *Representative Men* is now attributed to English heroes and leads to the social aristocracy that one finds in *The Conduct of Life,* which is, as Stephen Whicher has suggested, a "gospel for patricians."

What impressed Emerson most about the English was their power. As he discusses race and character, wealth and aristocracy, he reminds us that the English "assimilate other races to themselves, and are not assimiliated," that "the stability of England is the security of the modern world." He recognizes that the American system is more democratic, more humane; yet the American people "do not yield better or more able men or more inventions or books or benefits than the English." The English dominate the world, the most accomplished nation in modern European history, and Emer-

* Compare these observations with the famous declaration of intellectual independence in "The American Scholar": "We have listened too long to the courtly muses of Europe."

son's admiration is almost wholly devoted to those aspects of character that "have helped to make the English the leaders that they are." He does conclude, in a kind of afterthought, that the quality "which lures a solitary American in the woods with the wish to see England, is the moral peculiarity of the Saxon race—its commanding sense of right and wrong, the love and devotion to that—this is the imperial trait, which arms them with the sceptre of the globe"; but, in fact, as he notes early in the book, the English "are with difficulty ideal." His emphasis throughout *English Traits* is on the practical and not the ideal traits of the people, on their authority in the world and not their idealism. He is less concerned with what the English will become than with what they were and are. "The power of performance has not been exceeded," he reminds us finally, and the power of that performance is "the creation of value. The English have given importance to individuals, a principal end and fruit of every society. Every man is allowed and encouraged to be what he is, and is guarded in the indulgence of his whim."

Emerson's fascination with power and success becomes most manifest in *The Conduct of Life,* in which he asserts that life is, in effect, a search after power. The first two chapters, "Fate" and "Power," are in a mutual tension—"the antagonist of Fate is Power," Emerson states at the outset—and the reader recognizes the antipodal forces that Emerson conceives of as governing human nature. Although he admits that we are at the mercy of natural forces and that we are fated in many ways, Emerson insists that fate "can teach us a fatal courage," so long as we realize that the strongest power comes from Nature and that "There are sources on which we have not drawn. . . . For though Fate is immense, so is Power, which is the other fact in the dual world, immense. If Fate follows and limits Power, Power attends and antagonizes Fate."

The tone of these essays is patronizing, the attitude toward the common person condescending. Whereas the early work concentrated upon the moral virtues that stem from self-reliance, the later essays in *The Conduct of Life* are guides to practical success—and though they often use the same terminology, it now has a more secular, different purpose. Whereas self-reliance meant God-reliance in the early essays, now it means literally reliance on the individual self. Thought and the moral sentiment make us free so that we can transcend our fate and achieve a "sovereignty of power"; manners, whose basis is self-reliance, are a force and "impress us as they indicate real power"; power is what "men of esteem" want—"power to execute their design, power to give legs and feet, form and actuality to their thought"; man must learn not to spend but to "hoard for power." These statements, and they are representative of others in *The Conduct of Life,* reflect Emerson's conviction that "very few of our race can be said to be yet finished men"; and he concludes that man's purpose is now "to convert all impediments into instruments, all enemies into power" so that the organic effort of his human nature "to mount and meliorate" can be effected and "the corresponding impulse to the Better in the human being" can be achieved.

Emerson's work comes at a turning point in American culture. "The American Scholar" is one of the climactic expressions of nationalism and democratic idealism; the aristocracy of talent demanded in the early essay surrenders to a social aristocracy for whom Emerson prescribes the proper use of manners, behavior, culture, worship, and wealth—the proper conduct of life. The terms of this life, rooted as they are in power and force, have led to industrial, commercial, practical power and success—a pattern prefigured by the development of Emerson's own view. His waning interest in democratic idealism and his increased emphasis on the uses to which power can be put suggest the general direction that our society has taken; from a heritage of individualism we have developed into a centralized power state that reduces Emerson's early self-reliance to the realm of antiquated theory. Emerson's view is that only the "well born" can realize the self-reliance that he prescribes, and this view, which is increasingly pronounced in *Representative Men, English Traits,* and *The Conduct of Life,* is similar to the actualities of our so-called democracy today. Paradoxically, the individual whom he addresses in "Nature" and the "Divinity School Address" becomes the victim of twentieth-century literature, a victim to the kind of power advocated in *The Conduct of Life*—power in the political, commercial, and religious spheres of our life.

Emerson's concept of the hero as an emerging idealist struggling against the authority of tradition and conformity had a profound effect on his contemporaries and on Whitman.* But the fusion of the early concept, with its concentration on morality, and the later

---

* It has become increasingly apparent to critics that Emerson is in many ways the seminal writer of nineteenth-century American literature. Hyatt Waggoner's *American Poets, From The Puritans to the Present* (Boston, 1968), as a recent example, makes large claims for Emerson's centrality in the American poetic tradition.

concept, with its emphasis on manners, appears dramatically in the fiction of Henry James, F. Scott Fitzgerald, and other novelists. I do not mean to imply direct influence, but I would suggest that Emerson's shifting concept of the hero recurs in the work of these authors, embodying yoked and often irreconcilable opposites, and that it assumes a significant pattern in their writing. The idealist as wealthy and powerful man can be traced in one distinct portion of the literature since Emerson's time—from Christopher Newman of *The American* to Jay Gatsby of *The Great Gatsby*. There is a buoyant naïvety and self-reliance in the characters of James and Fitzgerald that is fused with their sudden acquisition of money or power—they are a little awkward with the money and the power, like Gatsby whose foot is never still. That awkwardness, which is still new enough to be decidedly idealistic, confronts the solid authority of European decadence (like the Bellegardes in *The American*) or the decadent rich in America (the Buchanans in *Gatsby*), and the larger conflict between idealism and authority is drawn. The hero of this fiction tends to be morally triumphant, even though he may end in defeat or death with his ideal yet unrealized; but the real meaning of his experience lies in the unresolved tensions between his ideals and the sudden authority he possesses. After Gatsby's noble failure American writers begin to conceive of idealism as crushed by a mechanistic culture, by the very power it has helped to create. The hero then becomes the victim or the cripple or the idiot or the dislocated adolescent, receding inwards into private meditations, lonely introspection, fantasies, searching for that moment when the idealistic attitude of his country or his region, his family or his personal life began to turn into cynicism or bitterness: thus the work of Faulkner, Carson McCullers, J. D. Salinger, Truman Capote, Tennessee Williams, and Edward Albee. But then, as if a cyclical law is at work in the development of our literature, the ideal hero emerges in the work of some of these same writers and in that of other important contemporaries.

For the reader of modern literature Emerson's ideological dogmatism, unchecked by an ambiguity and irony so congenial to the present sensibility, is perhaps antipathetic and the concentration on force in his later work hardly attractive, given the events of twentieth-century history. But Emerson remains, as Newton Arvin suggested years ago, "in some sense our bishop." His vision was more profound than any single expression of it. In a fundamental way he assumed the posture that has become distinctly associated with the American writer: the assertion of the author's character throughout his work rather than the creation of a world of individual figures—comic or tragic—in which the creator's personality is largely absent. Thoreau, Whitman, and Emily Dickinson speak in the first person, and much could be made of this American obsession with self in the work of many twentieth-century writers. But most significantly Emerson expressed fully and profoundly that strain of idealism which is deeply embedded in the American consciousness. And if we have achieved the empirical power that he himself had come to admire, if we have sometimes abused that power—as he could not foresee we would—we have still the element of idealism that reasserts itself insistently.

No one would question the significance of the Gothic tradition as it has been traced by D. H. Lawrence, Malcolm Cowley, and Leslie Fiedler; but Gothicism is, in most cases, checked by an idealistic strain that finds its roots in Emerson's writing; and, of course, the tragic vision of Hawthorne and Melville, responsive as it is to the optimism of Emerson and his followers, cannot be fully understood without a knowledge of Emerson's work.

NATHANIEL HAWTHORNE

The Absurdity of Heroism

As we read the fiction of Hawthorne and recognize its tragic dimensions, our deepest sympathies are inevitably modified by the potential if not actual absurdity implicit in every dark event. The evil rarely horrifies us, for it is attentuated by laughter, by irony, by paradox, by the playful ambiguity of the solid, socially-rooted figure of Hawthorne himself. Seldom does he permit us the ultimate purgation elicited by profound tragedy. In the prefaces to his romances he promises that he will take the privilege "awarded to the romancer," sensing the need to create an atmosphere which will permit him to render his compositions more than "painfully discernible," more than realistically true; but he rarely deals with the absolute consequences of evil and rarely offers us the complete satisfaction of a truly tragic vision.

Hawthorne's unwillingness to explore fully the implications of his conception—the hard-headed resistance that we feel in much of his work—suggests why he responded so critically to the ideological premises of transcendentalism. He deeply suspected the heroism

championed by Emerson and Whitman—not to speak of his contempt for the sentimental bravura in the popular fiction of his time—
and his suspicion expressed itself in the absurdity and the tough
literal-mindedness that often modifies and even mocks the heroism
of his tragic figures. In *The Blithedale Romance,* where heroism and
absurdity are in the most delicate balance, Zenobia states the principle explicitly: "There can be no truer test of the noble and heroic,
in any individual, than the degree in which he possesses the faculty
of distinguishing heroism from absurdity." Zenobia is defending the
idealistic reformer Hollingsworth, who has finally grown grotesque
in the skeptical eyes of Coverdale and society and the reader; there
is something ludicrous as well as pathetic in her fidelity to this
dangerous dreamer—there is a moral perversion in her willful misconception—for Hollingsworth has become an absurd hero in his
"blind enthusiasm." Hawthorne's position is clear and consistent in
The Blithedale Romance and throughout his fiction: heroism and
absurdity cannot be easily distinguished—Zenobia's decline is the
result of her unwillingness to accept that central truth—and much
of Hawthorne's work is testimony to the limitations of idealism,
of self-reliance, of nature, of faith, of any absolute abstraction to
which the hero is irrevocably committed. As Coverdale remarks at
the outset of the book: "The greatest obstacle to being heroic is the
doubt whether one may or may not be going to prove one's self a
fool."

The ordinary, mundane aspects of life form the subject of most
of Hawthorne's unremembered tales. Anthologies of his fiction tend
not to reprint "A Rill from the Town Pump" or "Sunday at Home"
or "The Toll Gatherer's Day" or "Buds and Bird Voices"; for the
modern reader Hawthorne is the serious, somber, and metaphysically
inclined author of "The Minister's Black Veil" and "Young Goodman Brown" and "My Kinsman, Major Molineux." Whatever
aesthetic justification we may claim for this choice, we should sense
that the choice itself distorts the historical, the actual Hawthorne
who wrote for the annuals and journals of the 1830's and 1840's.
When we look at a chronological listing of his publications and suspend a discriminatory judgment—when we become readers of *his*
time, an audience accustomed to the light essays of Irving or the
casual social observations of Nathaniel P. Willis and James Kirke
Paulding—we are struck by the pervasive presence of whimsy, of
comic attitudes, of absurdity in Hawthorne's work. As Henry

James reminds us, Hawthorne had, in early nineteenth-century America, "no Oxford, nor Eton, nor Harrow; no literature, no novels, no museums, no pictures, no political society, no sporting class—no Epsom nor Ascot!"; and the thin texture of his social world—expressed in sketches like "Main Street," "Sights from a Steeple," "Little Annie's Ramble," "David Swan," and "Snow-Flakes"—suggests why he needed the symbolic or allegoric tale when he wished to view the tragic frailties of man and why for him allegory was not a "lighter exercise of the imagination." But even in the more profound stories, however elaborate the formal structure may be, we sense an obeisance to actuality, a retreat to reality and the absurdity that always lurks somewhere on the edge of the darkest truth.

No clear or valid distinction of mind can be made between these tentative sketches and Hawthorne's more impressive tales; nor can we consider them as only the exercises of a younger writer in search of a subject and a tone and a point of view. "The Gentle Boy," "My Kinsman, Major Molineux," and "Roger Malvin's Burial" appeared in 1832 and "Jonathan Cilley" and "Chippings with a Chisel" were published in 1838. *Fanshawe,* written in 1828, was a self-confessed failure and we think of it as the imitative, awkward work of a young author; but we remember the abortive, trivial last romances: *Septimius Felton, Dr. Grimshawe's Secret, The Ancestral Footstep,* and *The Dolliver Romance.* As F. O. Matthiessen points out, there is no "progress in essentials" to Hawthorne's tales; and Hawthorne himself confessed, in his introduction to *The Snow-Image* (1851), that he was "disposed to quarrel with the earlier sketches . . . because they came so nearly up to the standard of the best that I can achieve now." The only distinction we feel repeatedly is in the kind of material that Hawthorne uses for each particular story.

The presence of whimsy and frivolity, of simple social observation in Hawthorne's anecdotes, sketches, and tales is more than a response to his audience, more than a natural reaction to eighteenth-century writers of the informal essay; it is the symptom of a deep instinct, a need to keep actuality near to him so that he can do more than "open an intercourse with the world." The sense of the actual forced Hawthorne to modify the intensity of his tragic vision and conditioned his attitude toward heroism. So recurrent is this self-conscious modification that it appears throughout his profound stories, written at the same time as the casual sketches, and helps to explain why Hawthorne is so attractive to our modern sensibility and what in fact constitutes his modernity.

Heroism, in its more vulgar aspects, is sharply censured in the scientific figures of Hawthorne's fiction: in Aylmer and Rappaccini most notably, but also in those other alchemists and scientists who quickly assume grotesque moral proportions. These idealists, who often elicit Hawthorne's partial admiration because of a bold, romantic imagination, are inevitably ludicrous in their singular and proud quest for some absolute. Their idealism is not tempered by the authority of the external world or of God—they have arrogated that authority to themselves—and because they have destroyed a necessary balance between idealism and authority, they strike the reader as awkward or absurd, closer to caricatures than to fully-rounded human beings. The hero is thus consumed by his own idealism in an active or romantic way that differs from the silent, introspective, more intensely ethical idealism which destroys someone like Dimmesdale: these scientists become the authority they ostensibly challenge, and their potential heroism turns to tyranny, to irrational pride. When Aylmer, whose inordinate pride in trying to remove his wife's birthmark has rendered him the perverted hero, hears his servant's "hoarse chuckle" and persuades him that he has "earned the right to laugh," he is acquiescing in his own absurdity; and indeed the "hoarse chuckling laugh" of Animadab is the lingering note at the end of "The Birthmark." Beatrice Rappaccini is capable, Hawthorne tells us directly, "of the height and heroism of love," but her father, an heroic man of science, destroys her through his "fatal love of science." The extreme attitude is the absurd attitude, although with figures like Chillingworth or Westervelt—who also represent progressively rigid forms of authority—absurdity can manifest itself in a sinister fashion that leaves no room for the sympathy or compassion of the author.

Hawthorne's suspicion of the heroic ideal is more subtly dramatized in those tales for which he is justly characterized as "modern." If we consider Reuben Bourne, Robin Molineux, Goodman Brown, the Reverend Hooper, and Ethan Brand in juxtaposition with one another, we recognize how limited they are—how intentionally limited they are—as heroes in an age of romantic and sentimental literary expression; we think of them as vulnerable in their earthly nature; and we remember them as either guilt-ridden human beings or ludicrous figures in a world where others mock or misunderstand them. In "Roger Malvin's Burial," for example, Hawthorne introduces two struggling and wounded men as part of an heroic "little band who gave battle to twice their number in the heart of the enemy's country." Unlike the writers of his time, Hawthorne does not treat this potentially sentimental subject sentimentally but explores the vulnerability of human nature, the limitations of heroism, the breakdown of Reuben Bourne because of his guilt-ridden, tortured mind. Hawthorne senses the human flaw in his hero and by creating a tale that is so completely a moral parable, so poetic in language and metaphoric in technique that it soon ceases to function on the level of reality or historicity—reality is seen through the distorted vision of Reuben Bourne—he succeeds in tracing the deterioration of a human being. Reuben Bourne's guilt over his inability to realize the heroic ideal is not demonstrated in this material world but in a romantic, poetic world that is compelling so long as it is metaphoric; but when Hawthorne wonders whose guilt has blasted the oak tree, when Reuben Bourne fires accidentally into his son and the "topmost bough of the oak" loosens itself and falls, Hawthorne is surely too literal, too explicit. He has forsaken the tragic implications of his tale and introduced a lesser reality that modifies and attenuates the effect of tragic truth. By externalizing the inward guilt of his declining hero, he loses aesthetic control of his material.

The technique of "My Kinsman, Major Molineux" permits Hawthorne to make a more overt criticism of idealism. Whereas the dramatic movement in "Roger Malvin's Burial" is almost completely in the deteriorating mind of the hero, the conflict of "My Kinsman, Major Molineux" takes place in the public world. Reality, which for Hawthorne so often means the discovery of evil, prevents the boy from escaping his limitations or those of his kinsman. Robin never emerges as more than a "country representative" or a "vagabond," mocked by those figures of social authority whose cynicism and corruption make any attempt at self-realization impossible and ludicrous. Indeed his own desire to rise materially, his reliance on his kinsman, his susceptibility to evil, disqualify him at the outset: he has no real understanding of idealism and authority, not even in the primitive sense of self-reliance coming to terms with brutal social conditions, and as a consequence he cannot be heroic. Robin's kinsman, who is also his hero, is finally absurd in his humiliation, thus forcing the boy to recognize his own quest as absurd. When Robin joins the laughter of those people who have scorned him and his kinsman, he is of course laughing at his own naïve moral assumptions and recognizing the evil which exists in the universe; but he is also confessing the severe limitations of heroic behavior in his actual world. So intense a lesson learned at so formative an age gives the tale its special pathos. There are pity and terror in the souls of Robin and his kinsman as they stare at each other, and there is the suggestion of purgation in the culminating laughter; but there is no moral triumph, no final understanding. There is only the sense of Robin's defeat and involvement in evil. He walks away a wiser boy, but we never know the nature of his wisdom—we can infer it, but we do not know the quality of his perception from what is told to us in the story—and thus we think of him as ordinary, as unheroic, as someone who has been shattered by a confrontation with evil but who has yet to comprehend the meaning of that confrontation. Robin's purpose is clear—his passion rises so intensely that it demands tragic realization; but there is no deep perception of his tragedy, and as a consequence the boy does not assume heroic proportions. He remains a figure in a tragic situation rather than a hero in a tragedy.

In "Young Goodman Brown" the presence of evil is equally impressive, attended as it is by the uncanny laughter of the forest and its satanic inhabitants. Hawthorne penetrates into the essence of evil, into that "blackness, ten times black" that Melville so admired; but, as in "My Kinsman, Major Molineux," he withholds from Goodman Brown the vision that we demand of genuine tragedy—and justly so, for his central figure is after all an ordinary man. Brown becomes a "stern, a sad, a darkly meditative, a distrustful" person who is unwilling and indeed unable, because of his common nature, to accept evil as a part of human experience; he fails to attain the understanding of the ennobled tragic hero and becomes a recognizable nineteenth- and twentieth-century man, a man incapable of traditional heroism.

There is this constant sense of only partial self-understanding in the fallen figures of Hawthorne's fiction—herein lies the human limitation that makes them appear particularly modern.* Wakefield,

---

* I say "appear" because in some final sense Hawthorne's fiction is palpably different from that of modern authors—and I do not mean in terms of style or form or technique. One can easily imagine the figures of Robin Molineux, Goodman Brown, and the Reverend

for example, possesses a crafty smile of a rather elementary kind: he has not even seen the evil that Robin Molineux and Goodman Brown acknowledge. He senses the absurdity of the world but only begins to sense the absurdity and inhumanity of his own actions. The Reverend Hooper, in "The Minister's Black Veil," smiles at his congregation because they do not understand the meaning of the veil; in their vulgar voyeurism they yearn to see under the veil, but they cannot comprehend its symbolic significance. No one—not even the Reverend's fiancée—asks him the meaning of the black veil, and Hooper dies with the knowledge that the people have only a partial glimpse into the reality of their lives; the people are absurd and limited, but Hooper, in his self-imposed isolation and ultimate madness, is absurd too. These tales, suggestive of Hawthorne's thematic approach throughout his fiction, inevitably interpose a symbolic device or humor or paradox or the reality of the social world itself between Hawthorne and the tragic conception he is developing. His description of the mother in "The Snow-Image" defines his attitude: "all through life she had kept her heart full of childlike simplicity and faith, which was pure and clear as crystal. And looking at all matters through this transparent medium, she sometimes saw truths so profound that other people laughed at them as nonsense and absurdity." Her husband, "with a most benevolent smile on his sagacious visage," represents the social, sensible reality that prevents her from articulating the truths she sees; he evokes Hawthorne's admiration, but it is clear that his "healthy" skepticism permits him to apprehend reality in only a partial manner—certain truths are beyond his capacity.

Hester Prynne has only a limited vision, also. Of all Hawthorne's important work, *The Scarlet Letter* would seem to satisfy the requirements of a romantic narrative in which heroism triumphs; for surely Hester converts the community from hatred to respect, from hostility to acceptance. But her conversion manifests

---

Hooper in modern dress, but there is a tragic finality to their lives that one does not find in modern fiction. Idealism is crushed in a way it never is in the work of Salinger, Bellow, Mailer, and other writers. Hawthorne's themes of isolation, manipulation, sin, and guilt are taken up by these authors; they too are fond of paradox, ambiguity, and irony. But they see the hero as someone who is unwilling to succumb to authority of any kind. One of the incidental paradoxes of our day is that in a world of greater authority, our writers are increasingly idealistic.

itself only in physical terms—indeed she succeeds primarily because, unlike Dimmesdale, she never attempts to explore or understand completely the nature of her sin. She thinks in concrete terms: her daughter's safety, her lover's health, her own practical future in this life. In the process of defying the community she has become a feminist and incurred an inevitable moral disintegration. Her attempt to escape her expiation, as Leslie Fiedler notes, gives her a moral weakness her lover never has. She does not share Dimmesdale's tragic vision—the scene in the forest indicates her limitations, her inability to understand completely the nature of her expiation. Only in a direct, physical, and superficially successful way does she triumph over the community.

The Scarlet Letter is an explicit statement of the limitations of heroism in an age when the popular American novel was dedicated to the romantic possibilities of the gentleman and his lady as they confronted some obvious villainy. Dimmesdale, who is the true "hero" of the novel, acts heroically twice in the book—when he refuses to leave with Hester and when publicly he confesses his sin; at all other times he is presented in terms of his fallability and frailty, a man of doubt and guilt, of hesitation and fear, a man so essentially weak that we, as modern readers, are compelled to believe in his humanity and reality. Crippled by his own sensitivity, he perceives his sin but cannot act upon it; he has tragic vision but not the necessary heroism. Not until his long-delayed confession, in which he needs the physical aid of Hester Prynne, does he assume extraordinary proportions; but he is already a dying man, and our memory of him is as a man with his hand on his heart, not as a transcendent, triumphant figure delivering an Election-day oration. In criticizing the moral rigidity of the community, which demands heroic behavior of its ministers, and in ironically contrasting Dimmesdale's deterioration with the growing admiration of the community for the minister, Hawthorne explores a range of psychological behavior that American novelists of his time were hardly willing to acknowledge.

It is through the figure of Dimmesdale that Hawthorne explores the delicate balance between idealism and authority. The reader of *The Scarlet Letter* is first struck by obvious contrasts: the idealism of Hester Prynne and the rigid authority of the community, the idealism of Dimmesdale and the predatory power of Chillingworth. The entire book functions in terms of social and moral correspondences. But as the revelations of character unfold, the most penetrating is Dimmesdale's unwillingness to modify his idealism before the authority of the community he serves. By having slept with Hester Prynne, Dimmesdale admitted implicitly the vulnerability of his ideals; by refusing to confess his weakness, he perverts idealism until it mocks the body that has yielded to its own humanity. The rigidity of Dimmesdale's idealism becomes its own authority and destroys the man. By not confronting the social authority of the community with his own tempered idealism, Dimmesdale has distorted the true nature of his ideals and destroyed himself. In the terms which W. H. Auden uses in *The Enchafèd Flood,* Dimmesdale is an ethical hero, "the one who at any given moment happens to know more than the others." Dimmesdale, in "desiring aesthetic admiration, is tempted to refuse to surrender his superiority and refuse to share his knowledge, treating it instead as a hermetic mystery, the consequences of which is that, thinking always of his relation to the ignorant, he ceases to think about the truth." Therein lies his tragedy; therein lies the vulnerability of his idealism before the social authority he fears. The power of his public revelation stems directly from the intensity of this fear, and his perception, as the last element of his tragedy, is worthy of the passion he has locked within himself.

The Scarlet Letter is a cogent drama of the limitations of heroism. In this sense the moral of the tale takes on particular significance and reminds us of how skeptical Hawthorne was: "Be true! Be true!" the author tells the reader. "Show freely to the world, if not your worst, yet some trait whereby the worst may be inferred!" This is the advice of a man who deeply distrusts the heroic ideal, who hedges even as he asks the reader to act with self-reliance. The commitment of the Emersonian hero to the ideal is filled with little ambiguity, however much it alters in its emphases; the vision of evil that Ahab has is blinding in its directness. Hawthorne prefers inference—inference determines his special strengths and weaknesses. Lionel Trilling is correct in suggesting that Hawthorne's vision is not truly tragic; but that very limitation gives Hawthorne's best work a distinctive power. The glimpse into evil has a force that may not be as cathartic as that of the tragic authors, but it casts its own peculiar magic. Hawthorne cuts across our emotional desire for an apocalyptic vision; he prevents us from entering the eye of the storm, keeping us off-center, as we are in life. One rarely completes a Hawthorne story with complete aesthetic satisfaction—there is too much realism in the author to surrender all he knows and feels to the purposes of formal tragedy.

Hawthorne felt that *The Scarlet Letter* suffered from excessive and unrelieved gloom and that *The House of the Seven Gables* was "more characteristic of my mind, and more proper and natural for me to write." This judgment is sound, for the potential morbidity or "gloom" of the latter work is controlled and mitigated by its constant recognition of the absurdity in human behavior. The figures of *The House of the Seven Gables* first appear as awkward, misplaced people who can scarcely function in the realistic world. Hawthorne confronts us with absurd metamorphoses: the patrician lady transformed into the plebeian woman; the gray-haired man reduced to childlike behavior; the villain grown inhuman with inherited pomposity; the innocent country girl dedicated to reforming two old people who are clearly beyond redemption. Holgrave is a boy whose externals change too rapidly for us to believe in his future— he is the only vital human being in the novel, but he is too often absurd to bear its thematic burden or to be considered a hero. The entire novel is a movement away from the pompous, the pretentious, the heroic: "if we look through all the heroic fortunes of mankind," Hawthorne warns us early in the narrative, "we shall find this same entanglement of something mean and trivial with whatever is noblest in joy or sorrow. Life is made up of marble and mud."

There is very little marble in *The House of the Seven Gables,* but the mud is constantly before those who wish to escape it. In the parable of the Italian organ grinder and his avaricious monkey, Hawthorne points the moral of his tale. The figurines that surround the organ grinder represent every variety of occupation—"the cobbler, the blacksmith, the soldier, the lady with her fan, the toper with his bottle, the milkmaid sitting by her cow,"—and Hawthorne wonders if "some cynic, at once merry and bitter, had desired to signify, in this pantomimic scene, that we mortals, whatever our business or amusement,—however serious, however trifling,—all dance to one identical tune, and, in spite of our ridiculous activity, bring nothing finally to pass. Clifford has taken a "childish delight" in this street show, but when the monkey reveals that he is no more than "the Mammon of copper coin," Clifford is shocked by his horrible ugliness, "spiritual as well as physical," and begins "to shed tears." Hawthorne explains his weakness as one "which men of merely delicate endowments, and destitute of the fiercer, deeper, and more tragic power of laughter, can hardly avoid, when the worst and meanest aspect of life happens to be presented to them." The poetic sensibility, which most of Hawthorne's heroes possess, refuses to and ultimately cannot confront the reality of life—the scene in which both Clifford and Hepzibah seem most queer and yet credible is their flight from the house, their awkward confrontation with the "interior life of the railroad." It is the pathetic frailty, the human inaction, the oppressiveness of the past that distinguishes *The House of the Seven Gables*. We listen to the remarks of Holgrave and Phoebe, but they take the form of speeches and even sermons rather than actual dialogue spoken by actual people; we witness the delicacy of Hepzibah and Clifford—their absurd relationship to the real world—and we are convinced of their decline, of their inability to bring anything "finally to pass."

The work which most clearly and self-consciously demonstrates the limitations of heroism, however, is *The Blithedale Romance*. Its movement is in terms of revelations and meetings, which can permit the conflicting figures to offer their various philosophical and social views; and the author's view, expressed directly by his narrator and obliquely by the other characters, is the great danger of a belief in any absolute principle. The book is Hawthorne's clearest and most overt statement of the absurdity implicit in any obsessive commitment to heroism.

As the narrator, Coverdale imposes an attitude of cynicism on everything he reports. He realizes before he even goes to Blithedale that it is an act of "heroism" for him to leave his "comfortable quarters" in the city "in quest of a better life"; and he quickly reminds the reader that "The greatest obstacle to being heroic is the doubt whether one may not be going to prove one's self a fool; the truest heroism is to resist the doubt: and the profoundest wisdom to know when it ought to be resisted, and when to be obeyed." Coverdale himself has little choice, for he is a victim of his own frailties. He arrives at Blithedale and becomes a patient before he functions as a worker; he admits to being a mediocre poet; he sees himself as a crotchety, aging bachelor, ineffectual in love; he watches passively the adventures of other more active people; and he finally agrees with the negative judgment of outsiders: "Meeting former acquaintances, who showed themselves inclined to ridicule my heroic devotion to the cause of human welfare, I spoke of the recent phase of my life as indeed fair matter for a jest."

Coverdale's awareness of human fallability is not restricted to himself. He sees the ostensible idealists at Blithedale in terms of their peculiarities and limitations so that we are never allowed to forget the juxtapositions of their transcendental theories and their actual mundane existence. Coverdale emphasizes their absurdity: Silas Foster's request that someone "must go to next Brighton fair, and buy a dozen pigs"; Hollingsworth's entrance in "his shaggy great-coat all covered with snow"; Zenobia's cooking—"her gruel was very wretched stuff"; the picture of these Arcadians as "a gang of beggars, or banditti, than either a company of honest laboring men, or a con-clave of philosophers." These idealists appear absurd and awkward and entirely misplaced in nature because, in Coverdale's view, "in-tellectual activity is incompatible with any large amount of bodily exercise. The yeoman and the scholar . . . are two distinct individ-uals, and can never be melted or welded into one substance."

Those sympathetic visitors to Blithedale are equally absurd in their enthusiasm. "It was absolutely funny," Coverdale remarks, "to observe what a glory was shed about our life and labors, in the imagination of these longing proselytes." So unreal does the entire experiment in Utopian living seem to Coverdale that he is ultimately forced to admit its practical failure: "I suddenly found myself pos-sessed by a mood of disbelief in moral beauty or heroism, and a con-viction of the folly of attempting to benefit the world. Our especial scheme of reform, which, from my observatory, I could take in with the bodily eye, looked so ridiculous that it was impossible not to laugh aloud."

Coverdale protects himself from any absolute commitment to the Utopian experiment by always characterizing it in skeptical terms. When he fears that he is "getting quite out of . . . reckoning, with regard to the existing state of the world," he leaves Blithedale for the city. "No sagacious man," he concludes, "will long retain his sagacity, if he live exclusively among reformers and progressive people, without periodically returning into the settled system of things, to correct himself by a new observation from that old stand-point." Coverdale's need for "the actual world" expresses his fear of more obsessive, more intense people. Like so many of the other central figures in Hawthorne's narratives, he must withdraw from the dream—from the "foolish dream"; for we come to realize, as the characters lose their sense of actuality at Blithedale, that we are again involved in a tale of traditional morality, a tale not very different from all those more obvious excursions into the past that Hawthorne has taken. Coverdale looks at the three people who have come to dominate his life and sees "in Hollingsworth all that an artist could desire for the grim portrait of a Puritan magistrate holding inquest of life and death in a case of witchcraft; in Zenobia, the sorceress herself, not aged, wrinkled, and decrepit, but fair enough to tempt Satan with a force reciprocal to his own; and in Priscilla, the pale victim, whose soul and body had been wasted by her spells. . . ."

Hollingsworth is presented as an absurd dreamer. He "must have been originally endowed with a great spirit of benevolence," but we see him only as a man who has wasted "all the warmth of his heart" in his attempt to reform his criminal brethren; we see him as a defeated fanatic, estranged from the world, who no longer is able to love other human beings; we see him, in his fallen condition, as the ultimate perversion of the hero, someone gone mad in a world where his transcendental type of heroism is less than real, less than human—the idealist victimized by his own moral rigidity. He possesses a measure of self-scrutiny in the beginning of the novel as he recognizes that the "most marked trait" in his character is "an inflexible severity of purpose"; but he soon loses the sense of his relationship to the outside world—the authority he challenges fades as the authority of his fanaticism obsesses him—and with it the stature that we demand of a hero. He is a type before he is a character, and though he appears momentarily menacing in his treatment of Zenobia and Priscilla, he too often appears as the caricature of a concept.

And insofar as Hollingsworth forsakes the tragic dignity of the hero, Zenobia foregoes her claim to heroism, too. She is forever the character *in potentia*. "With all her faults," Coverdale suggests, "she possessed noble traits and a heart which must, at least, have been valuable while new." But we see her as a passionate, earthy woman among cerebral transcendentalists, an exotic feminist who has tended to the laundry and made the gruel and, in spite of her heroic possibilities, has submitted to the mad control of Hollingsworth. The pathos of her decline grows out of her inability to make the very distinction she insists the genuine hero—or heroine—must make: "A great man," she tells Coverdale, "attains his normal condition only through the inspiration of one great idea. As a friend of Mr. Hollingsworth, and, at the same time, a calm observer, I must tell you that he seems to me such a man. But you are very pardonable for fancying him ridiculous. Doubtless, he is so—to you! There can be no truer test of the noble and heroic, in any individual, than the degree in which he possesses the faculty of distinguishing heroism from absurdity." Ultimately Zenobia is able to see the absurdity of Hollingsworth and accuse him of considering only the self, of having embodied himself "in a project" to so great an extent that his disguise has become a "self-deception"; but, of course, by this time she is close to her own suicide. She perceives the absurdity of Hollingsworth's heroism and admits her misconception. When she remarks to Coverdale that her own defeat "is a genuine tragedy, is it not?" she follows her comment with a light laugh that indicates her own disbelief—Hollingsworth was never a hero and she, because of her devotion to him, was no genuine heroine; Blithedale itself was more the setting for a comedy—or at best a tragic comedy—than a tragedy. Her later remark—"It was, indeed a foolish dream!"—is more apt and accurate, recalling as it does the comment in the preface to the novel—the episode at Brook Farm, Hawthorne notes, was "essentially a day-dream and yet a fact,"—and the questions that cast doubt upon the reality experienced in other narratives, in especially "Young Goodman Brown" and "My Kinsman, Major Molineux." No tragedy has been possible in these narratives—especially not in *The Blithedale Romance*—because the realities of the world have limited the heroic vision of the central figures. In *The Blithedale Romance* actuality has mocked theory and reduced it to absurd proportions.

"It was too absurd!" Westervelt concludes, in judgment of Zenobia's suicide—"to drown herself for yonder dreamy philanthropist." Westervelt is a repugnant man, the grotesque symbol of authority, of that evil aspect of the western world which seeks to manipulate frailty to its own end. Westervelt represents the perversion of heroism and, as Coverdale tells him, "is Zenobia's fate." He is the fate that broods over the other characters as well—over Priscilla, quite obviously, but over Hollingsworth, too, for Hollingsworth ultimately grows to depend upon Priscilla. Hollingsworth and Westervelt symbolize the moral polarities of the novel—idealism and authority in their crudest forms—and by assigning Westervelt the role of fate, Hawthorne underscores his deep distrust of the ideal hero.

Westervelt judges Zenobia in her death and Hollingsworth in his defeat; and it is the judgment of the self-reliant man, corrupt in his dedication to absolutes. His judgment nevertheless is correct; Zenobia's death is absurd and precisely because she has failed to distinguish between heroism and absurdity.

Heroism is the concept that Hawthorne measures with his scorn and skepticism in *The Blithedale Romance*. He is concerned with transcendental doctrines in general—with friendship and love, self-reliance, prudence, spiritual laws and the other ideas that Emerson considers in his first collection of *Essays* and that appear in *The Dial* and the lectures of contemporaneous thinkers. But the special irony that he achieves is in terms of the heroism of the mind as estimated by the potential and actual absurdity of reality—a recurrent theme in his fiction, whether one considers his casual sketches or the profound works which explore the nature of evil.

"Heroism feels and never reasons, and therefore is always right." Who else, in mid-nineteenth-century America, could be more obviously the author of this proclamation than Emerson? Where else could it seem more incongruous than in an appraisal of the cynical, self-conscious, ever-doubting texture of Hawthorne's work? The passion of heroism—whether it take the form of the Reverend Hooper's self-appointed judgment of his congregation; the ambition of Robin Molineux; the distorted idealism of Arthur Dimmesdale; the aristocratic pretensions of the Pyncheon family; or the absurd idealism of Hollingsworth and Zenobia—is forever the object of Hawthorne's earthy criticism. In an age of transcendental idealism, of Whitmanesque optimism and self-conviction, of a broad belief in democracy on the part of popular writers, Hawthorne is the first serious and artistic critic of the possibilities of heroism. He was persistently aware of man's limitations—those limitations that reduce the hero to human proportions, that make him real rather than the creation of a concept, the projection of a hope or of a dream—and his awareness prevented him from ever creating his characters in truly tragic terms. The ever-present laughter; the cynical observation; the ambiguity; the stubborn, realistic vision; the doubt, and finally the unceasing *respect* for the mysteries of human nature restrained him from exploring those mysteries in any complete and absolute way. We are frustrated by his refusal to commit himself, to say no in thunder, but his recognition of the dangers of self-reliance and heroism now seem like historical prophecy as well as the acute criticism of his age. We return to him, even as we try to escape the finality of his judgment and write a literature of accommodation to authority, a literature in which heroism is not altogether absurd, not necessarily doomed.

We can never embrace the Emersonian hero in all his confidence, largely because of the intervening century but also because the fiction of Hawthorne is somewhere in our minds, conditioning that self-reliant figure, pointing to his potential absurdity, reminding us of life as it is lived, not as it might be lived.

HERMAN
MELVILLE

The
Nature
of
Authority

We can find
many reasons for the attraction of Herman Melville's work in our generation. His use of myth and symbolism, of satire and irony, of fantasy and dream appeals to our imagination; his relentless uncertainty about eschatalogical problems commands our ambiguous and doubting minds; his response to natural and primitive forces, his sympathy for human limitation, his scorn of cant and hypocrisy, his recognition of and attempt to understand the sources of evil in an age when philosophical thinkers shun the problem—all these attitudes, as expressed by a genuinely honest and open intelligence, persuade us that Melville's vision of the world is essentially ours.

But Melville seems relevant in an even more direct, thematic way. At the center of his fiction is his criticism of Emersonian self-reliance, his deep skepticism about the nature of confidence and optimism—and authority. Much of the tension in Melville's work grows out of his fear of power: power controls the significant figures of his novels and stories; power lurks behind the most innocent of his tales when it is not directly manifest; and the number of victims that groan beneath the heavy weight of authority is of course legion. In tracing Melville's changing attitude toward power and authority we witness the development of a prominent concept in his work; and we notice, moreover, a movement of even larger cultural proportions, one that suggests a major direction in American literature itself. We see a nineteenth-century Romantic, whose early ideas are at one with those of his literary predecessors and his contemporaries, become a skeptic whose views anticipate those of twentieth-century writers. Melville's withdrawal into cynicism and disenchantment permits us to measure the surrender of an early nineteenth-century belief in heroism and idealism to an ultimate acceptance—one is tempted to say an ultimate need—of skepticism in our own time, although most contemporary authors seek to transcend the comic negation so evident in a book like *The Confidence Man*. Writing in the middle of the nineteenth century, Melville expressed a growing distrust in power, and the quality of that distrust points toward what surely must be the dominant theme of modern American literature—the nature of authority.

The novels that precede *Moby Dick* seem innocent enough; they share with so much of the literature of the time an impressionism that is their charm as well as their limitation. We accept as natural the Romantic qualities of *Typee* (1846) and *Omoo* (1847), for example—those qualities undoubtedly give the tales their chief significance. The tone is amiable, and Melville has no profound commitment to any single idea; but we sense even in these travel books the brooding power that lies in the hands of authoritarian figures. However generous Mehevi may pretend to be to the narrator of *Typee*, there is no doubt that the white man is a captive to the chieftain's power. Melville may rhapsodize that there are "no foreclosures of mortgages, no protest notes, no debts of honour in Typee"; he may elaborate upon the festivals or the natives' health or the beauty of Fayaway, but it is clear that *Typee* develops in power as the narrator grows to see the situation in terms of his imprisonment. Moreover, the exercise of authority seems motiveless: "For what conceivable purpose did they thus retain me a captive?" the narrator asks; "what could be their object in treating me with such apparent kindness, and did it not cover some treacherous scheme?" The questions are never answered, although the narrator becomes "desperate" once he is convinced of the natives' "determination to retain me a captive." The questions cannot be answered, for Melville never explores the mind of the Typees; but the purposeless captivity, on a rather rudimentary, inchoate level, provides whatever tension is in the novel.

This conflict between the figure of authority, so often characterized as a potential or actual tyrant, and his victim is less focused in *Omoo*, although the missionaries come to represent for Melville dictatorial people who deny the reason, who, in the name of religion, forbid the natives their spiritual freedom. More pertinent to the development of Melville's concern with power and its abuses is *Redburn* (1849), where the nature of authority becomes the overt central theme. As William H. Gilman points out, the book functions in two periods of time, neither of which is clearly divorced from the other. The immediate present traces Redburn's development as an ingratiatingly naïve, expansive, romantic boy; and the retrospective moments suggest that an older man is recounting his youthful adventures. Because the book has the intrinsic, artistic quality of having been written years later—of having been written twice, as it were—the adventures seem unreal, the attitudes often incompatible with the boy who is expressing them.

The present in *Redburn* is full of bouyancy, patriotism, naïveté, optimism, and idealism; the young narrator searches for heroes to worship but finds none; and he experiences disillusionment—but a kind of literary, Romantic disillusionment—as his ideals are shattered by the evil in the world. Evil, however, is in the mind of Redburn; it exists *a priori*, without any real reference to actuality, without any genuine dramatic proof. The scenes in Liverpool, which are the most moving in the book and almost Dostoevskian in their compassionate concern with suffering, seem interpolated by an older, wiser man—one whose moral comment is implicit in his description. But they do not substantially affect the boy Redburn; for all their dramatic effectiveness, they seem artificially placed in the novel. A more obvious example of unrealized evil—an evil that Melville knew existed but somehow could not yet render in persuasively concrete terms—is Jackson, who, as a "tyrant over much better men than himself," is a "dictator" possessing an "evil eye" which Redburn cannot escape. Ultimately Redburn concludes that "the extraordinary dominion of this one miserable Jackson, over twelve or fourteen strong, healthy tars, is a riddle, whose solution must be left to the philosophers." Jackson's tyranny is a riddle because it is only real as it exists in the mind of Redburn. Melville had not yet found the fitting symbol of dominance, but in writing of a boy's emergence into the world, he felt it necessary to confront Redburn with evil, expressed in terms of inexplicable power or authority. He is careful to indicate that though Redburn "hated this Jackson," he also "pitied him"; but his pity is equally abstract, belonging to the retrospective level of the book that is so unreal. Redburn hates and pities and fears Jackson because he needs Jackson's nihilism—without it the essential confrontation between the victim and his tyrant loses its force and its meaning.

The same polarities exist in *White Jacket* (1850), although the idealistic young man who narrates the story sees tyranny in descriptive rather than dramatic terms. Like *Redburn,* this novel grows out of the author's optimistic faith in human nature and his firm belief in the political experiment of America. "True heroism is not in the hand, but in the heart and the head," the narrator remarks at one point, reaffirming our belief that he is thoroughly Emersonian in his conception of idealism and self-reliance. There is no irony in those patriotic passages that describe America as the country elected by God for future greatness, and except for the awkward and rather simplified phraseology—no different in its essential jingoism from that of the popular writers of Melville's own age—the ideas are a curious mixture of Calvinistic predestination and Emersonian idealism:

> God has predestinated, mankind expects, great things from our race; and great things we feel in our souls. The rest of the nations must soon be in our rear. We are the pioneers of the world; the advance-guard, sent on through the wilderness of untried things, to break a new path in the New World that is ours. In our youth is our strength; in our inexperience, our wisdom. At a period when other nations have but lisped, our deep voice is heard afar. Long enough have we been skeptics with regard to ourselves, and doubted whether, indeed, the political Messiah had come. But he has come in *us,* if we would but give utterance to his promptings. And let us always remember that with ourselves, almost for the first time in the history of earth, national selfishness is unbounded philanthropy; for we can not do a good to America but we give alms to the world.

The idealism of this passage will soon yield to skepticism and bitterness. By 1851 Melville's Romantic effusiveness begins to change into a more sober, less simplistic attitude, and by the mid-fifties, in

Israel Potter (1855), *The Piazza Tales* (1856), and *The Confidence-Man* (1857), it finds its expression in confidence men of various kinds; at the same time his idealism—a disintegrating, frustrated idealism—takes the form of mad or lonely or silent figures: Pierre, Hunilla, Benito Cereno, Bartleby, the deaf-mute of *The Confidence-Man,* and finally Billy Budd. But the idealistic point of view controls the writing of *White Jacket* and the novels that precede *Moby-Dick,* even though we can see in *White Jacket* the developing authoritarian figure of the captain.

Like Redburn, the narrator of *White Jacket* is in search of a hero, and he finds himself confronted with two distinct types that represent for Melville, in his early writing, a sort of Manichean vision of authority: Jack Chase fulfills White Jacket's wishes and needs; Captain Claret tyrannizes over this "world in a man of war"—this actual world. Jack Chase—the handsome sailor—grows increasingly unreal as the novel develops, however ideal he may remain in the mind of White Jacket; and Captain Claret assumes greater importance as the boy is forced to confront the reality of his own life.

The distrust of Captain Claret is reinforced by those sections of the novel in which Melville condemns the abuses of the Articles of War and the excessive dominion generally enjoyed by ship Captains. At an early point in the book, White Jacket protests the flogging aboard a man-of-war: "If there are any three things opposed to the genius of the American Constitution, they are these: irresponsibility in a judge, unlimited discretionary authority in an executive, and the union of an irresponsible judge and an unlimited executive in one person." Later in the novel, there is the sense that Captain Claret has become that unlimited executive and that White Jacket, an idealistic victim before the authoritarian figure, has come to accept his reality: the hero Jack Chase has receded before the increasing reality of the tyrannical Captain. "In our own hearts, we mould the whole world's hereafters," Melville observes in one of those sententious passages that function like a gloss upon the dramatic incidents in the novel; "and in our own hearts we fashion our own gods. Each mortal casts his vote for whom he will to rule the worlds; I have a voice that helps to shape eternity; and my volitions stir the orbits of the furthest suns. In two senses, we are precisely what we worship. Ourselves are Fate." Melville surely did not cast his vote for the tyranny of Captain Claret, but he recognized and dreaded his real presence in the world.

Melville's most brilliant expression of the abusive effects of power and manipulation is, of course, *Moby-Dick;* indeed the novel is a series of confrontations between an individual—or a group of individuals—and some authoritative force that threatens to destroy or at least control the human spirit. Father Mapple states the theological terms of the novel when he warns his congregation that Jonah's sin was "in his wilful disobedience of the command of God . . . if we obey God, we must disobey ourselves; and it is in this disobeying ourselves, wherein the hardness of obeying God consists." This large conflict, translated dramatically into the tension between Ahab and Moby Dick, subsumes other conflicts which involve the willful use of power and which lend support to Ahab's personal struggle against unyielding authority.

On the simplest level, Ishmael and the other crew members grow to feel imprisoned and controlled by Ahab's power. From the moment that he is fully described, Ahab is characterized as "the supreme lord and dictator" of the crew; and Ishmael adds, with the awe that stems from his own fear and respect and even admiration of the isolated Captain, that "there was an infinity of firmest fortitude, a determinate, unsurrenderable wilfulness, in the fixed and fearless, forward dedication of [Ahab's] glance." Ahab takes on the extraordinary qualities of the epic hero—"his whole high, broad form, seemed made of solid bronze, and shaped in an alterable mould, like Cellini's cast Perseus; the brand that descends his tawny scorched face and neck" has been incurred—so the Gay-Head Indian superstitiously asserts—"not in the fury of any mortal fray, but in an elemental strife at sea"; and his barbaric "white leg" gives him, in Ishmael's eyes, "an overbearing grimness." These and other characteristics—most notably his morbid, brooding silence—suggest that Ahab possesses a dimension of inhumanity which awes, in its very resistance to habitual behavior and common piety, those sailors who are dominated by him. As Ahab himself confesses, the "lovely light of the world, it lights not me; all loveliness is anguish to me, since I can ne'er enjoy. Gifted with the high perception, I lack the low, enjoying power; damned, most subtly and most malignantly! damned in the midst of Paradise! . . . I'm demoniac, I am madness maddened!" At this early point in the novel, Ahab is aware—of his own human limitations and of his potential power, his capacity to manipulate the crew members, all of whom have sworn "Death to Moby Dick" and have lifted their "long, barbed steel goblets" in communal vengeance. " 'Twas not so hard a task," Ahab remarks to himself. "I thought to find one stubborn, at the least; but my cogged circle fits into all their various wheels, and they revolve. Or, if you will, like so many ant-hills of powder, they all stand before me; and I their match." The manipulation of the crew is underscored when a reluctant Starbuck admits that he has surrendered his will, that his "soul is more than matched; she's over-manned; and by a madman!" Melville returns to these relationships throughout the book—they form a rather sardonic commentary on the corrupt will of the sailors —until finally, on the third day of the chase, Ahab is able to tell his dominated crew: "Ye are not other men, but my arms and my legs: and so obey me."

Ahab's unrelenting control of his crew is the abuse of power on the human level; but as Ahab grows increasingly demonic he too is dominated by forces over which he has no control—and, because of those epic, preternatural qualities that have made him apparently invulnerable, his own eventual submission to domination is especially uncanny. Only necromantic or inhuman forces like Fedallah and Moby Dick possess the necessary attributes to challenge Ahab and assert themselves over him. "Certain it is," Melville warns us, "that while the subordinate phantoms soon found their place among the crew, . . . yet that hair-turbaned Fedallah remained a muffled mystery to the last. Where he came in a mannerly world like this, by what sort of unaccountable tie he soon evinced himself to be linked with Ahab's peculiar fortunes; nay, so far as to have some sort of a half-hinted influence; Heaven knows, but it might have been even authority over him; all this none knew, but one cannot sustain an indifferent air concerning Fedallah."

The pagan domination of Ahab—a domination that is a perversion of the human relationship and a corruption of human values— assumes significant proportions as the Pequod approaches Moby Dick. The Parsee is awake at the same time as Ahab, indeed he observes Ahab as he rises from his sleep; his morbid glance seems permanently fixed upon the captain. In secret communion, he assures Ahab that "though it come to the last, I shall still go before thee my pilot." And Ahab accepts his subordinate position: "Well, then, did I believe all ye say, oh my pilot!" In the sections preceding the chase, Melville emphasizes Fedallah's control over Ahab so that we are especially alert to the hero's rejection of human reason and human compassion: "But did you deeply scan him [Ahab] in his more secret confidential hours; when he thought no glance but one was on him; then you would have seen that even as Ahab's eyes so awed the crew's, the inscrutable Parsee's glance awed his; or somehow, at least, in some wild way, at times affected it . . . his wan but wondrous eyes did plainly say—We two watchmen never rest."

Fedallah's success in luring Ahab away from humanity is unmistakable in the last sections of the novel; and when he dies, "lashed round and round to the fish's back . . . his distended eyes [are]turned full upon Ahab." Melville attempts to assert Ahab's freedom, *his* authoritative force—"Ahab seemed [to his subordinates] an independent lord, the Parsee but his slave"—for the hero of the novel cannot be truly tragic unless he appears to be truly free; yet the repeated allusions to Fedallah have suggested too firm a control over Ahab for us to believe in the captain's independence.

Ahab possesses extraordinary energy and Fedallah undefined, supernatural power; but both of them, as well as the crew, are in turn dominated by an authority they do not fully understand. It is precisely this partial knowledge of Moby Dick that gives him his awful power, for the whale is filled with the awe of a religious being—and not only because of his huge presence in the sea or his capacity to destroy or even his indifference. Moby Dick's dignity and beauty and power stem from man's inability to comprehend his total being. The persistent, methodical, quasi-scientific inquiry into the anatomy of the whale only emphasizes his ultimate elusiveness. Chapters that deal with "The Monstrous Pictures of Whales" or "Of Whales in Paint; in Wood; in Sheet and Iron; in Stone; in Mountains, in Stars" reinforce his aloof independence—it is Moby Dick who seems to be "the independent lord" and Ahab "his slave." The whale is never understood. He becomes whatever each human being believes him to be, a partial refraction of the individual's need for evil or lust or piety or avarice; he is felt—not known or comprehended—as an inscrutable power; and Ahab speaks for all the crew when he confesses on the third day of the chase that "Ahab never thinks; he only feels, feels, feels; that's tingling enough for mortal man! To think's audacity. God only has that right and privilege." It is difficult to discover another major novel in American literature that depends so little on the mind, that creates its tensions almost entirely in terms of the will. No one thinks in *Moby-Dick,* and yet the novel is meaningless unless considered intellectually; it is a profound book about the destruction of the mind by the overreaching self-reliance of the will. Heroism finds itself crucified on the flank of the whale; and the will of the sailors—potentially corrupt at the outset—dies because of their submission to the vitiated will of their leader.

Moby Dick is dominated too, not by human but by natural authority—by the sea, by the wind. Melville warns us that "man has lost that sense of the full awfulness of the sea which aboriginally belongs to it." He underscores its absolute and final power: "not only is the sea such a foe to man who is an alien to it, but it is also a fiend to its own off-spring; worse than the Persian host who murdered his own guests; sparing not the creature which itself hath spawned. Like a savage tigress that tossing in the jungle overlays her own cubs, so the sea dashes even the mightiest whales against the rocks, and leaves them there side by side with the split wrecks of ships. No mercy, no power but its own controls it. Panting and snorting like a mad battle steed that has lost its rider, the masterless ocean overruns the globe."

It is particularly significant that Melville should characterize the sea—not man, not Ahab, not even Moby Dick—as the uncontrollable authority of the globe; it expresses his deep understanding of the ultimate power of natural forces and of their potential destructiveness. At the end of the novel Ahab confesses his subservience to another natural force—the wind—just before his last encounter with Moby Dick. "Were I the wind," Ahab reflects, "I'd blow no more on such a wicked, miserable world. I'd crawl somewhere to a cave, and slink there. And yet, 'tis a noble and heroic thing, the wind! Whoever conquered it? In every fight it has the last and bitterest blow. . . . Would not the wind but had a body; but all things that most exasperate and outrage mortal man, all these things are bodiless, but only bodiless as objects, not as agents. There's a most special, a most cunning, oh, a most malicious difference!" In nature lies the ultimate authority, the ultimate power, and though Melville is aware that the sea and the wind can be benevolent as well as cruel, he respects their force because they are capable of destruction and because they are dangerous insofar as they are "agents" and not "objects"; they are more than mortal and thus inaccessible intellectually, although they lure us on precisely because of their inaccessibility. In a key passage at the conclusion of the chapter entitled "Brit," Melville makes his meaning clear: "Consider the subtleness of the sea; how its most dreaded creatures glide under water, unapparent for the most part . . . Consider also the devilish brilliance and beauty of its remorseless tribes . . . Consider once more, the universal cannibalism of the sea; all whose creatures prey upon each other, carrying on eternal war since the world began. . . . Consider all this; and then return to this green, gentle, and most docile earth; consider them both, the sea and the land; and do you not find a strange analogy to something in yourself? For as this appalling ocean surrounds the verdant land, so in the soul of man there lies one insular Tahiti, full of peace and joy, but encompassed by all the horrors of the half known life. God keep thee! Push not off from that isle, thou canst never return!"

These remarks are not only a direct commentary on the choice that Ahab makes; they are Melville's personal prophecy, too, for his next novel—one is tempted to say his subsequent body of fiction—could have been subtitled "the horrors of the half known life" as well as "the ambiguities." Melville had deep respect for the man who was willing to "dive," but there are no epic heroes of Ahab's dimensions in the later fictions, and the work of the 1850's is marked by a series of victims who are "encompassed by all the horrors of the half known life," who are embittered or isolated or maddened or crippled —almost always they are crippled—by a ruthless force that attempts to stifle the human spirit. In *Pierre* the hero becomes a victim and deteriorates into madness and a paralysis of the will because of parents who have provided no stability or even sanity. In "The Encantadas" the Chola woman loses her husband and brother because of the cruelty of nature—the very absence of any reason renders her especially pathetic; Oberlus, the figure in Sketch Ninth of "The Encantadas," is also deserted; and the "runaways, castaways, solitaries" are seen as people who have had a "sullen hatred of the tyrannic ship." Throughout the fiction after *Moby-Dick*, Melville writes of afflicted people who no longer are able to challenge authority—forgotten people, lost people—or victims who have become tyrants in one gesture of rebellious madness. In his most successful stories of this period—"Benito Cereno" and "Bartleby, the Scrivener" —Melville traces the attenuation of the will, the breakdown of a sensibility before some adamant form of authority.

"Benito Cereno" develops the theme of misused power in a stark, elemental manner. Captain Delano's innocence is born of his inability to perceive evil or corruption; he seems excessively naïve, but in this respect he is genuinely American, and his attitude toward master and slave on the San Dominick is the American attitude toward racial relations—he sees no more than exists at the moment, and he refuses to regard the Negro as a human being until the Negro insists upon his humanity. But we as readers see more than Delano, and what we see is the eternal desire of the slave to be master. F. O. Matthiessen criticizes Melville for "raising questions" that are never answered, for failing to consider the fact that the Negroes "were slaves and that evil had thus originally been done to them." But it would seem that the very absence of specific motivation provides the terror that we feel in the story; Babo, Atufal, and their followers have been in the kind of bondage that needs no documentation other than that supplied by our imagination. When Captain Delano asks Benito Cereno "what has cast such a shadow upon" him and the Spanish Captain answers, "the negro," Melville is commenting upon the intrinsic guilt and hatred and fear that the master—the white man in the western world—must have vis-à-vis his slave. From the American point of view, we need not pursue W. J. Cash's thesis of the guilt that has developed in the Southern mind as a result of slavocracy; nor need we elaborate upon the defensive attitude so pervasive among Southern authors like Thomas Nelson Page and Joel Chandler Harris in the nineteenth century; nor, to consider momentarily an opposing attitude, do we have to catalogue the explosive bitterness of current Negro writers—more than a century after Melville's story—who have achieved a dominance in their art if not in their lives, who can utter banalities—often irresponsible banalities—in the name of liberalism. It is obvious that Melville's story is not only a penetrating paradox of the psychological manifestations of authority—the master as slave, the servant briefly triumphant while a dull, white American watches; "Benito Cereno" is also an acute commentary on the potential terror of the racial problem in the West, a terror that when it explodes resembles the transitory domination of Babo and his followers. Babo's favorite word is "master" and the words used by Delano to describe the Negro are "fidelity" and "trust." The paradoxical nature of these words provides the essential irony of the tale, although there is little irony when we consider how Babo has succeeded in destroying Benito Cereno's will, his capacity or desire to live. Victimization in "Benito Cereno" has the profound power that attends the triumph of primitive passion over civilized vulnerability. But the most disturbing aspect of the story is the insensitivity of Delano, for he seems to remind us of our own complacency, our own indifference to misused power until that power becomes an irrevocable fact that affects our private lives.

"Bartleby the Scrivener" is equally concerned with the attenuation of the will, and in terms that are more familiar because they are more confessional, more introspective, even more embarrassing. Most interpretations of this story tend to concentrate on the figure of Bartleby, on his growing madness, isolation, and forlornness; these approaches are fruitful, but often they neglect the significance of the employer himself. Melville is not so concerned with Bartleby as he is with Bartleby's effect on the employer; and in dramatizing the deterioration of the boy, he also defines the atrophying will of the man. The story is about impotence, and the impotence of a good-natured, amiable, "safe" man: the employer suffers "twinges of impotent rebellion against the mild effrontery of this unaccountable scrivener"; as he admits, it is Bartleby's "wonderful mildness chiefly, which not only disarmed me, but unmanned me as it were. For I consider that one, for the time, is somehow unmanned when he tranquilly permits his hired clerk to dictate to him."

The impotence of the employer is suggested at the outset when he admits that, in effect, he cannot control the people working for him. Turkey prefaces his remarks to the employer in mock-deferential words—"With submission, sir"; but in fact the employer submits to both Turkey and Nippers by catering to their peculiar working habits. When Bartleby refuses to submit to the employer and "prefers" not to work, the employer turns to his other workers and asks their disinterested opinion; but he has already admitted that Turkey and Nippers are psychologically crippled, that they are unable to function completely in the real world. His need of their justification is a confession of his own weakness, his own limited vision. Bartleby senses his weakness, and without great difficulty soon dominates him.

The process of domination provides the chief interest in the story. It begins when the employer assumes responsibility for Bartleby. "If I turn him away," he reasons, "the chances are he will fall in with some less-indulgent employer, and then he will be rudely treated, and perhaps driven forth miserably to starve. Yes. Here I can cheaply purchase a delicious self-approval." Once the employer admits his need for a human relationship with Bartleby—"both I and Bartleby were sons of Adam"—he surrenders his will to this boy who, in his turn, refuses to accept all human contact. Bartleby's forlornness becomes the employer's; Bartleby's victimization to an "incurable disorder" affects the older man—"my contact with the scrivener had already and seriously affected me in a mental way." The employer admits that he is weak and that "the inscrutable scrivener" has gained a "wondrous ascendancy" over him; what worries him most is that this passive boy has denied his authority and undermined his own capacity to function. By the end of the story the mode of domination is clear: Bartleby controls the employer by making him responsible for another human being—and, in this case, a human being who has gone mad.

The employer has been searching to express his own humanity, and the pathos of the last line, "Ah, Bartleby! Ah, humanity!" lies in the fact that he is unsuccessful. He has let Bartleby control him, as Turkey and Nippers did in their own way, in the unconscious hope that he will be brought back to a fuller humanity. But Bartleby demands a "diver"—to use Melville's term—and the employer is merely a "safe man." The older man releases himself from Bartleby by letting him die; only by doing so can he be released, for in life Bartleby controls him.

The breakdown of the will that is at the thematic center of "Benito Cereno" and "Bartleby the Scrivener" reaches its fullest intensity in *The Confidence-Man,* in which the various caricatures are seen almost exclusively as paralyzed victims. This novel, whose informing idea is so promising and provocative but whose formal meaning and structure are finally more suggested than fulfilled, carries Melville's fiction to the extreme point of despair that began with *Pierre,* was successfully articulated in "Benito Cereno" and "Bartleby, the Scrivener," and was anticipated by those other works that are concerned with confidence and its abuses—"The Lightning Rod Man" and *Israel Potter.* Whatever criticisms we may make of *The Confidence-Man* as a novel, we should recognize that it suggests the vision of many twentieth-century American authors in its distrust of idealism, of optimism, of any abstractions like Faith or Hope or Charity. "No Trust," the barber's sign reads, and if we alter the mannerisms and the locale in only superficial ways, we can find ourselves in the modern world, observing the skepticism of the young Hemingway of "In Another Country" and *A Farewell to Arms;* the ironic death of Gatsby's idealism before "the last and greatest of all human dreams"; the disillusionment of Quentin

Compson in *The Sound and the Fury* or Ike McCaslin in *The Bear* as the formal abstractions of a heritage collapse before their inquisitive eyes; or, in more contemporary literature, the pathetic skepticism of Holden Caulfield in *The Catcher in the Rye,* for whom the world is populated by confidence men of various descriptions. Melville's portrait of the Confidence Man, selling optimism as though it were a product, is an acute criticism of nineteenth-century American thought; and in its rejection of abstractions, it anticipates the main direction of serious twentieth-century American literature.

Saul Bellow has recently noted the limitations of the tragic view of history; he criticizes one "of the dominant ideas of the [twentieth] century, accepted by many modern artists—the idea that humankind has reached a terminal point," and goes on to point out that "the termination did not fully terminate. Civilization is still here. The prophecies have not been borne out. Novelists are wrong to put an interpretation of history at the base of artistic creation—to speak 'the last word.'" This reservation is a sane corrective—indeed a necessary one—in our time. In terms of the dominant direction of American literature since 1857, the year in which *The Confidence-Man* was published, there has been a growing disbelief in the validity of abstractions, a disgust with and reaction against the optimism of earlier authors, and a search for some private source of comfort—the phrase suggests fragility because much of the fiction is so delicately stated—in a world where authority seems to rest in the hands of fewer and fewer people. The Emersonian hero appears incredible if not absurd and, as a significant counter-weight, Melville's praise of Hawthorne seems to take on heightened relevance: "There is the grand truth about Nathaniel Hawthorne. He says No! in thunder; but the Devil himself cannot make him say *Yes.* For all men who say *Yes,* lie." For many modern readers, the final scene of *The Confidence-Man,* in which the cosmopolitan, that last avatar of the confidence man, extinguishes the old man's lamp and leads him to his stateroom in the darkness is an appropriate metaphor of the possible consequences of confidence and self-reliance in American culture. But we should not be too quick to assent to Melville's misanthropy—it has not been borne out, as Bellow's argument reminds us, historically.*

* Bellow's own fiction is testament to that fact. Although he often presents Melville's cynical view of human nature in modern dress,

Melville's own work in the last thirty-five years of his life suggests that he was not satisfied with the bitter pessimism—the cynical termination—of *The Confidence-Man;* that novel comments sharply on the grotesque masks that manipulation may take, but it does not represent Melville's final statement on the nature of authority. His poetry—especially *Battle-Pieces* (1866) and *Clarel* (1876)—indicates his continued quest for faith, his desire to say yes without lying; but as a poet Melville suggests more than he states, hopes more than he believes, and it is *Billy Budd,* written thirty-two years after the publication of *The Confidence-Man,* that represents Melville's truly considered coda to the problem of authority in his world.

The absence of choice on the part of Captain Vere is perhaps the most striking characteristic of *Billy Budd.* Although he "is a conscientious disciplinarian," the captain, Melville assures us, is "no lover of authority for mere authority's sake"; and yet he never hesitates in his knowledge that Billy must die for his crime. Vere defends the need for authority, however much he may regret its specific consequences in the case of Billy Budd.

We can measure Melville's attitudes most clearly by considering the scene in which Billy murders Claggart. The only thought that has taken shape "in the young sailor's mind," before he enters the captain's cabin, is that Vere "looks kindly" upon him—Billy Budd has complete confidence in Captain Vere. But in spite of Vere's benevolence, Billy becomes an impotent victim when he is confronted by unaccountable evil. Although Melville has earlier described "the form of Billy Budd" as "heroic," in this critical scene the boy's human limitation controls him—he can neither understand nor overwhelm the authority of evil in the world. Billy's "lurking defect" is intensified "into a convulsed tongue-tie; while the intent head and entire form straining forward in an agony of ineffectual eagerness to obey the injunction to speak and defend himself, [gives] an expression to the face like that of a condemned vestal priestess in

---

Bellow refuses to accept Melville's conclusion—bleakness is not the note struck at the end of his fiction. Nor is it the mood we feel in the most recent work of Salinger, Mailer, Baldwin, and Ellison. As we shall see in a later consideration of these authors, they often say yes—perhaps a more precise description would be that they often murmur yes—and they put their affirmation in a realistic, thoroughly sober context which does not permit us to feel that they lie. One need only contrast the early and the later writing of the contemporary authors I have cited to demonstrate a significant trend away from Melville's misanthropic conclusion to *The Confidence Man.*

the moment of being buried alive, and in the first struggle against suffocation." In his compassion Vere remembers a "bright young schoolmate of his whom he had seen struck by much the same startling impotence," and he treats Billy Budd like a son, but when the young sailor kills Claggart, "the father in" Captain Vere, "manifested toward Billy thus far in the scene, [is] replaced by the military disciplinarian." Law prevails rather than love; the father must sacrifice the son to the absolute authority of the universe; and Vere, whose first words after Billy's blow to Claggart, are "fated boy," never hesitates in his judgment: "Struck dead by the angel of God. Yet the Angel must hang!"

Melville has not sacrificed completely the skepticism of *The Confidence-Man*. In the conclusion of the story, he presents the distorted newspaper version of the murder—Claggart "was vindictively stabbed to the heart by the suddenly drawn sheath-knife of Budd,"—and adds that this item "is all that hitherto has stood in human record to attest what manner of men respectively were John Claggart and Billy Budd." But those sailors who served with Billy and who "instinctively felt that Billy was a sort of man as incapable of mutiny as of wilful murder," preserve the spirit of the "handsome sailor" in the closing ballad; they offer a final judgment that suggests Billy's transcendence.

In *Billy Budd,* spiritual transcendence triumphs over the authority of the secular world. Billy accepts the judgment of Captain Vere, and his last words—"God Bless Captain Vere"—imply that he himself has gone beyond personal judgment; he realizes instinctively that Vere is in his way a victim of legal authority and of his own limitations, his inability to challenge or alter that authority. Captain Vere is compelled to have Billy hanged, but he himself recognizes the young man's spiritual superiority to actuality, and his final words, "Billy Budd, Billy Budd," indicate his belief in the permanence of the human spirit. The facts of *Billy Budd*—the death of innocence, the historical distortion of Billy's actions, the sudden, ostensibly meaningless slaying of Vere by the *Atheiste*—prepare us for a melancholic, bitter conclusion; but the final tone is not depressing, and largely because of the tragic terms in which the story is conveyed. In the deaths of Billy Budd and Captain Vere, Melville expresses his faith in the human spirit, however skeptical he may be about humanity, however muted is his faith.

But when we consider the aspect of Melville's thought that impresses itself upon our imagination, we are compelled to regard Captain Vere as the ideal, not the actual, authoritarian. His dramatic decision, which is a resolution of the inevitable tension between secular and divine authority, represents Melville's own intellectual conclusion—as if Melville had to suppress the lifelong ambiguities that develop from the mind's insistence upon one mode of action and the heart's unwillingness to submit to that insistence, as if he had to freeze his thought in the form of allegory in order to stifle the realistic ambiguities so natural to him.

We praise this testament of faith—we note *Billy Budd's* formal excellence, its justifiably high position in the Melville canon—but we believe the fiction of despair—*Moby Dick,* "Benito Cereno," "Bartleby the Scrivener," and *The Confidence-Man*—even as we are unwilling to accept the finality of that despair. Perhaps this reaction represents our limitations as readers, but perhaps it also suggests the verisimilitude of the works of Melville's mid-career. The disillusionment that pervades the fiction of the 1850's is a convincing reaction against the earlier idealism of the 1840's. *Billy Budd* is prayer; it speaks of the authority that ought to be—and Melville grudgingly assents even to that authority—whereas his earlier work traces his ever-increasing distrust of power and speaks of the authority that actually exists. We remember Melville as a profound critic of misused self-reliance in its various forms—the apocalyptic dominance of Ahab, the quiet tyranny of Bartleby, the naked aggression of Babo, the tyrannous cunning and duplicity of the Confidence Man—and as we become more aware of the dangers of the singular will, of ruthless power and authority, we find the image of ourselves reflected in the mirror of Melville's fiction and seek to escape that image.

4

**WALT
WHITMAN**

*The
Putative
Hero*

The poetry
of Walt Whitman may finally be understood and felt in its original
terms, for it speaks directly to the deepest concerns of the contemporary reader. It reaches across a century of indifferent if not hostile
criticism and expresses the desire of that man who Whitman knew
embodied the genuine reflection of America, that putative hero who
was and still remains America's representative man: the common,
simple man of our democracy. Now that the cultural dominance of
T. S. Eliot, Ezra Pound, and the variety of "new critics" is waning,
Whitman can be seen as the poet who sought to destroy all forms
of authority and assert the heroic ideal. Pound's poem, "A Pact,"
with its condescending tribute to Whitman ("It was you that broke
the new wood;/ Now is a time for carving") seems old-fashioned
and almost precious when compared with Whitman's gregarious
insistence upon equality, freedom and idealism. In his first and most
important phase as poet of the common man, Whitman refused the
role of teacher, although not of guide; the function of leader, but
not of hero; the position of authoritarian for that of an idealist who
encourages the American to realize his uniqueness, diversity, and
human spontaneity. These various roles turn more self-conscious **51**

and arch as Whitman grows older; they harden into the roles of prophet and mentor, leader and guru as Whitman strikes his prolonged pose for history, that carefully created pose of the good gray poet which is too often confused with the genuine poetic performance of *Song of Myself*, "Out of the Cradle Endlessly Rocking," and "When Lilacs Last in the Dooryard Bloom'd." In the first ten-year period of his career, the years from 1855–1865 so charged with hope and then so abruptly clouded over by personal doubt and despair, Whitman touches upon the most profound emotions of today's bewildered American; he is, to use the charismatic word of our generation, the most relevant as well as the greatest of all our poets.

The poet who speaks with the confidence of *Song of Myself* has surely begun "a great career" which, to continue in Emerson's famous words, "must have had a long foreground somewhere." Many critics have sought to discover that foreground, particularly the period from 1848 until 1855, and I do not wish to rehearse their numerous theories. The most direct and influential source of Whitman's early poetry—apart from any sexual self-discovery which still must remain conjectural—is the writing of Emerson himself, as Whitman recognized in a phrase which needs no amplification: "I was simmering, simmering, simmering; Emerson brought me to a boil." Emerson's central concepts of nature, correspondences, and self-reliance are felt everywhere in *Song of Myself*, and they are given a dramatic focus through Whitman's distinctive form and point of view—through, finally and most forcefully, Whitman's formidable personality. In its form Whitman's poem breaks with all tradition—especially with the poetic tradition in American literature; in its point of view—not to speak, for the moment, of the elements within the poem itself—*Song of Myself* is different from Emerson's work. Emerson always seems to stand behind a lectern, descending to meet the people he addresses; Whitman invites us "to walk with" him, and he stops "somewhere waiting for" us. Whenever Whitman resorts to oratory, which is his form of sentimentality, and assumes the Emersonian pose of lecturer or his own pose of bardic singer, he loses the spontaneity of his best verse. And this self-conscious point of view sets in very early in his career—by the time of the third edition of *Leaves of Grass*. But in *Song of Myself*, the various roles of guide, hero, and idealist are emergent and tentative, caught in the music of Whitman's denial of authority and his assertion of heroism. The power of the poetry is instinctive and that instinctive power is offered to and shared with the reader.

The form and point of view of Whitman's first important poem need to be clarified before we can speak of his assimilation of Emerson's ideas or his bold and engaging personification of the heroic ideal. Before Whitman's time, American poets expressed their faith in democracy through the epic form. Their poems, written in the late eighteenth and early nineteenth centuries, are sentimental tributes to the rising Republic in which the new nation becomes the epic hero. Whitman sensed that America needed a radically different poem, and he rejected the forms—and specifically the form of the epic—that were more compatible to other countries and other times. In the preface to the 1855 edition of *Leaves of Grass,* he states that "the expression of the American poet is to be transcendent and new. It is to be indirect and not direct or descriptive or epic. Here the theme is creative and has vista." By adopting a free form that is organic to his subject—"the United States themselves"—and by avoiding the abstract tributes to the new nation that blur the epics of the Revolutionary writers, Whitman is able to achieve a truly indigenous poem, one in which the power of the country is within the individual American himself. The form reflects the diversity upon which Whitman insists in his preface and permits the poet to weave a song in which external authority is almost wholly absent. Here in America, Whitman writes, "is the hospitality which forever indicates heroes." Nothing in this new country forbids the flowering of the ideal hero—nothing but the individual himself; and *Song of Myself* becomes a dialogue between Whitman and his self. From the opening words ("I celebrate myself and sing myself") until the concluding lines ("It is not chaos or death—it is form, union, plan—it is eternal life—it is Happiness"), Whitman seeks to resolve the dissociation of sensibility that he felt was at the center of American life, the conflict that radiated outwards, like the circles of Emerson's essays: the conflict between God and the poet, between nature and the individual.

But *Song of Myself* is more than a dialogue between Whitman and his self; it is an invitation to the reader. This point of view is established, once again, in the first lines ("And what I assume you shall assume/ For every atom belonging to me as good belongs to you"), rises to an overt statement at the end of the second section

("Stop this day with me and you shall possess the origin of all poems,/ . . . You shall listen to all sides and filter them from your self"), and controls our feeling at the end of the poem:

> Who wishes to walk with me?
> . . . Failing to fetch me at first keep encouraged,
> Missing me one place search another,
> I stop somewhere waiting for you.

Still the point of view is more heavily orchestrated. Whitman not only confronts himself and the reader; he observes his country, God, and nature—he widens the circle to include the universe. Through this rhythmic, elastic point of view—enlarging and contracting, contracting only to mirror still larger elements—Whitman adapts Emerson's ideas concerning nature, correspondences, and self-reliance to his own poetic use.

Nature is the setting of *Song of Myself*—the entire poem is in the open air, the entire poem is an answer to the child's question, *What is the grass?* The initial answers have a comic tone ("I guess it must me the flag of my disposition, out of hopeful green stuff woven/ Or I guess it is the handkerchief of the Lord"); soon they assume a more tender aspect in which the grass suggests an innocence that defies death ("Or I guess the grass is itself a child"); and finally, fundamentally, they speak of the grass as both cosmic ("I believe a blade of grass is no less than the journey-work of the stars") and concrete:

> And [I know] that a kelson of the creation is love,
> And limitless are leaves stiff or drooping in the fields,
> And brown ants in the little wells beneath them,
> And mossy scabs of the worm fence, and heap'd stones, elder,
>   mullein and pokeweed.
> . . . I bequeath myself to the dirt to grow from the grass I love,
> If you want me again look for me under your boot-soles.

The variousness and specificity with which Whitman describes nature is greater than one finds in Emerson. The essayist, we remember, concentrates upon sight; Thoreau, his other disciple, is particularly sensitive to sound; Whitman is the poet of touch. This is evident everywhere in *Song of Myself,* as all of Whitman's senses tend to merge and find their definition and greatest feeling in specific human contact; but it rises to a frenzied pitch in the sexual description of sections 28 and 29. In these impassioned verses—which can be heterosexual, homosexual, or in fact autoerotic—Whitman releases all inhibitions, all indirections, and confesses his complete ecstasy:

> Is this then a touch? quivering me to a new identity,
> Flames and ether making a rush for my veins,
> Treacherous tip of me reaching and crowding to help them,
> . . . Blind loving wrestling touch, sheath'd hooded sharp-tooth'd
>   touch!
> Did it make you ache so, leaving me?

Whitman thinks of himself as a poet of all the senses, as he speaks in section 39 of emanations that "descend in new forms from the tips of fingers/ They are wafted with the odor of his body or breath, they fly out of the glance of his eyes." But touch is his most alert sense and it marks one of the chief distinctions between Emerson and himself: Whitman sees nature as a way of revealing the natural condition of man, of making the individual conscious of his physical self. And here, once again, is his great relevance to that modern man who expresses an aspect of his idealism by withstanding the authority of his technocracy and returning to the natural, even primitive roots of his behavior. Whitman can locate his natural self among the leaves of grass, in a landscape fused with the landscape of his soul—he celebrates nature as well as himself, he issues no protest against the denudation of the American scene. It is no accident that Allen Ginsberg, the one contemporary poet who most resembles Whitman—however different in inward intensity and stature the two poets obviously are—, should call his first poem "Howl"; no song of his self, Ginsberg's poem howls against the destruction of the self by mechanized authority. And Ginsberg's later poetry—as well as that of other poets in this oral, bardic tradition—is a desperate, sometimes hysterical, attempt to return to the roots of their being.

Beginning *Song of Myself* "in perfect health," Whitman promises "to speak at every hazard,/ Nature without check with original energy," finding "every organ and attribute" welcome, believing that "Not an inch nor a particle an inch is vile, and none shall be less familiar than the rest." This "turbulent, fleshly, sensual, eating, drinking and breeding" Walt Whitman is never far from us in *Song of Myself,* and though he abjures the epic form as well as other purely literary forms as unsuitable to a democracy, Whitman emerges as the democratic version of an epic hero—an extension and an enlargement of that Emersonian hero whose characteristics are described in the essays of the first and second series. Beginning "in perfect health," Whitman refuses to let the reader be less fragile than himself ("No doubt, not disease shall dare to lay finger upon you,/ I have embraced you, and henceforth possess you to myself"); and he concludes on the same note of heroic confidence:

> If you want me again look for me under your boot-soles,
> You will hardly know who I am or what I mean
> But I shall be good health to you nevertheless
> And filter and fibre your blood.

Thus, in the most intimate way, Whitman links his celebration of nature and the natural man with that other highly significant Emersonian concept—the theory of correspondences. As in the essays of Emerson, correspondences function on many different levels—spiritual, physical, and social—spiraling outwards from the soul of Whitman. The clue is in the affirmative title *Song of Myself,* for this is a poem of Whitman's self, corresponding to Whitman's physical person. It is a poem of the Me (and now, like Whitman, I am using the actual language of Emerson's *Nature*) as correspondent to the Not Me, of the Seal as correspondent to the Print. Whitman establishes these fundamental correspondences in the first four sections of the poem, culminating with his full recognition of "sickness and ill-doing," of "battles, the horrors of fratricidal war, the fever of doubtful news, the fitful events," but claiming that "they are not the Me Myself." From this point, which has established not only a correspondence between Whitman and his soul but correspondences between the poet and the teacher as well as the poet and nature, Whitman becomes more conscious of his social self; from sections 8 through 14 he relates himself to the people and the animals of America, culminating with the democratic confession that "What is commonest, cheapest, nearest, easiest, is Me." The core of the man has come to represent the ideal hero of America—the common man. This correspondence with society rises to its most elaborate expression in sections 15 and 16, in which Whitman celebrates the wonders of America romantically, reminding us that he is "One of the Nation of many nations, the smallest the same and the largest the same" and glorying in his own diversity. That diversity—once again expressed in spiritual, physical, and social terms—determines Whitman's sense of correspondences, and from section 21 until the end of the poem, he states the many variations of the theory of correspondences which he embodies and personifies:

> I am the poet of the Body, I am the poet of the Soul, . . .
> I am the poet of the woman the same as the man, . . .
> I am not the poet of goodness only, I do not decline to be the poet of wickedness also . . .
> I am the man, I suffer'd, I was there.

Whitman's correspondence with society is most succinctly stated in the famous lines which he put at the beginning of *Leaves of Grass* in 1867 ("One's self I sing, a simple separate person,/ Yet utter the word Democratic, the word En-Masse"), but it is, of course, implicit everywhere in *Song of Myself*. He is insisting upon his individuality, indeed his eccentricity (and in this sense, as Richard Chase suggests, the poem is decidedly comic); yet he wants the diverse elements of America bound together—he wants a unity of sensibility. All of the correspondences upon which he elaborates, all of the "miracles" of seeing, hearing, feeling, of "the flesh and the appetites," are brought into the possibility of union at the end of the poem:

> There is that in me—I do not know what it is—but I know it is in me
> . . . I do not know it—it is without name—it is a word unsaid,
> It is not in any dictionary, utterance, symbol,
> . . . Do you see O my brothers and sisters?
> It is not chaos or death—it is form, union, plan—it is eternal life
> —it is happiness.

But these lines are not the conclusion to the poem. The significance of nature and of correspondences is focused finally upon Whitman and the reader—the point of view is reasserted in the clearest sense. At the end of the poem—as at the end of most of Emerson's essays—self-reliance is invoked and the reader is urged to share Whitman's confidence. Earlier he had said, "And nothing, not God, is greater to one than one's self . . . And there is no trade or employment but the young man following it may become a hero." In the last lines Whitman transcends whatever contradictions may have seemed present between himself and Nature, himself and God, himself and the reader he addresses. Through his largeness, he encourages the reader to emulate his confidence. There is a marvelous arrogance in the famous lines—"Do I contradict myself?/ Very well then I contradict myself,/ (I am large, I contain multitudes)"—and in those that follow: "I too am not a bit tamed, I too am untranslatable, I sound my barbaric yawp over the roofs of the world." But in identifying with the grass and in placing himself beneath the reader's "boot-soles," in stopping and waiting for the reader, Whitman rejects the role of teacher for that of a guide who simply points the way. And it is because of this role, this close and compassionate relationship with the reader that we may consider Whitman's early poetry so significant to contemporary America. On the open road awaits the heroic ideal, as large and compelling as the idea of America itself, rooted in the self of this new nation where authority is always suspect, whether in the form of a Calvinistic church or a foreign philosophy or the false supremacy of color or a huge and monstrous machinery that threatens man's self-confidence: so long as authority can be levelled by this idealism there remains the hope that Whitman offers at the end of *Song of Myself.*

Song of Myself—and I would add "Song of the Open Road" and "Crossing Brooklyn Ferry" as other obvious examples—is a song of freedom and openness. Inspired by Emerson, Whitman expressed his belief in the infinitude of the private man: "I know I have the best of time and space, and was never measured and never will be measured." His belief in the common American compelled him to deny all forms of authority except that of the individual himself and this Whitman, who believed deeply in the heroic ideal, is most effectively dramatized in *Song of Myself;* it is this aspect of his multi-faceted personality that spans the century and speaks of an important trait within the American character itself. This Whitman—and there are other Whitmans, there are many Whitmans—is the one who has been raised to the role of patron saint by our contemporary generation. Yet it would be misleading—it would be a distortion of his total achievement—to present Whitman as a poet who sought only to deny authority. "Be radical, be radical, be not too damned radical," he warned Americans; and we ought to remember his words to Horace Traubel whenever we think of this early phase of his career: "I am not afraid of conservatism, not afraid of going too slow, of being held back: rather I often wonder if we are not going ahead too swiftly—whether it's not good to have the radicalities, progress, reforms, restrained. The fact remains that we must hold our horses, that we must not rush aimlessly ahead." Whitman did grow more conservative, as Milton Hindus has suggested, by the time he wrote *Democratic Vistas* (1871) and his later poetry. But his lyrics of the seventies and eighties—even his ambitious poem, *A Passage to India*—do not have the moral urgency or the striking imagery of *Song of Myself*. Behind his first poem lies the implicit authority of the past, those religious strictures and cultural attitudes that imprison the American imagination—Whitman is so bold because his readers have been so timid, and his boldness strengthens the verse itself. Not only is *Song of Myself* more relevant to the American tradition of the heroic ideal and thus to the contemporary American; the poem is intrinsically superior to the later work because it expresses the tension, on the personal as well as the cultural level, that is locked within Whitman and that finds its release in the affirmative burst of language that caused Emerson—and causes the modern reader—to rub his eyes "a little, to see if this sunbeam were no illusion."

There have been many efforts to view Whitman as a developing poet whose nationalistic vision in *Song of Myself* expanded into a more mature consideration of internationalism in *Passage to India* and the later poetry. Scholars have burdened Whitman with a wealth of sources—to read the *Whitman Handbook* is to be bewildered by a forest of influences that do not always clarify the essential poet. That essential Whitman would appear to be an emerging artist in his thirties who has been liberated and given confidence by Emerson and who creates an ideal hero—an Emersonian hero—indistinguishable from the common man. Whitman created his greatest poetry within a ten-year period and its greatness, we should emphasize, does not lie in its specifically American character; as John Kinnaird has pointed out, in an excellent essay, "*Leaves of Grass* and the American Paradox," "we find" in *Song of Myself* "that we are really never in a consciously American world, but always within the purely magical universe of Whitman's 'self' and its strange visitations." Even when he retreated from the assertiveness of *Song of Myself* and composed his most impressive lyrics—

"Out of the Cradle Endlessly Rocking" and "When Lilacs Last in the Dooryard Bloom'd"—he wrote within that same period of time and he wrote within the framework of his private rather than any specifically American experience. Now, however, authority takes the form of death, and idealism finds its personal antagonist in the end of youth or in the death of the hero.

These poems are songs of physical limitation and express Whitman's deepening tragic sense, his more tempered, subdued, and reticent realization of final things. The intense feeling of "Out of the Cradle Endlessly Rocking" springs from the wrenching of the child —who is innocent and idealistic—away from love into a sudden, shocking sense of death and an equally powerful awareness of his poetic calling: death is balanced by the birth and permanent life of art. That turning point comes after the boy has listened to the birds sing to one another:

> Till of a sudden,
> Maybe-kill'd, unknown to her mate,
> One forenoon the she-bird crouch'd not on the nest,
> Nor return'd that afternoon, nor the next,
> Nor ever appear'd again.

From this moment until the end of the poem, the boy is drawn to death—"silent, avoiding the moonbeams, blending [himself] with the shadows," listening to "death's carols," listening to the sea,

> Delaying not, hurrying not
> Whisper'd me through the night, and very plainly before day-
> break,
> Lisp'd to me the low and delicious word death,
> And again death, death, death, death,
> Hissing melodious, neither like the bird nor like my arous'd
> child's heart,
> But edging near as privately for me rustling at my feet,
> Creeping thence steadily up to my ears and laving me softly all
> over,
> Death, death, death, death, death.

But the boy is also drawn to the *song* of death, to himself as a solitary singer who will perpetuate the bird, to his inescapable destiny as a poet. Thus Whitman focuses on that moment when the man recalls both his awareness of death and his vision of himself as being born a poet. The setting of "Out of the Cradle" is of little consequence; the birds, the sea, the sand, the moon, the stars are all creations of the imagination, gestating within the mind of the poet until they lead to the overwhelming realization that the lyric impulse has been born within him. There is no real specificity to the ambience, despite the few names—Paumanok and Alabama—which Whitman uses. The images are literary and their oppositions are yoked within the boy himself: love and death; the land and the sea; day and night; union and separation; the death of the bird and the birth of song within the human being.

Setting is of greater importance in "When Lilacs Last in the Dooryard Bloom'd," especially in the beginning when Whitman evokes the country through which Lincoln's coffin travels; but it is still of secondary importance. The authority of death and its impact on the mind of the poet is the subject of the lyric. Death, which has "cruel hands" and holds the poet "powerless" and "helpless," is a harsh surrounding cloud that will not free [his] soul"; and the poem, although inspired by the personality of Lincoln and given release by the imminence of his passing, is a meditation on death more than a eulogy on the death of a hero:

(Not for you, for one alone,
Blossoms and branches green to coffins all I bring,
For fresh as the morning, thus would I chant a song for you
O sane and sacred death.

All over bouquets of roses,
O death I cover you over with roses and early lilies,
But mostly and now the lilac that blooms the first,
Copious I break, I break the sprigs from the bushes,
With loaded arms I come, pouring for you,
For you and the coffins all of you O death.)

Although Whitman does refer specifically "to the large sweet soul that has gone" and wonders "what shall my perfume be for the grave of him I love," he becomes increasingly concerned with the impact of death upon himself. The first half of the poem, until the end of section 14, is dominated by Whitman's sharp grief, his identification with the hermit thrush who expresses that grief, and his own confused question: "how I shall warble myself for the dead one there I love?" After contemplating this question and the country he loves, in section 14, he concludes that "lo, then and there,/ Falling upon them all and among them all, enveloping me with the rest,/ Appear'd the cloud, appear'd the long black trail,/ And I knew death, its thought, and the sacred knowledge of death." From this point, the poem is a meditation on death, first chanted by the bird and then by Whitman himself.

> Come lovely and soothing death,
> Undulate round the world, serenely arriving, arriving,
> In the day, in the night, to all, to each,
> Sooner or later delicate death.
>
> Prais'd be the fathomless universe,
> For life and joy, and for objects and knowledge curious,
> And for love, sweet love—but praise! praise! praise!
> For the sure-enwinding arms of cool-enfolding death.
>
> . . . Over the tree-tops I float thee a song,
> Over the rising and sinking waves, over the myriad fields and the
>   prairies wide,
> I float this carol with joy, with joy to thee O death.

The hermit bird sings of death and its chant is certainly for Lincoln the fallen hero of America—"For the sweetest, wisest soul of all my days and lands"—but "the call of the bird" is also for "Comrades mine . . . and their memory ever to keep, for the dead I loved so well": Lincoln's death drives the poet to the contemplation and recognition of death in general, it leaves Whitman alone, "There in the fragrant pines and the cedars dusk and dim." "When Lilacs Last in the Dooryard Bloom'd" is thus a meditation on death and, more specifically, a dialogue between the bird who sings of death and Whitman himself. Lincoln has no character in the poem; he is the emotional catalyst, the symbol who has liberated the poet's sense of his own finite feeling and caused him to chant this song of limitation.

Individual poems in the broad Whitman canon have justly been considered individually memorable, and I do not want to leave the impression that I am restricting Whitman's achievement to only three poems. I have simply isolated these poems to emphasize two major aspects of his best work: the assertion of the heroic ideal and its sharp modification by his poetic awareness of death. In addition to *Song of Myself,* "Out of the Cradle Endlessly Rocking," and "When Lilacs Last in the Dooryard Bloom'd," the roster of great lyrics is impressive and would have to be carefully considered by any-one attempting a more comprehensive survey than I offer in this brief essay: "As I Ebb'd With the Ocean of Life," "There Was a Child Went Forth," "Song of the Redwood Tree," "Prayer of Co-lumbus," "Whispers of Heavenly Death," "Chanting the Square Deific," and many others. These poems come at different moments in Whitman's career; but, in general, the great intensity of that ten-year period from 1855–1865 is not so sharply felt in the later poetry, that tension between the heroic ideal of *Song of Myself* and the implied timidity of the common American, that tension between the idealism of "Out of the Cradle" and "Lilacs" and the authority of death. This is the Whitman to whom we return when we seek to find ourselves in his writing, the Whitman who precedes the prophet, the poseur, and the self-conscious poet; for it would appear, as we measure the meaning of Whitman to this generation of Amer-icans, that two of the major strands of contemporary American poetry—the confessional and the idealistic—find their genesis and their ever-returning power in Whitman's early work.

More than any other poet of his time, Whitman is a confes-sional poet. It is true, as Richard Chase has pointed out, that he never really speaks about himself intimately—he never confides in the reader as Robert Lowell does in *Life Studies;* it is also true, as Leslie Fiedler suggests in his perceptive essay, "Images of Walt Whitman," that Whitman was a poet who wore many masks and remained in a fundamental sense anonymous. But he directed the reader inward, away from the sentimentality of his age and toward the romance of the self; and if he could not speak specifically of himself—as Emerson could not concretize many of his most passion-ate ideas—he came closer than his contemporaries, he pointed toward the intimacy of body and mind, he confessed far more than *his* culture ever sanctioned. Whitman's center may be a "pun on the self," as Fielder reminds us, his poetry "a continual shimmering on the surfaces of concealment and revelation that is at once pathetic and comical." But he is neither pathetic nor comic when he states his existential credo in *Song of Myself:*

> Creeds and schools in abeyance; . . .
> I have no chair, no church, no philosophy,

I lead no man to a dinner-table, library, exchange,
But each man and each woman of you I lead upon a knoll,
My left hand hooking you round the waist,
My right hand pointing to landscapes of continents and the
  public road.

Not I, not any one else can travel that road for you,
You must travel it for yourself.
. . . No shutter'd room or school can commune with me,
But roughs and little children better than they.
. . . I bequeath myself to the dirt to grow from the grass I love,
If you want me again look for me under your boot-soles.

This statement as well as others throughout Whitman's early poetry suggests the second and more important connection, at least for our purposes, between Whitman and contemporary poets: the defiance of all forms of authority. One need only compare Whitman's openness with T. S. Eliot's announcement in 1928 that he is "a royalist in politics, a classicist in literature, and an Anglo-Catholic in religion" to realize how close Whitman is to the modern sensibility. Eliot's recourse to authority and tradition seems antiquated when compared with Whitman's openness; it seems more European, more detached from the American experience, more self-conscious and literary. "The Love Song of J. Alfred Prufrock," like *Song of Myself,* is an invitation to the reader to make a journey; Eliot's poem, apart from the obvious differences in tone, expresses the loss of the heroic ideal and concludes on the most despairing note, whereas *Song of Myself* encourages the reader to assert his heroism. "Prufrock" is a poem of impotence, *Song of Myself* a celebration of physical strength. "Prufrock" is terminal, *Song of Myself* invites the reader to the open road. "Prufrock" and other early poems by Eliot share the disenchantment in the heroic ideal that is reflected, as we shall see, in the prose of Hemingway and Fitzgerald; *Song of Myself* has more in common with the mood of American literature after the Second World War, particularly with the literature of the sixties. Whitman, we must remember, was an artist whose criticism grew from within himself—like that of Norman Mailer; Whitman celebrated the senses and spoke for a liberation from all inhibitions—like Allen Ginsberg. What Whitman shares with Mailer, Ginsberg, and the host of contemparary cult heroes is a candor, a romantic spontaneity, and a deep distrust of tradition and authority. His song is of himself, of his strength, his importance, his potential heroism as a single, separate person. As he wrote later in his life, *Leaves of Grass* was his attempt to put a single person of the nineteenth century down on paper. And in *Song of Myself*—more successfully than in any other poem he wrote, more authoritatively than in any other poem in American literature—he affirmed the intrinsic worth of the human being, full of contradictions, yet large and diverse, in love with natural experience and with his fellow man.

Still, an important distinction must be made between Whitman's poetry and that of contemporary writers. When Allen Ginsberg asks, "Where are we going, Walt Whitman?" in "A Supermarket in California," and then goes on to seek guidance, "The doors close in an hour./ Which way does your beard point tonight?" he is of course referring to the prophetic, oracular Whitman of Camden, New Jersey—the good gray poet. This Whitman, as Roy Harvey Pearce and others have noted, is the man who rendered his ideas explicitly and overtly, who stated in his prose works and much of the poetry after 1865 what his ideas were and imposed those ideas on his poetry inorganically. He is not the man who created the great early verses, for that Whitman is a poet whose heroic ideal is always putative, always in the process of realization rather than ever being realized; and because it is putative, it carries a charged tension absent from the later work. The central perception of D. H. Lawrence still holds: Whitman was the first American writer who broke with "The tight mental allegiance given to a morality which the passional self repudiates. . . . He was the first to smash the old moral conception, that the soul of man is something 'superior' and 'above' the flesh." Whitman's utterance, in *Song of Myself*, is instinctive—the body has been released from the prison of its mind. This spontaneous overflow of emotion runs through the entire poem and is in striking contrast to many later, far more self-conscious proclamations and in contrast with the overt statements of a poet like Ginsberg, who celebrates—perhaps advertises is the more appropriate word—his body, his homosexuality, and his autoeroticism more flagrantly than Whitman because a readership sympathizes if it does not always sanction his attitudes. The influence Whitman sought, Ginsberg has won; and this is not essentially a matter of talent, it is a matter of the moment in American history. Ginsberg can be direct because his audience permits directness; and to the extent that he is direct, unafraid or unperplexed, untroubled by his sexuality—to the extent that he invokes the bearded Whitman as his prophet—he is least effective as a poet and has missed the element in Whitman that sparked his most impressive poetry. The implicit tension of *Song of Myself,* of a man bursting through the inhibitions of his society and himself is gone, and with it the power of poetry. Whitman speaks in the present and future tense: "I celebrate myself and sing myself/ And what I assume you *shall* assume"; Ginsberg and others who only howl at the authority of America write in the past tense, in a context of assumptions that have clearly been formulated and have thus become lifeless because they are too available, too obvious—the currency of common protest. Similarly, in the poems on death— "Out of the Cradle Endlessly Rocking" and "When Lilacs Last in the Dooryard Bloom'd"—the sudden awe of death strikes one as genuine because the self-confident poet has been arrested in time, suspended in the midst of a revelation that strikes at the root of his private being and shatters the boldness of his expanding self.

America will never be what it was when Whitman wrote his early poetry—certain poetic possibilities are gone forever, as civilizations and languages and religions vanish from the mind of man. His own experiences in the Civil War and his disenchantment with the rapacious aspect of a growing industrialism tempered his idealism so that his later work contained only sporadic moments of lyric beauty and power. The war that followed Whitman's death only deepened the disillusionment in the writers of the 1920's—doom was the note of their poetry and fiction, and the heroes were the impotent or terrified figures of Hemingway; the wealthy decadents of Fitzgerald; the vacillating, tortured idealists of Faulkner. The dissociation of sensibility was terminal in these writers, and some form of death or suicide concludes most of their finest work. But the contemporary author desperately searches for a unified sensibility among common Americans: a return to the natural and even the primitive; a renewal of diversity and complexity that challenges the monolithic state; a quixotic if not more assertive heroic ideal, a bridging together of the two halves of America, the dream and the reality, the hope and the actual, the promise and all that still remains unfulfilled within Americans.

This search for "form, union, plan" is the great legacy Whitman has bequeathed to us; it is in this quest for the heroic ideal that we find his connection with our own moment in history. At times Whitman the man is confused with Whitman the poet, and he becomes a caricature of the ebullient prophet; but at his finest, he is a man of contradictions who cherishes those contradictions, a man of enormous compassion for the suffering and the maimed who, despite his recognition of death and injury and human limitation, seeks to share with the reader—not as a prophet but as a guide—the quest for idealism. In our fractured America, where idealism and authority tangle desperately, no connection between our lives and the literature of our greatest poet would seem to be more relevant.

HENRY JAMES

The Illusion of Freedom

In the fiction of Henry James the conflict between idealism and authority achieves its most intense and effective dramatic form. The Emersonian hero strides through James's early fiction, convinced that his innocence is his idealism and that freedom is a native blessing. He is a free man—"free," as Emerson wrote, "even to the definition of freedom." But with each new novel that James wrote during the 1880's and 1890's, freedom is more searchingly questioned—a greater distinction is made between innocence and idealism—and by the time we read *The Ambassadors* (1902), we are prepared for Strether's *cri de coeur:* "Still, one has the illusion of freedom; there, don't be like me, without the memory of that illusion. . . . Live!" And we know, as we witness the existential despair of Strether's remark—as we feel an ambivalence in his exhortation which we do not experience in Emerson's work or indeed in James's early writing—that we are listening to the sound of the twentieth century.

The central figures in James's work are romantic heroes out of a nineteenth-century America with which he himself claimed little personal attachment—his not being a New Englander was, as he said, "a danger after all escaped"—but without which one important aspect of his work would be inconceivable. James's important characters possess all the necessary qualities for heroism. They are attractive, courageous, active, social, and likeable, and above all they are willing to make the greatest private sacrifices for an ideal which they pursue with intensity. But inextricably bound to their idealism is their innocence. James presents his self-willed heroes in terms of the present and the future; the past, which is usually American, is scarcely defined, but it is a burden of innocence that his heroes never wholly escape. The complex fate of being American is, after all, the innocence of being American. It can take the form of Christopher Newman's "good nature," of Isabel Archer's distorted vision, of Strether's initial parochialism. Whatever its form and however little it is dramatically defined, it conditions the hero as he encounters the authority which challenges his idealism: American innocence is, in a fundamental sense, the "comic flaw" of Henry James's heroes.

The conflict between idealism and authority can be seen most clearly by measuring its dramatic rendition in certain novels and stories—*The American* (1877), *The Portrait of a Lady* (1881), "The Pupil" (1890), "The Beast in the Jungle" (1900), and *The Ambassadors* (1902)—which come at significant moments in James's career and which view the conflict with progressive complexity. The freedom that Christopher Newman and Isabel Archer assume constitutes their American legacy, their birthright into a Europe that defies their innocent and idealistic behavior. Strether is not free, although he is innocent; his ability to renounce, in middle-age, the forms of authority which have restricted him and kept him innocent enables him to assert his idealism and to achieve his freedom—or, to use his more accurate phrase, the "illusion of freedom." Between *The American* and *The Ambassadors* falls the shadow of an era—Newman's confidence and Strether's ambivalence characterize the American in the nineteenth and twentieth centuries.

In *The American* idealism and authority are personified in the crudest form. It was Madame de Cintré's authority "that especially impressed and fascinated" Christopher Newman; and by authority James means "the sense of an elaborate education, of her having passed through mysterious ceremonies and processes of culture in her youth, of her having been fashioned and made flexible to certain deep social needs." But the basic paradox of *The American* is that cultural authority—this civilizing element of the European woman—is a restrictive force which prevents the European from achieving the kind of ideal that Newman naturally assumes and aggressively demands of life. Rather than liberating the human being and making her "flexible to certain deep social needs," culture in this case has atrophied her will; it has affected the moral nature of her mother and brother, and it has not prepared Madame de Cintré herself for the world. The real world is Christopher Newman—his physical presence, his moral force—and the central characteristic of Newman is his idealism.

Madame de Cintré recognizes Newman's bold idealism, and she cringes before its demands. "Depend upon it. I don't come up to the mark at all; your mark's much too high. I'm not all you suppose; I'm a much smaller affair. She's a magnificent person, the person you imagine. Pray how did she come to such perfection?" And Newman answers simply: "She was never anything *but* perfection." By the end of the novel, Madame de Cintré is not merely engaged and fascinated by her suitor's idealism; she is terrified by it and retreats in a pathetic capitulation to the authority of her family. Newman refuses to adjust his innocent moral vision to the deep need of the Bellegardes for power. His vision is ironic because he is a "commercial person" aware of the open realistic world, but it is nevertheless tenacious and restrictive—his innocence is the comic flaw in his character. When Madame de Bellegarde tells him that "we've used authority" in changing Claire's mind, Newman cannot really understand her. "Ah, you've used authority!" he says. "They've used authority! . . . What in the world is their authority and how do they apply it?"

The American is too simply conceived, too melodramatic in its telling, too polarized in its moral distinctions; but the undeniable power in the book is present despite these faults, and it stems from the irreconcilable confrontation of American idealism and European authority. Newman loses his innocence but not his idealism; indeed idealism has been strengthened by the repressive and essentially moribund demonstration of authority by the Bellegardes. Given Newman's "good nature," his virtue, he could never have exposed the Bellegardes—his idealism had to assert itself; given the will of Madame de Bellegarde—it was the terrible strong will she put into her eyes, we are told, that had killed her husband—she could never have permitted Newman to marry her daughter. Our interest in

Newman's decision is motivated by the deeper conflict between these representatives of two cultures—Newman's complex fate is his inability to understand the nature of Madame de Bellegarde's authority, her success in manipulating her daughter.

The American is an early example of James's tendency to dramatize romantic figures realistically, a thesis which Richard Chase develops cogently in *The American Novel and Its Tradition.* Unlike *The Portrait of a Lady,* in which Isabel Archer's romanticism as a character is qualified by James's realistic presentation as a novelist, *The American* makes little distinction between the point of view of Newman and James. Realistically Madame de Bellegarde would simply have taken Newman's money, whatever elaborate reasons she might have given—on this level the novel lacks verisimilitude. But there is a romantic conflict between Newman and Madame de Bellegarde that commands our primary attention—a naked struggle of the will, a war between American idealism and European authority. The tone of the book is comic, as Constance Rourke and Richard Poirier have demonstrated, and largely because James senses that the neat conflict between idealism and authority can no longer be created in a novel—as opposed to a romance—without the qualification of art. Romanticism now surrenders to realism, although not completely —Newman's idealism is still James's. Both of the opposing characters are a little ludicrous because their dramatic postures are antiquated: Newman as the self-reliant Emersonian hero—that antebellum figure —and Madame de Bellegarde as a kind of Gothic villainess are histrionic figures more compatible with past than with future fiction. James preserves credibility on the realistic level of the novel by smiling at his characters and by making Newman's innocence seem a comic rather than a tragic flaw—his infectious idealism is rendered credible by his comic innocence. Thus the ending of the book is not depressing even though the hero does not win his lady, even though that lady is a victim of the morbid use of authority.

The Portrait of a Lady is also a comic novel, although only if the word comic is used in the broadest sense—as it is, for example, in speaking of Chekhov's plays. The source of comedy, once again, is the distinction made between innocence and idealism, and the roots of this distinction are buried in the American heritage of Isabel Archer. In the beginning of the book, James creates a brief but vivid picture of Isabel Archer as a young American girl. It is an affectionate glimpse of the naïve adolescent before she begins the active pursuit of her ideal, but James is careful to suggest that Isabel's American education and upbringing are responsible for her distorted vision, the fundamental innocence that causes her to make the wrong decisions in her later life: all of her later choices are measured against an innocence that is peculiarly American. Her father, who had an aversion to unhappiness, shielded her from suffering; like James's own father, he had rejected the tragic view of life and had come to feel that unhappiness was a "disease." Although James himself renounced his father's mysticism, his attraction to the transcendental ideas of Emerson and especially Emanuel Swedenborg, he shared the moral premises of idealism upon which the elder Henry James lived; and there is a sympathy for Isabel that stems in part from James's own place in the tradition of idealism. Innocence and idealism are fused together in Isabel's American character, and her special triumph is to renounce her innocence without sacrificing her idealism.

In these early scenes James presents Isabel in a room which is given the title of "the office" and which possesses for the young American girl the "mysterious melancholy" of Romance that protects her from the "strange, unseen place on the other side—a place which [has become] to the child's imagination, according to its different moods, a region of delight or terror." At the moment that Mrs. Touchett first meets her, Isabel is "trudging over the sandy plains of a history of German Thought"—a student of the idealistic philosophy that had such an impact on the American Transcendentalists and upon James's own father. Isabel confesses to Mrs. Touchett that she knows nothing "about money"—which is to say she knows nothing about reality—and that she has a "great desire for knowledge." She also admits to having "too many theories" about reality and we soon learn that there is a great and dangerous disparity between her romantic concepts and the actuality of her life. As the novel develops, Isabel withdraws from experience—she sees rather than feels, as Ralph Touchett tells her—and is as theoretical about life as the exigencies of her life will permit her to be. When Lord Warburton, in his turn, says that he "never saw a person judge things on such theoretic grounds," he too touches upon a central tendency in her character.

Isabel is always the heroine—beautiful, young, audacious, extroverted, cold yet impulsive and courageous—but she pursues an ideal that, in a fashion never completely articulated, she really hopes will not be realized. The exchange with Mrs. Touchett, early in the book, warns us of Isabel's fundamental fear of reaching any decision in her life:

> ". . . . You're too fond of your own ways."
> "Yes, I think I'm very fond of them. But I always want to know the things one shouldn't do."
> "So as to do them?" asked her aunt.
> "So as to choose," said Isabel.

Although it may seem that Isabel wishes to act perversely throughout the novel, to contradict the next logical step and to defy all forms of authority, this is not the case; she really wants to choose not to act. The very act of choice, in scene after scene, is the act of no decision: her every choice involves ultimately no choice. The one decision she does make—her marriage to Gilbert Osmond— is profoundly mistaken because she has not made any previous decision: her perception is distorted by inexperience, by the self-willed perpetuation of her innocence. Isabel is a mid-nineteenth-century girl who has been privately affected by the idealism of western thinkers and particularly by the innocence of her American childhood and thus can be duped into the acceptance of evil. She does not see because she has not felt; she has not trained herself to know and thus to resist the temptations of Mme Merle and Osmond. In a dramatic sense, James's book is a portrait of a lady but not of a woman; the marriage of Isabel to Osmond is possible because of Isabel's romantic idealism, her vulnerable innocence, her unwillingness to see life from any other vantage point than the ideal which, until she perceives the horror of her marriage, is confused in her mind with innocence. She victimizes herself more than becomes the victim of Mme Merle and Osmond, and if she is manipulated by any force in the novel, it is the force of an idealistic tradition that, as Richard Chase points out in his analysis of the novel, distorts her vision: "Isabel subscribes to the American romance of the self. She believes that the self finds fulfillment either in its own isolated integrity or on a more or less transcendent ground where the contending forces of good and evil are symbolized abstractions . . . In Isabel's unhappy career we estimate the tragic implications of an idealism that in effect directs one to seek the rewards of the fully 'lived life' without descending from one's high pedestal into its actual conditions."

That idealistic tradition to which Isabel allies herself is never clearly defined because it is not clear in Isabel's own mind; as James suggests, "Her thoughts were a tangle of vague outlines which had never been corrected by the judgment of people speaking with authority." But it is no less powerful for being vague, and from one point of view *The Portrait of a Lady* is a dramatic criticism of the idealism—insofar as idealism is debased into innocence—which Isabel inherits from her Puritan past and the Western thinkers she has read. Like Hawthorne and Melville—although obviously in a very different style—James is measuring the preconceptions of the mind against the realities of the flesh, he is pointing to the empirical dangers of an Emersonian idealism that is dangerously simplified. But he is by no means wholly critical. The most attractive features of Isabel Archer stem from her idealism and the most unattractive qualities of Osmond are bound to his perversion of the idealistic spirit, his belief in authority. James gives Isabel all the Emersonian virtues—self-reliance, heroism, aesthetic sensitivity—but he sends her into the real world, which in this case is the world of Europe, and illustrates both the limitations of American innocence when it confronts an unsympathetic antagonist like Gilbert Osmond and the triumph of Emersonian idealism when it is asserted in the full knowledge of evil.

The portrait that James draws is one in which the lady is poised between two worlds, one dying and the other born but not fully matured. The deliquescent American tradition of idealism—the past —is represented most sympathetically by the Touchetts, both of whom are moribund, and in its crudest form by Mme Merle and Osmond; their idealism has turned into the most rigid form of authority. In both cases idealism bears a morbid aspect: frailty and death or, in the case of Osmond, the lack of genuine passion. Contrasted with this dying idealism is the aggressive, commercial, gregarious, and powerful American reality—the future, the twentieth century—as typified by Henrietta Stackpole and Caspar Goodwood. Ralph Touchett advises Isabel, after she has compared Henrietta's aggressiveness to "the great country [of America] stretching away beyond the rivers and across the prairies, blooming and smiling and spreading till it stops at the green Pacific!" to distinguish herself from her American friend. "I'm not so sure the Pacific's so green as that," he tells her; "but you're a young woman of imagination.

Henrietta however, does smell of the Future—it almost knocks one down!"

Ultimately Isabel succeeds in distinguishing herself from Henrietta and from the other characters in the novel. In spite of her realization that idealism has perished in those Europeanized Americans she meets and in spite of her resistance to the demands of Henrietta Stackpole and especially Caspar Goodwood, she is able to assert a personal idealism that transcends the corruption surrounding her. She remains loyal to her idealistic vision, although the husband to whom she returns scarcely deserves her loyalty. More profoundly she has surrendered her innocence, that peculiar American quality that causes so many heroes in our literature to appear comic, and has emerged an idealistic heroine. James cannot even permit Isabel a dénouement; he must end his book with her idealistic gesture—the imminent clash of her newborn idealism with Osmond's recalcitrant authority can only lead to a bitterness or a disenchantment which we find at the conclusion of fiction by Hemingway and Fitzgerald.

Comparison with Fitzgerald is particularly fruitful at this point, for the twentieth-century writer is clearly in the idealistic tradition of James and yet his resolution of the conflict between idealism and authority is significantly different. The sacrifices of self to a transcendent self-image informs *The Great Gatsby* as deeply as it does *The Portrait of a Lady,* although Gatsby's death is tragic whereas *The Portrait* concludes on a note of acceptance and accommodation. The differences in time explain the shifting tone, point of view, and vision of the two books: Fitzgerald could not treat his hero as seriously as James treats Isabel Archer—a war had intervened and the word idealism could never again be spoken with the same confidence or belief. Gatsby is credible precisely because he is, to a great extent, incredible. Nevertheless both characters have the same idealistic conception of success. As Isabel tells Mme Merle: " 'It's to see some dream of one's youth come true.' "

The difference between Isabel and Gatsby is that she perceives, in the brilliant 42nd chapter of *The Portrait,* the perversion of her own American dream whereas perception in *The Great Gatsby* is reserved for another man who is not the hero. Isabel sees—and now the act of seeing *is* the act of feeling—that her innocence has caused her to confuse Osmond's love of the conventional, "of harmony and order and decency and of all the stately offices of life," with what it really was—a slavish dedication to authority that thinly masks his own egotism and envy. Isabel sees the mistake that she has made, but her insight does not defeat her—she seeks neither escape nor death. She renounces her innocence and asserts a mature and reasoned idealism, accepting whatever evil is in her private world and maintaining a belief in the conceptual—the heroine and the concept of heroism are fused at the end of the book. The lady does not become a woman but returns to become an even more ennobled lady. This fusion of the individual and the concept he embodies is absent from the work of Fitzgerald as well as that of Hemingway, and its absence creates the special tensions in novels like *The Great Gatsby* and *The Sun Also Rises.* Most modern readers never question Gatsby's death, which is very close to melodrama, but they may feel that Isabel's return to Osmond appears incredible—and incredible not because it is simply an obstinate and foolish gesture but because Isabel is acting on an idealistic assumption, presented in the most serious way, that does not square with the facts of her existence. For Isabel—for the romantic figure of the nineteenth-century world—the concept of idealism lost none of its power because of the mean authority of her husband; for the twentieth-century reader the concept is dead—and the character who attempts to realize it must die—unless it materializes into concrete action.

Isabel Archer's idealism is dramatically defined and heightened because of its juxtaposition to the authority of Mme Merle and Gilbert Osmond—without their rigid obeisance to authority, Isabel's idealism would be nothing more than a kind of petulant willfulness, as it seems in her rejection of Lord Warburton. Both of these Europeanized Americans appear to exhibit ideal behavior. Mme Merle is "too perfectly the social animal that man and woman are supposed to be" and, as Mrs. Touchett tells Isabel, "she hasn't a fault"; Osmond, as he warns Isabel, is "convention itself." But the essence of these two figures is their commitment to authority—the authority of tradition and manners, of religion and aestheticism—and their willing submission is passed on to their daughter Pansy, who is "evidently impregnated with the idea of submission, which was due to anyone who took the tone of authority." At one point in the book, Mme Merle confesses to Isabel that she has no romantic "ideal" in life, that "the whole envelope of circumstances" around a person is of greater significance to her. "There's no such thing as an isolated man or woman; we're each of us made up of some cluster of appurtenances. What shall we call our 'self'? Where does it begin? where does it end? It overflows into everything that belongs to us—and then it flows back again. I know a large part of myself is the clothes I choose to wear. I've a great respect for *things!* One's self—for other people—is one's expression of one's self; and one's house, one's furniture, one's garments, the books one reads, the company one keeps—these things are all expressive."

As the lives of Mme Merle and Isabel develop, she is perfectly correct: both of them must recognize that they are not isolated, that they must accept their fates as mistress and wife of Osmond; Mme Merle must accept the consequences of her "great respect for *things!*"; Isabel must live with her distorted preconception—her innocent notion—that "Mr. Osmond makes no mistakes! He knows everything, he understands everything, he has the kindest, gentlest, highest spirit."

Isabel's idealistic loyalty and obligation to "the very fact of marriage" if not to Osmond himself is rendered extreme and even faintly ludicrous by Osmond's devotion to authority. Osmond maintains that he has ideals in terms of the church, of marriage, of art, of child-rearing, of life itself; but in fact he cannot conceive of any situation beyond his own needs—institutions and their conventions govern him until whatever idealism he once may have possessed is stifled by the limitations of authority. For James this is a central question—one is tempted to say it is the essential question of all his fiction—and he makes it Isabel's great burden. When she sees Pansy in the convent to which Osmond has sent her, she reflects that Pansy's presence "seemed to represent the surrender of a personality to the authority of the Church." As the girl bows "her pretty head to authority and only [asks] of authority to be merciful," James makes his ultimate indictment of Osmond and all that he represents. The triumph of authority is that it has stifled the potential humanity and freedom of innocence—it has not permitted innocence to mature into idealism. Pansy's surrender to authority is a kind of living death, and Osmond's manipulation of his daughter is a cardinal sin in James's moral universe. Isabel's final trip to Ralph Touchett is toward a more actual death—the death of the cousin who once sought to translate her idealism into some form of actual life. *The Portrait of a Lady* concludes on the dual note that, as Isabel says, "the world's very small": it is a place governed by the authority of an Osmond, but, in the nineteenth century, it still allows for idealism, even if that idealism assumes the perverse character of Isabel's return to her husband. The past belongs to the Touchetts, Osmond, Mme Merle, and Isabel; the future is commanded by Henrietta Stackpole and Caspar Goodwood, and it is fitting that they, in their youth, should speak the last words of the novel.

Although I am concentrating on *The American, The Portrait of a Lady,* and *The Ambassadors,* the complex fate of innocence and its emergence in the form of either idealism or authority is central to all of James's work. America and Europe offered James the proper cultural and social distinctions for this theme—the environment of the characters almost always conditions their choices. But even though the setting may be more limited in scope and the subject may be feminism or anarchism, murder, art, or aestheticism, the fate of innocence recurs. *The Bostonians* and *The Princess Cassamassima* as well as other large novels of the eighties and nineties clearly develop this theme, but my point can be made most simply and directly by examining two of James's finest stories, "The Pupil" and "The Beast in the Jungle," before turning to his elaborate examination of idealism and authority in *The Ambassadors.*

As in many of James's stories concerning the moral superiority of children over their parents, the pathos of "The Pupil" lies in the death of innocence before it is permitted to flower into idealism. Morgan Moreen is an extraordinary little person, a hero in a modern tragi-comedy whose first name suggests his magical possibilities but whose inherited surname implies the fate that his corrupt family has bequeathed him—the fate of a diseased heart. The greatest spiritual evil of the Moreens is their irresponsibility, the self-absolvement of their position as parents, the way in which they force Pemberton to assume responsibility for Morgan, and, more specifically, for Morgan's salvation. Pemberton is too weak to save his pupil and Morgan is too young to transcend the authority of his parents; like other tragic heroes the boy struggles against his fate, and with the help of his tutor exhibits a certain noble behavior before he dies, but his exquisite sensibility succumbs to the cruelty and selfishness of his family. We might conclude by saying that "The Pupil" is a powerful tragedy of unrealized idealism—that would seem to follow from our analysis—but we would be misrepresenting not only the tone of the story, which is comic, but the antagonists as well—Morgan's heart attack is viewed through the absurdity of his parents. We can call the Moreens' irresponsible behavior immoral, even evil, but

James prevents us from viewing it as only tragic by reducing the stature of the Moreens through their child-like absurdity. It is fitting that Mr. Moreen's reaction to his son's death should be the last note struck in the story: "Mr. Moreen was trembling all over and was in his way as deeply affected as his wife. But after the very first he took his bereavement as a man of the world." The note is ironic, the flaw of moral innocence at the center of the Moreen character is comic. Idealism flickers for "an instant" as Morgan turns with "boy-ish joy" to Pemberton, but it is quickly extinguished by the tutor's weakness and the Moreens' corrupted nature. Morgan's death is not precisely comic, but it is conveyed in ironic terms which dull the impact of what ordinarily would be a profoundly tragic climax to a tragic story. If incongruity, as George Meredith defines it, is central to the comic vision, then "The Pupil" is a good example of that definition; and the most incongruous of events is the young boy's death itself.

Incongruity is the technique which also gives "The Beast in the Jungle" its special quality. John Marcher's innocence seems almost absurd when one considers the age of the man—indeed he is rendered more real because James makes him appear quixotic. As in the case of Isabel Archer, Marcher's innocence is his selfishness. The Beast that lurks within him is an idealism that he could never grasp, although it had always taken the form of May Bartram's love; the Jungle is the willful innocence of Marcher's life, which in its selfishness has become an aspect of authority, a closed world. James deplores, in the most impassioned prose, Marcher's inability to transcend his innocence, his frail submission to the authority of his limitations; and he grants Marcher only the final vision of how he has failed to assert the idealism that would have given his life meaning.

The innocence of these heroes frustrates the freedom they seek so desperately; they struggle with the contending forces of idealism and authority, searching for freedom from their own constricting characters. Nowhere is this conflict more clearly defined than in *The Ambassadors,* a novel in which one aspect of the innocence of nineteenth-century America is personified by Mrs. Newsome, the other by Lambert Strether. In the growing disagreement between these two nineteenth-century figures over what will happen to the innocence of Chad, one has a brilliant image of the conflict between idealism and authority and a broad suggestion of James's fears about the twentieth century.

When Strether tells Maria Gostrey, for no apparent reason, that he comes from Woolett, Massachusetts, she quickly interprets his statement: "You say that . . . as if you wanted one immediately to know the worst." Strether consciously wants her to know his innocence—"it sticks out of" him, as he says—but the worst revelation of innocence is what he is announcing on a deeper, less conscious level. In this first scene, he is Mrs. Newsome's spiritual as well as physical ambassador and is stubbornly in accord with her; but he is a naïf, even at the age of fifty-five, whereas Mrs. Newsome possesses an innocence that is dangerous because it expresses itself as authority. Her innocence and narrowness constitute the American parochialism which James laments in *Hawthorne* and which Emerson criticizes throughout his essays. When Strether distinguishes between the Newsomes and himself, he assures Miss Gostrey that he doesn't "touch the business" but edits the Review, which is colored green and which is Mrs. Newsome's "tribute to the ideal." For Mrs. Newsome the ideal represents dignity and grace, but in fact it scarcely conceals the authority of the Newsome business, the source of which Strether has suggested is corrupt or at least indescribable; furthermore, the Review is only her tribute—one of "the good works of Woolett," as F. W. Dupee suggests. Strether does the editing and insists that "It's exactly the thing that I'm reduced to doing for myself. It seems to rescue a little, you see, from the wreck of hopes and ambitions, the refuse-heap of disappointments and failures, my one presentable little scrap of an identity."

The phrase with which Strether facetiously characterizes Mrs. Newsome's condescension to the arts—her "tribute to the ideal" *— goes far in explaining the cultural rigidity of the Newsomes in general. Later in the novel—in Chapter II of the Ninth Book— Strether uses the phrase again, only now it refers to the daughter of Mrs. Newsome, Sarah Pocock. For the moment Sarah has an attraction to Paris, experiencing freedom from the authority of her prejudices: "That's *her* tribute to the ideal," Strether remarks, "—we each have our own. It's her romance—and it seems to me better on the

* This phrase—"tribute to the ideal"—is clearly a clue to James's intentions. It occurs frequently throughout the book in regard to each of the characters. In describing Waymarsh, at the outset of the novel, for example, James speaks of his bad relations with his wife: "One might one's self easily have left Mrs. Waymarsh; and one would assuredly have paid one's tribute to the ideal—covering with that attitude the decision of having been left by her."

whole than mine. To have it in Paris too . . . on this classic ground, in this charged infectious air, with so sudden an intensity: well, it's more than she expected. She has had in short to recognize the breaking out for her of a real affinity—and with everything to enhance the drama." Ultimately she cannot surrender to Paris, and she stands at one with Mrs. Newsome as she condemns the moral ambivalence of Strether: " 'What is your conduct but an outrage to women like *us*? I mean your acting as if there be a doubt—as between such another—of his [Chad's] duty?' "

Chad's own tribute to the ideal, his love affair with Mme de Vionnet, is more elaborate than that of his mother or sister, but he lacks imagination, as Strether reminds him, and he lacks heroism— "He habitually left things to others," James remarks, and one remembers him as a passive figure, led by a French woman into what is after all an adulterous affair, and commanded by American women into the authority of American business. Chad speaks of his leaving Mme de Vionnet as a great sacrifice—"It will be the greatest loss I ever suffered. I owe her so much"—but in fact he leaves her quite willingly, unable finally to honor beauty and human variousness. He returns to America unchanged, his vision still unimpaired by its confusion of art and utilitarianism. Chad's affair belongs to the nineteenth-century demi-monde, although Mme de Vionnet's charm and subtle grace raise it from vulgarity. His final observations on his future career in advertising belong to the twentieth century: "Yes," he tells Strether, "advertising affects the object being sold extraordinarily; really beyond what one had supposed. I mean of course when it's done as one makes out that, in our roaring age, it *can* be done. . . . It's an art like another, and infinite like all the arts. . . . In the hands, naturally, of a master. The right man must take hold. With the right man it c'est un monde."

Strether becomes, of course, the hero—"The hero of the drama," as Miss Barrace says—and the nature of his heroism is the clue to the meaning of *The Ambassadors* and to much of James's fiction. Like Christopher Newman, who surrenders a wife for an ideal, and Isabel Archer, who sacrifices a life of freedom for her loyalty to idealism, Strether forgoes a fortune and a comfortable old age because of his belief in a life beyond the utilitarian. "That, you see, is my only logic," he remarks. "Not, out of the whole affair, to have got anything for myself." And it is through Strether's final act that we begin to see a central theme of James's work: Renunciation and sacrifice of material gain, of private comfort and selfishness, for the commitment to an ideal become the criteria of character in James's works. This sacrifice rarely leads to mundane happiness, but it does lead to well-being. If the purpose of the innocent Jamesian hero is the pursuit of experience and his passion becomes the movement from one kind of experience to another, then his greatest perception lies in his sacrifice, his renunciation, and his ability to convert his innocence into an idealism that opposes the authority of his antagonist. Maria Gostrey expresses this idea to Strether in powerful and cogent terms: "What I hate is myself—when I think that one has to take so much, to be happy, out of the lives of others, and that one isn't happy even then. One does it to cheat one's self and to stop one's mouth—but that's only at the best for a little. The wretched self is always there, always making out somehow a fresh anxiety. What it comes to is that it's not, that it's never a happiness, any happiness at all, to *take*. The only thing is to give. It's what plays you least false."

Strether gives, and his sacrifice does not play him false. He transfigures his innocence into idealism whereas Chad, who has only taken, succumbs to the authority of the American future—his innocence becomes the perversion of idealism. Strether's famous lament is pathetic in its context—"Live all you can; it's a mistake not to. It doesn't so much matter what you do in particular, so long as you have your life. If you haven't that what *have* you had? . . . What one loses one loses; make no mistake about that. . . . One lives in fine as one can. Still, one has the illusion of freedom; therefore, don't be like me, without the memory of that illusion. . . . Do what you like so long as you don't make my mistake. For it was a mistake. Live!" It is a pathetic lament that gains its existential strength and meaning by Strether's ultimate decision to free himself of the Newsomes; but it takes on an even greater significance when we remember that Howells was the model for Strether and when, as a consequence, we place James's exhortation in the cultural context of nineteenth- and twentieth-century American literature.

The idealistic tradition in American literature begins—taking into account all of the variations that individual authors demand—with Revolutionary writers like Crèvecoeur, Barlow, and Brackenridge; reaches its most forthright statement in Emerson, Whitman, and the transcendentalists; develops into a dramatic ambivalence in Twain and James; rises to tragic commentary in Fitzgerald and

Hemingway; and reappears in a comic form in Bellow, Salinger, and Mailer. James spans the nineteenth and twentieth centuries—James points in both directions. The moral triumph of Christopher Newman, Isabel Archer, and Lambert Strether is essentially that of the nineteenth century; it rests upon the belief in abstractions and especially the abstraction of heroism. For the last magnificent moment in our literature, the hero and the concept that informs his character are linked—Christopher Newman is the American, Isabel Archer is the Lady, Lambert Strether is the Ambassador; and for the last time an author can speak of sacrifice and idealism and heroism without qualifying the moral premises of his remarks. However subtle and ambiguous James's perception of human character may be, the moral framework of his art is absolutely lucid. Innocents like Christopher Newman, Isabel Archer, and Lambert Strether may not see the authority and rigidity of their ultimate antagonists, but James does; their final perception coincides with that of James, and their decision to act ideally is given James's blessing.

Innocence in twentieth-century American literature is not honorific; it rarely flowers into idealism. Daisy Buchanan of *The Great Gatsby* may have been named after James's heroine, but her passivity and innocence are absorbed into the authority of her unscrupulous husband, who carries on the heritage of the Newsomes; the Buchanans, the Warrens (of *Tender Is the Night*), and Brady (of *The Last Tycoon*) are figures of authority over whom the idealistic heroes cannot triumph. In Hemingway's work the "innocence" of America is presented even more brutally: in a story like "Soldier's Home" or through Robert Cohen and other Americans of *The Sun Also Rises*; in the stories which feature Nick Adams; and in *The Green Hills of Africa*—"Our people went to America because that was the place to go then. It had been a good country and we had made a bloody mess of it. . . . Let the others come to America who did not know that they had come too late." The innocence of the Hemingway hero is destroyed early in life; it never has the opportunity to manifest itself in idealism—it never has the "illusion of freedom," which James considers so important—and therein lies an important reason for the pathos and the terror one feels in Hemingway's work.

The illusion of freedom. In that phrase one begins to understand the meaning of that other phrase which has meant so much to so many Americans and which has been spoken with seriousness and with scorn—the American dream. Freedom was real to the Revolutionary writers, to Emerson, Whitman, and Henry James—and it contained the possibility of achieving the ideal, the dream. For James freedom became an illusion, but the meaning of Strether's plea is that it is a true illusion; as conscious as James is of the "form" that controls our "consciousness" and our limitations, he demands the illusion of freedom—and the power of *The Ambassadors* is that Strether, at the age of fifty-five, with nothing to gain materially from that illusion, seizes it. In *The Ambassadors* James strains the meaning of active idealism to the breaking point—he pays his allegiance to the nineteenth century. But the fact that he can still make a faith in idealism psychologically credible suggests how much he owes to the twentieth century. For Fitzgerald and Hemingway idealism is retrospective and realism omnipresent. In Bellow, Salinger, Mailer, Baldwin, Ellison, and other contemporary writers idealism is either quixotically conveyed or it is so abstract it has little to do with human character. Many of these authors are deeply indebted to James artistically, but few of them—as novelists—can realize his moral assumptions concerning the triumph of idealism over authority. They speak of idealism in their essays and at times through characters in their fiction, but it is an emergent, abstract, potential idealism and not a matter of character, as in Christopher Newman, Isabel Archer, and Lambert Strether. The shadow of American idealism surrenders to the sword of its authority, and the hero is disenchanted or, in our present moment, quixotic. The Emersonian hero, so serious and so certain, belongs to the nineteenth century.

TWO

The
Southern
Hero

1

The Code of Southern Heroism

If there is any truth to the indictment that literary criticism and scholarship have become notoriously parochial, then surely the commentaries on American literature are among the most specialized, the most limited imaginatively; and of all the tedious research into our national culture, the investigation and exploration and exhumation of Southern letters are most vulnerable to the indictment. In a kind of rearguard action that bursts forth sporadically, that blurs esthetic standards in its defense of texts that have, as the saying goes, "historical significance," the Civil War of American literary criticism is still being fought.

A recently published volume, *Southern Writers: Appraisals in Our Time*,* suggests the limitations of most scholarship that has traditionally shaped our conception of Southern literature. The essays range in scope from "Poe in Richmond: The Double Image" to "The Youngest Generation of Southern Fiction Writers"; and

---

* *Southern Writers: Appraisals in Our Time,* edited by R. C. Simonini, Jr. (Charlottesville, 1964).

though there are intelligent estimates of Southern culture—Willard Thorp offers an illuminating account of "The Writer as Pariah in the Old South" and Louis D. Rubin, Jr., writes sensibly of "The Civil War in Southern Fiction"—too many of the essays suffer from a provincialism that has characterized the criticism of Southern letters for more than a century. We read, for example, that Mary Johnston's *The Long Roll* and *Cease Firing* are "the nearest thing we have in American literature to *War and Peace*"; we learn that James Branch Cabell was indeed critical of the South, but "one may be quite sure that Cabell himself would be the first to spring to the defense of his homeland should any stranger seek to malign it"; we are assured that "Poe, Glasgow, Faulkner, the *Fugitive-Agrarians,* Styron—these writers are Southern; for they run counter to the stream of writing in most other sections of the nation but they have a common home in the tradition of Southern literary art." It is certainly true, as the editor announces in his foreword, that creatively "the South today is the most dynamic region of our country"; but one wonders why, in 1964, a group of critics feels it necessary to speak so defensively, so extravagantly—so irresponsibly—about the literature of the South.

We can attribute this kind of unsophisticated "appraisal" to a narrow chauvinism, or simply to low critical standards, or to the solemnity that attends most criticism when it is in the business of resurrecting so-called neglected writers of the past. But the reasons are less obvious and more significant than may first seem apparent; for the failure of self-criticism in Southern letters suggests some of the reasons for the limited value of the literature itself, the literature that antedates Faulkner and the contemporary generation of writers. We begin to see why so few important works of art appeared in all of nineteenth-century Southern culture; and this failure is not one of talent or ambition or diligence but of a deep habit of mind, of a certain pervasive attitude toward human nature on the part of the nineteenth-century Southern author.

That habit of mind can be discerned by observing the literary attitudes and achievements of some representative nineteenth-century Southern writers and by examining the work of two prominent, rather typical authors of the antebellum and postbellum periods—William Gilmore Simms and Thomas Nelson Page. A suggestive approach is offered by Page himself, in an essay entitled "Literature in the South Before the War," which he published in

1889. Page calls the roll of antebellum Southern authors and cites John Pendleton Kennedy, William Gilmore Simms, and John Esten Cooke as writers who were popularly Romantic; he notes their great dependence on Scott's fiction, and offers judicious and temperate estimates of their work. The essay is written in the impressionistic manner of the period, and though there is little attempt to give the literature a dimension it does not have, Page automatically assumes an apologetic tone and suggests the reasons for the absence of genuine literary activity in this period. He observes that before the war there was a practical interest in agriculture, an absence of large cities (where culture usually thrives), political activity, and the great concern over slavery; these conditions, he suggests, caused the South to have a very small reading audience, which in turn discouraged potential artists.

Page's observations are traditional. One can find them anticipated in the correspondence of Simms or Paul Hamilton Hayne, although these authors are understandably less dispassionate than Page; one can see their modern version in *The Cambridge History of American Literature, The Literary History of the United States,* and most significantly in Jay B. Hubbell's *The South in American Literature.* But when one reads the fiction of the period; when one reads John Pendleton Kennedy's *Horseshoe Robinson* (1835), William A. Caruther's *The Cavaliers of Virginia* (1835), Beverley Tucker's *The Partisan Leader* (1836), John Esten Cooke's *The Virginia Comedians* (1854), or Simms' *The Forayers* (1855)—and these novels represent some of the finest fictional achievements of the antebellum South—one wonders whether their severe limitations can be attributed to the agrarian conditions of the South, or to the concern over slavery, or to the lack of an audience. Were Northern authors so indifferent to racial problems? Was a typical Southerner like Simms so concerned with slavery in the 1830's and 1840's? Was Hawthorne or Melville or Whitman—or the Southerner Poe, who barely survived in the North—so greatly encouraged by a wide audience of sympathetic readers? Was it not possible for Simms or any other talented author to have his work published and distributed by a Northern press? It must be true that the social milieu of the antebellum South was not conducive to artistic survival, and the pathetic lamentations of Paul Hamilton Hayne and of William Gilmore Simms certainly have foundation in fact. But these antebellum Southern writers cannot be seen as merely victims of an indifferent society, even though they often saw themselves this way; the mediocrity of their achievement suggests the limited vision, the blunted sensibility, the pre-conditioned mind that they brought to the writing of literature. There were simply certain cultural positions that nineteenth-century Southern authors did not dare to take. Not only were they writing in obeisance to a sentimental literary tradition that was inevitably a deliquescent variation of Scott; not only were they bound by certain rigid views of sexuality. These authors were championing a civilization that forced them to see heroes rather than human beings, to think in epic modes even though their form demanded realism. When we consider the finest work of Northern writers—"The Divinity School Address," *The Prairie, Walden, The Scarlet Letter, Song of Myself* and *The Confidence-Man*—we recognize at once the tension involved in the rejection of a past belief or a present attitude; we respect the mind that has called its religious and cultural and personal assumptions into question. One of the reasons why Simms, for example, never achieves the dramatic dimension of Cooper is that his work lacks the significant conflict that we find in any of the Leatherstocking novels, the tension inevitably involved in the breakdown of a civilization, the surrender of one way of living for another. The writers of the antebellum period were controlled by no essential thematic conflict as they pursued the past glories of Virginia or South Carolina, and in their treatment of character they adopted a code of heroism which is so rigid, so mannered, so *unreal,* that it infects the fiction until it seems like little more than a defense of the Southern way of life. The idealism of the Southern hero scarcely challenges the authority of the family, the church, or the South, and when this hero defends his institutions against the British or against the Northern gentleman, he becomes simply a sentimental figure in a novel whose realism lacks power because it lacks genuine tension. The code I speak of was a natural development of antebellum social conditions, and its effect was fundamental and far-reaching; it offered the Southern writer a set of values which dictated the form and thematic approach that his fiction was to assume, and in the nineteenth century no Southern writer, with the exception of Mark Twain, challenged it.

The code of Southern heroism involved a moral attitude in which truth and honor and loyalty are constant; a military discipline in which fencing and riding and hunting are necessary accomplishments; an inflexible social posture that represents the quintessence of manners, courtesy, and hospitality. Other characteristics of the code that inevitably develop as the hero matures are the idealization of woman, which, as W. J. Cash has suggested, amounts to "gyneolatry"; extravagant oratory; a sectional chauvinism, which flowers into Southern nationalism—or, as in the case of Simms, a nationalism which becomes increasingly sectional; a great emphasis on heraldry and ancestry, and the consequent glorification of the past; and, finally, a desire to establish a political state like that of Pericles' Athens, a free state based on a slave proletariat. All of these elements are put to the service of an idealistic moral attitude that implies when it does not overtly celebrate the superiority of the Southern hero.

We should not assume that Southern authors who adopted this code held the same social and political beliefs. Beverley Tucker was a staunch secessionist and John Pendleton Kennedy a Unionist; William A. Caruthers disliked slavery—at least the kind of slavery that existed in South Carolina where the slaves were, in his words, "plantation life-stock"; Simms always believed in slavery and the inferiority of the Negro, even though he opposed Nullification— and later in his career, when sectional pressures grew intense, he turned more militant and became an even greater advocate of secession and slavery. Most authors of the antebellum period, how- ever, did have similar literary attitudes, and in the fictional re- creation of their mutual past, they used and re-used the code of Southern heroism. They shared a romantic—more often a senti- mental—approach to character and setting; they championed a Southern literature; they glorified a past in which an aristocracy prevailed, in which a rigid code of behavior defined the actions of the various characters—the Southern gentleman, the lady, the squatter, the yeoman, and the slave. These writers—with the notable exception of Poe and Simms—thought of authorship as an avoca- tion; they did not concern themselves with form or style, and their individual works, written in great haste, suffer from formal limita- tions that often make them unreadable. But finally it is the adoption of the code of Southern heroism—sometimes overtly expressed but more often unconsciously felt, and therefore more profound, more rigid—that suppresses the deep, internal tensions and conflicts necessary to the creation of great literature. In a fiction where the slave and master always occupy the same role, where the lady is revered, the squatter reviled, there is little room for human differences; and the masochism of a Dimmesdale or the disillusionment of those victims of the Confidence Man is impossible if the authors are consecrated to the glorification rather than to the understanding of the Southern past, of the Southern character.

William Gilmore Simms and the Antebellum Writers

The first professional scholar to explore the effects of this code—although his approach was partially distorted by the obvious bias that he brought to nineteenth-century Southern culture—was William P. Trent, in his critical study of William Gilmore Simms. The term critical study has a two-fold significance when applied to *William Gilmore Simms* (1892), for Trent's book not only offers a fine criticism of Simms—it is still the most thorough single account of the man and his work—but it is critical in the sense that it suggests a totally new way of looking at nineteenth-century Southern literature. With all its obvious and glaring faults, *William Gilmore Simms* is a classic of American criticism and scholarship.

Many recent scholars have been quick to remind us of the limitations of Trent's study; indeed readers are immediately warned of Trent, as though he is a kind of Southern Judas for assuming his particular approach to Simms. In a highly contentious and chauvinistic essay that serves as an introduction to *The Letters of William Gilmore Simms,* Donald Davidson denounces Trent for writing "one of the least objective biographies ever written," for "openly and patronizingly deploring and condemning the principles of Simms and the principles of Simms' South Carolina and Simms' South," for feeling "that great works of literature were actually impossible in the South." J. V. Ridgely, author of *William Gilmore Simms* (1963), offers a more tempered but still unfavorable estimate of Trent's volume, and notes that "Trent, a fervent proponent of the 'New South' movement of his day, had as his subject a man who for a life time had championed a diametrically opposed ideal . . . Trent's biography is consequently marred by his view that the old South was 'primitive and retrogressive.'"

There is no question that Trent's work is limited by prejudice, by the frequent attempt to see Simms as a symbolic rather than an individual author. Trent does distort the significance of Simms' lower social condition in Charleston; he does become excessively melodramatic in the description of the father's sudden departure from his family and its effect on young Simms; he does commit errors in fact, although they are generally insignificant, and his critical judgments tend to be colored by the Victorian insistence that all literature be "ennobling"; and lastly, most crucially, he is too eager to denounce many aspects of the South. But Trent's thesis that Simms "owes the fact that he never rose to the front rank, even of his own country's writers, to the limitations imposed upon him by his Southern birth" is fundamentally accurate; his view that Simms was inhibited artistically because "the models before him were those of statesmen and men of action" is sound; his repeated assertion that the Southern people, down to 1861, were living a primitive life in terms of literature and the arts seems justified—not only because of similar statements made by Simms, Hayne, and other antebellum writers but because of the more tempered historical appraisals of our own time.

Trent concludes his book in the sentimental fashion that was so popular in nineteenth- and early twentieth-century American criticism: "Yes. [Paul Hamilton] Hayne was right. The man Simms 'is worthy of all honor!' Whether as a literary toiler, working successfully under most harassing conditions; whether as a misguided patriot, striving for what he believed to be his section's good; whether as a defeated, worn-out spirit, laboring to relieve the distresses of his children and his friends, the man Simms ceases to be a mere man and assumes proportions that are truly heroic." Indeed Simms emerges in Trent's biography as a kind of tragic hero—a nineteenth-century martyr—whose artistic flaw is his assumption of a narrow sectional chauvinism, his intense belief in Southern white supremacy. And as we reconsider Simms' career, we begin to see that Trent's judgments are essentially correct. The code of heroism that Simms automatically assumed when he wrote his early novels developed into an elaborate defense of the South; the glory of the Revolutionary era, when Southerners had contributed to a successful rebellion against England, was used implicitly to justify the anticipated secession from the Union; the moral idealism of the hero serves the social authority of the South, and fiction becomes inevitably propaganda. As Simms grew more self-conscious and defensive about slavery, the more rigid did the code of heroism become.

Simms began to write fiction in 1833, when he published *Martin Faber,* a crime novel that was influenced by William Godwin's *Caleb Williams.* From 1833 to 1856, Simms brought a dedication to his writing that is unmatched in its intensity by any other nineteenth-century Southern author. He published seventeen novels, innumerable short stories, plays, poems, criticism, biography, and histories; he was the editor of a daily newspaper, the *Charleston City Gazette,* and of various magazines—*The Magnolia* (1842–1843), *The Southern and Western Magazine* (1845), and *The Southern Quarterly Review* (1849–1855)—in which he championed the South and published the work of promising Southern authors; he was active in the various political and literary movements—Northern as well as Southern—of the times; and, as the five-volume edition of his letters suggests, he was a devoted correspondent to his Northern and Southern friends. His most significant achievement, however, was his fiction, and particularly the Revolutionary novels: *The Partisan* (1835), *Mellichampe* (1836), *The Scout* (1842), *Katherine Walton* (1851), *Woodcraft* (1852), *The Forayers* (1855), and *Eutaw* (1856). These novels not only demonstrate Simms' distinctive qualities but also indicate his changing attitude toward the place of the antebellum South in American culture; even though his social attitudes toward Negroes never fundamentally changed—he always believed in white supremacy and maintained a paternalistic attitude toward the Negro until the Reconstruction period—Simms grew more tendentious as he approached the Civil War. It may be true, as Donald Davidson reminds us, "that of Simms' large list of fiction only one book, *Southward Ho!* confronts directly the theme of slavery and secession"; but it is impossible to read the Revolutionary novels without realizing that Simms' attitude toward social issues and the concept of heroism is deeply modified by his increasingly defensive view of slavery and secession and sectionalism.

When Simms published *The Partisan, Mellichampe,* and *The Scout,* he was a nationalist. He had supported the Union in the Nullification controversy of 1830, and throughout the late thirties and early forties he advocated a national literature, scoffing the narrow parochialism of many Southern authors and sympathizing with the Young America group—Cornelius Matthews, Evert A. Duyckinck, J. T. Headley, and others. He brought to the creation of his first three Revolutionary novels—and to all the other works of this early period—a typically sentimental view of literature: his heroes are predictably mannered, his heroines vapid, his villains stock types. In *The Partisan,* Major Singleton is the aristocratic gentleman who loves the aristocratic lady, Katherine Walton, and serves heroically in the army of General Marion; for him " 'war is not a sport, but a duty, and we should not love it. It is a cruel necessity, and only to be resorted to as it protects from cruelty.' " Other figures—notably the scouts in *Mellichampe* and *The Scout*—exhibit a realistic heroism in defiance of the British, and the action of the three novels develops from these obvious confrontations. Simms was inevitably affected by the literary sentimentalism of his time, but unlike his contemporaries, he succeeded in creating realistic Southern types of the Revolutionary period. There was a certain coarseness in his character, deplored by some of his contemporaries, that gives his work a strength attractive to the modern reader; in any case, his interests were more historical than psychological, more patriotic than personal, and thus he avoids—although not completely—the mawkish relationships that burden the novels of sentimental writers. *The Partisan, Mellichampe,* and *The Scout* are celebrations of South Carolina, the natural tribute of a politically conscious author to his native state; and Simms automatically attributes to his central figures the various characteristics of the code of Southern heroism. Mellichampe learns from the scout Thumbscrew Witherspoon the need for honor and justice in combat; Clarence Conway, the passionate and virtuous hero in *The Scout,* accepts the sensible advice of "Supple Jack" Bannister, although Conway demonstrates in his own private and public life the various characteristics of the code.

By the time he wrote *Katherine Walton* and *Woodcraft,* however, Simms had altered his vision of the Revolution because of his growing concern over slavery in the South. In the first three novels he uses the Revolution as the historical period when the partisans of South Carolina defy the domination of the British, when the various figures act out of a natural romantic heroism—the idealism of these Southern heroes is a clear challenge to the authority of the British and the balance, although rather superficial and obvious, is clear and credible. But in *Katherine Walton,* as J. V. Ridgely points out, Simms identifies "his Revolutionary patriots with rebellious South Carolians of the 1850's; once again his state should stand against all tyranny from without." We can feel the overtly defensive, chauvinistic attitude in the introduction to *Katherine Walton,* as Simms reflects upon the Revolutionary series in general and anticipates the particular novels that he will now begin to write: "My friends denounced my waste of time upon scenes, and situations, and events, in which they beheld nothing latent—nothing which could possibly (as they thought) reward the laborer. Now, South Carolina is regarded as a very store house for romance. She has furnished more materials for the use of art and fiction, than half the states in the Union." In *Katherine Walton* Simms does not demonstrate the romantic resources of his native state, although he attempts to deal with manners more than he does in any of the other Revolutionary tales; the "scenes, and situations, and events" of *Katherine Walton* are set in Charleston, but they do not seem peculiar to that city, they do not evoke any unique sense of local color. Simms does emphasize, however, the need for the code of Southern heroism. His two adversaries—the British Major Proctor, who is finally a convert to the Southern way of life, and Major Singleton, the same figure who had appeared in *The Partisan*—reiterate the significance of truth and honor and loyalty. Both men are incomparable soldiers who have learned the art of warfare; both are well-mannered; and both believe in the validity of white supremacy. Whatever idealistic behavior the British or the Southern hero exhibits must now serve the authority of Southern society; one senses that the freedom necessary to human complexity has faded with the imposition of a social fate upon the hero.

The need to justify the present by championing the past becomes increasingly noticeable in Simms' fiction of the 1850's. In *Southward Ho!* (1854) he has various orators speak upon the Negro question and one Southern chauvinist offers flatulent and hysterical defenses of secession; and in the last two Revolutionary novels—*The Forayers* (1855) and *Eutaw* (1856)—he suggests the ways in which the code of behavior will protect the new nation: the parallels between the Revolution and the anticipated Civil War are self-evident. This code, with its emphasis on loyalty, on physical accomplishments and military discipline, on reverence for the lady and devotion to a host of moral abstractions, on the rigidly controlled social behavior of the individual in this world, is the Southern version of an Arthurian code—without, one should add, the attendant mythology, without the historical and religious context that gives imaginative validity to the supernatural. Caste is still significant—Negroes, of course, are automatically slaves, appendages to the white man, and the ancestry of the hero often determines his bravery; but the hero—like Willie Sinclair in *The Forayers*—must not only be to the manner born but must also demonstrate that he is capable of obeying the code of heroism. The more Simms considers the problems of slavery, the more tortured he feels by the demands of an egalatarian society, the more he speaks of the code as peculiar to Southern people.

Once in his career Simms was able to defend the caste system in the South by attempting to present it in less than heroic terms, by making the one really human being in his fiction—Lieutenant Porgy—the spokesman for the Southern way of life. The Revolutionary novels are cluttered with the stock devices of sentimental fiction —they suffer from their dependence on conventional people in conventional situations; but in *Woodcraft,* published one year after the appearance of *Uncle Tom's Cabin* (1851), Simms offers the most persuasive defense of his position.

Although *Woodcraft* is Simms' finest novel, it is by no means free from his usual faults: the book is prolix, mannered, sentimental, and intellectually unrewarding. But there is a certain heavy truth in Simms' evocation of the Revolutionary struggles in South Carolina, and the novel has pictorial moments—Porgy's melancholic return to his plantation, the impoverished plantation itself, the home of the squatter's victimized family—which relieve a pervasive sentimentality that has become by 1852 a habit of Simms' mind. Originally the novel was entitled *The Sword and the Distaff; or "Fair, Fat, and*

Forty," *A Story of the South, at the Close of the Revolution,* which is a far more fitting if more prosaic description of its action. The sword and the distaff immediately suggest the fixed attitudes that Simms brings to his central subject—the defense of Southern heroism, of Southern womanhood, and of Southern slavocracy—and the subtitle, "Fair, Fat, and Forty," prepares the reader for the tone of the book.

Simms' relative success is achieved through his comic approach to character. Lieutenant Porgy occupies center stage, a figure who is not just a caricature in a vast panorama of the Revolutionary South but a defender of slavocracy—pathetic rather than farcical, human rather than bestial. In *The Partisan* Porgy almost never rises above the sensual level—he is interested only in satisfying his appetite, and Tom his Negro cook fulfills that function. By presenting the white man in a comic yet primitive condition, Simms persuades the reader of the primitivism of the Negro; for their friendship would be impossible without Porgy's willingness to descend to the Negro's level, and though Tom is seen in a kindly, paternal way, he assumes his abject role in a clearly defined Southern hierarchy: Porgy may be swinish in *The Partisan,* but there is never any question that he is always Tom's master. In the following novel, *Mellichampe,* Porgy "sits upon a fallen tree, his belt undone, his sword across his lap"; and in *The Forayers* and *Eutaw,* written twenty years later, he is essentially the same comic caricature—Simms does not use him for any overt, didactic purpose.

Only in *Woodcraft* does Porgy dominate the action of the novel. Now he is a gentle, awkward, defeated man whose primitive qualities are not recorded but only remembered. "He was a *fast* youth," Simms reminds us, "who fatally learned the pleasures of dissipation"; but Porgy's past belongs to the prehistory of the novel—his grossness is never really part of his present character—and in *Woodcraft* we see him as "a ruined man" whose numerous Negroes have been "carried off by the enemy"; we see him as someone who still has "a taste for pleasure" and who still grows "wise over his wine," but he is "already past middle age" and Simms informs him with too much pathos for us ever to consider him purely a caricature. His preparation in courting Mrs. Eveleigh, a widow of sense rather than of sensibility, is presented in a mock-heroic manner—"talk of the iron garments of ancient chivalry!" Simms remarks, indicating the absurdity of this fat, maladroit knight-errant who never really believes that he will be successful in love—but this kind of mock-heroism serves as a relief to the pathetic poverty that Porgy represents, so he is never merely the buffoon. Simms has created a character who is poised between comic and despairing attitudes, one whose unheroic nature and humorous self-appraisal prevent him from becoming sentimental, self-pitying, and mannered. If the critical cliché that Simms is a romantic realist has any meaning any more, it is demonstrated by the truth of Porgy's character as it develops against the backdrop of war and the aftermath of military conflict.

Porgy now represents a position Simms is defending quite openly—the position of white supremacy. And the defense is more successful here than anywhere else in his work because he has couched his argument in historical and comic terms rather than in the rigid association of the hero's idealism with that of Southern grandeur. The novel does not suffer from the messianic quality one finds in *Southward Ho!* or in those letters of the 1850's and 1860's that Simms wrote to Beverley Tucker and to his friend, James Henry Hammond—even though *Woodcraft* is, as Simms pointed out to Hammond, "probably as good an answer to Mrs. Stowe as has been published." The book is ostensibly concerned with the Revolution— with the "South at the close of the Revolution"—but the emphasis on Porgy's relation with his servant Tom and the various proclamations in defense of slavocracy indicate that Simms is writing a tract for his own time. By focusing our attention on that period when slavery first became an institution in the South, by presenting a banal, semi-ludicrous, and in many ways "typical" relationship between a white Southerner and a Negro, he champions white supremacy and suggests the human differences between white and Negro, the social necessity for the white man's guidance of the Negro. Idealism takes a comic turn and seems compatible with the social authority of slavocracy.

Porgy's attitude toward Tom is characterized by love—and by paternalism. "Tom is certainly a negro," he tells a friend, "Tom is certainly mine. . . . I love Tom. Tom is virtually a free man . . . the poor fellow has faithfully served a gentleman. He shall never fall into the hands of a scamp. I'll sacrifice him as a burnt-offering for my sins and his own. Tom, I'm thinking, would rather die my slave than live a thousand years under another owner." Porgy's friend assures him that "He *does* love you, captain," but Porgy further insists upon his own devotion to Tom. "The old rascal, I do love him. He makes the finest stew of any cook in Carolina. He shall cook for me as long as I'm able to eat: and when I'm not, we shall both be willing to die together."

The relationship of master and servant, based solidly on love and paternalism, is convincing precisely because of the pathetic juxtaposition of love and service—precisely because the relationship assumes a ludicrous aspect. On the lips of this "plethoric captain," this unmannered, unheroic middle-aged man—this combination of Falstaff and Don Quixote with a Southern accent—these attitudes are inoffensive so long as we can forget the realities of history, so long as we can suspend our disbelief; Simms has humanized and thus justified white supremacy. But *Woodcraft* was published in 1852 and is in part a rebuttal of *Uncle Tom's Cabin*; even Porgy loses his comic aspects as he becomes a mouthpiece for Simms' racial views. As Simms ceases to treat the captain and gentleman with condescending humor, Porgy grows preposterous in the reader's eyes. "Nothing but death shall ever part us," Porgy promises Tom. "When I die, you shall be buried with me. We have fought and fed too long together, Tom, and I trust we love each other quite too well, to submit to separation. When *your* kitchen grows cold, Tom, I shall cease to eat; and you, Tom, will not have breath enough to blow up the fire when mine is out! I shall fight for you to the last, Tom, and you, I know would fight to the last for me, as I am very sure that neither of us can long outlast the other." The Negro pledges absolute loyalty—he hardly has any other choice—but he cringes before his master's mad possessiveness. "Tom," Porgy warns, "sooner than have you be taken off by these vermin, I will shoot you! . . . But it may be, that I shall not have the opportunity. They may take advantage of my absence—they may *steal* you away—coming on you by surprise. If they should do so, Tom, I rely upon you to put *yourself* to death, sooner than abandon me and become the slave of another."

Simms is purposely farcical in this exchange; Porgy's absurd exaggerations grow partially out of the exaggeration in his own character; but his condescension toward the Negro, his gentle mocking of Tom—regardless of the tone with which that mocking is conveyed—simply reaffirms the need for the perpetuation of white supremacy. When Tom expresses his reluctance to commit suicide rather than live under another master, Porgy accuses the Negro of selfishness. "Is it possible that you could wish to live, if separated from me? Impossible, Tom! I will never believe it. No, boy, you shall never leave me. We shall never part. You shall be my cook, after death, in future worlds, even as you are here . . . I shall cry out, at your elbow, 'My coffee, Tom!' in a voice that shall shake the very house!" Simms closes the scene by suggesting Tom's rather primitive reaction to the promise of eternal domination: "Tom turned gloomily to the fire, not a little bewildered. The bravest negro is the slave of superstitious fancies, and Tom was a devout believer in ghosts, and quite famous in the kitchen for his own ghost experience."

The point that Simms wishes to make is that the Negro does not comprehend the intensity of this love affair; he only feels it, in much the manner that the Negroes out of the mythologies of Thomas Nelson Page and Joel Chandler Harris feel their devotion to their loyal masters. Porgy understands the proper relationship between white and Negro; like a reliable guardian he recognizes and satisfies the Negro's need; and though Simms presents the relationship in terms of mutual regard, of master and slave, he also suggests that the Negro's fidelity is less intense than the master's, that Tom cares fundamentally for his earthly comfort and consequently needs the white man to define a higher code of civilization for him. Porgy's attitude is the one that Simms wishes us to accept, and its good sense is confirmed by the vulgar position of another less enlightened Southerner who argues that "The Injin was born to clear the woods of the varmints for us; and the nigger to clean up after we've eaten—that's the philosophy." That is not Porgy's philosophy —that is not Simms' view. Porgy is described as a kind of knighterrant and a ludicrous lover—a pathetic Southerner quite different from all those gentlemen who populate the sentimental novel of the nineteenth century; but he has fundamentally a healthy if paternalistic attitude toward the Negro, rendered more convincing because of his own human limitations. *Woodcraft* is Simms' most convincing defense of white supremacy, written before the author's views have hardened and narrowed and become intolerably adamantine.

In his last two Revolutionary novels—*The Forayers* and *Eutaw* —Simms continues to see the Negro as irresponsible, mercurial, and completely dependent upon his white master; and whatever praise he accords the slave is modified and attenuated by a pervasive, increasingly embittered condescension. "Ah, the dear black, dirty scamps of negroes, big and little, on one of the old ante-revolutionary plantations! They acknowledge loving necessities as the fleas do; are as free in their intimacies as the frogs of Egypt; will blacken sunshine upon your walls with the pressure of their affections; and carry real, genuine hearts, full of sympathy for all the family, in spite of their rarely-washed visages." This ambivalent attitude, shifting from affection to contempt, from compassion to revulsion, marks Simms' fiction and correspondence of the 1850's; and as he retreated further from his earlier concerns as a novelist, as he became more self-consciously dedicated to white supremacy, more chauvinistic and parochial, more defensive of slavery, more impatient with Northern industrialism, the less he was able to view human nature with understanding. In the last years of his life he had neither the energy nor the desire to create fiction—he was a victim of the war to which he had dedicated himself. Simms' fascinating correspondence, which in many ways is his most impressive single achievement and a significant document in American cultural history, indicates quite clearly his developing bigotry, his increasing parochialism, his loss of sympathy for the Negro. In the 1850's he maintains a paternal and affectionate regard for his slaves; during the Reconstruction period, after he realizes that his paternalistic attitude has failed, he looks upon his Negroes or, more precisely, his ex-slaves as ungrateful parasites who refuse to work.

Ultimately Simms could not write fiction at all. He had projected another Revolutionary novel, but he never wrote it, and his last days present the bleak picture of a defeated Southern patriarch who has foresaken his early heroic conception of the South as one of the champions of the American Revolution for a narrow parochialism with which he defends the heroism of South Carolina. Throughout his letters of the 1850's and 1860's are scattered invidious comparisons between South Carolina and Virginia, between South Carolina and timid Southern states who refuse to take on the burden of secession; and when John T. Trowbridge visited South Carolina in 1867, Simms, in one of his more mystical moments, was able to claim that "Charleston, sir, . . . was the finest city in the world; not a large city, but the finest. South Carolina, sir, was the flower of modern civilization. Our people were the most hospitable, the most accomplished, having the highest degree of culture, and the highest sense of honor, of any people, I will not say of America, sir, but of any country on the globe. And they are so still, even in their temporary desolation." Thus far can the authority of social commitment devour the heroic ideal of a talented author who, under other circumstances, could be asking questions, challenging shibboleths, feeling free to explore the moral and cultural assumptions upon which his life is based.

It is no wonder that significant art became all but impossible when the sensibility turned so self-conscious, so arch, so mannered. All that was left for the nineteenth-century Southern writer was panegyric—or, a local color movement in which character was reduced in importance, in which Southern ladies and gentlemen and Negroes were part of the landscape, like figures in a frieze, eternally arrested, but in no way alive. The mawkish view of Southern heroism on the part of Caruthers, John Esten Cooke, or Tucker was inherited by ladies like Augusta Evans and Mary Jane Holmes; and, after the war, the children of Confederate soldiers, who had seen in their adolescence the effects of Reconstruction, continued the legend, speaking of a golden age spun out of memories, and sometimes—as in the case of Thomas Nelson Page—spun out of fading memories that quickly became incandescent dreams. In "The Morals of Slavery," Simms maintained that the "people of the South" possessed "a superior refinement" to that of Northerners. "Their grace of manner, courteous bearing, gentleness of deportment, studious forbearance and unobtrusiveness—their social characteristics, in general —all assumed to spring from the peculiar institution of Negro Slavery, as affording superior time, as well as leisure, to the controlling race—are usually admitted without question." Northerners, of course, refused to accept so biased a formulation in 1852; but by 1887, when Thomas Nelson Page published *In Ole Virginia,* they were prepared to honor or at least respect the most direct and sentimental kind of Southern chauvinism—never were Southern authors so hospitably received by Northern journals than in the eighties and nineties. The code of Southern heroism became more rigid and elaborate than it had been in the fiction of the antebellum writers. It now became a ritual.

3

Thomas
Nelson
Page
and
the
Postbellum
Writers

Nowhere in postbellum Southern literature is this formal perpetuation of Southern chauvinism more clearly articulated than in the fiction of Thomas Nelson Page; indeed Page's conception of character and place and time is controlled by his slavish dedication to an idealization of the code of Southern heroism. He fuses the sentimental literary tradition and the glorification of the Southern past, and gives them a special significance, a special poignance, in the postbellum period when the South is suffering what he felt was the ignominy of Reconstruction. By idealizing the historical South and transmuting it into a civilization that is parochial and self-sufficient and intensely chauvinistic, Page makes the various types in his fiction—the gentleman, the lady, the Negro servant, the poor white—distinctly Southern. Throughout the stories of *In Ole* **105**

Virginia (1887), essays such as "Social Life in Old Virginia Before the War" (1892) and "The Old South" (1889), and novels like *Red Rock* (1898), *Gordon Keith* (1903), and *John Marvel* (1909), Page has the types represent that vanished era when the South was essentially a static society; and once he defines the types for us, the ceremonial celebration of the Southern past follows inexorably. Page sees the code of Southern heroism in retrospect as the armature of a great and fallen civilization. More than any of the postbellum Southern authors, he raises the code to mythical proportions. His heroes must learn to live by the code—most of his stories are basically concerned with that process of learning; his Negroes admire only those whites who enforce the code; and his Ladies insist upon the hero's demonstration of the code before they submit themselves in marriage. Page adheres to the code so rigidly that his best fiction —the stories of *In Ole Virginia*—takes on the qualities of a narrow but quite forceful epic. One feels that his heroes and heroines, who are given ideal dimensions, are perpetuating the noble qualities of a great race. His worst fiction—protracted, rambling novels like *Gordon Keith* and *John Marvel*—uses the code as a substitute for characterization and plot development.

In "Marse Chan," Page's first and best-known story, we can measure the degree to which this sentimental writer, who wanted his work "to bring about a better understanding between the North and the South," depends upon the code of Southern heroism: nowhere else in postbellum Southern literature are the various characteristics of the code so clearly dramatized and idealized than in this minor American classic.

The origins of "Marse Chan" are significant, for as Page remembers them in the Preface to his Collected Works, they prepare the reader for the mythical and sentimental world that he is entering; they condition the mind of the reader to a certain way of thinking:

> In the autumn of 1880 a letter was shown [to Page] which had been taken from the pocket of a dead private in a Georgia regiment on one of the battle-fields around Richmond. It was written in an illiterate hand on coarse blue Confederate paper, and was from a young girl in Georgia to her sweetheart. In it she told him that she had discovered since he left that she loved him, and that she did not know why she had been so cruel to him before he went away; that, in fact, she had loved him ever

since they had gone to school together in the little school-house in the woods, when he had been so good to her and that now if he would get a furlough and come home she would marry him. This was all, except, of course, a postscript. As if fearful that such a temptation might prove too much even for the man she loved, across the blue Confederate paper were scrawled these words: "Don't come without a furlough; for if you don't come honorable, I won't marry you.

The soldier dies in battle—"he got his furlough through a bullet"—and Page remarks that the "idea took possession of me, and in about ten days I had written 'Marse Chan.' This story was promptly accepted, but was not published until something over three years afterwards. It was then followed by the other stories in 'In Ole Virginia,' and later by the remaining tales in this edition."

The ingredients of the Southern local color story—honor, loyalty, love, the dangers of battle, death, the evocative past that the hero and heroine have shared—are all present in this incident upon which "Marse Chan" is based; and they are completely compatible with Page's own interest in Southern literature and life. All that Page needs to convert life into literature is the proper and authentic point of view. In choosing the slave as narrator he gives his story its most memorable quality, a voice that is a haunting and convincing echo, which, like the chorus of Greek tragedy, judges and interprets as well as reports the tragedy. Furthermore, the Negro narrator frees Page from "the necessity of being specific"; he is a spectator rather than a participant in the action," as Page's most thorough critic, Harriet Holman, has observed, and can "therefore relate the whole story without either obvious self-glorification or undue reticence." By using a Negro narrator, Page successfully creates his idyll, a sentimentalized past which no one can refute; for the Negro, romantic and superstitious and nostalgic, summons up that past with complete recall: he was there, and though at times he seems a bit of a voyeur with a phenomenal memory, he is credible as the witness of that vanished era of glory.

Sam, the Negro, tells his story to a white man, who may be Southern or Northern—we are never certain—who may be Page himself or the reader. This man meets the isolated Negro in the postbellum South—the time is the autumn of 1872—and sees a shattered, disoriented ex-slave who now is suffering the horrors of Reconstruction. Cleverly Page puts the reader in the position of the author as someone listening objectively to recorded history, a history that takes on special significance since Sam is the only survivor of the wasted plantation and now bears the burden of accuracy.

Although the general outline of the story has been given to him, Page wants the reader to feel the full pathos of his hero's death, and he provides a background—what is to be the archetypical background for all his Southern fiction—to Marse Chan's life. Seen from the point of view of the Negro Sam, this life is highly ritualistic and even mythical, as we follow the development of the Southern hero, the boy who will later defend a civilization, the innocent youth who must learn and adhere to the code of Southern heroism, which, in Page's eyes, is as impressive as that of any knight in King Arthur's court.

Chan's birth is a time of great festivity—"jes' like in de Chris'mas," the narrator reminds us—and Page makes it clear that this birth is holy and significant, like that of Christ; eventually we discover that the boy is a martyr to the Southern cause, someone crucified in a war that for Page was as religious and moral as it was civil. The father gives his infant son a body servant and elects the Negro boy Sam for that sacred role, thus promoting a love relationship between the two that stems from birth. Throughout childhood the white and Negro boys attend school together, although, as Sam quickly assures his listener, only Marse Chan studies. Sam assumes his servile condition; indeed he is proud of it and wears his slavery like a badge of honor and distinction. He is no rebellious, discontented slave but a servant happy to share his master's life, feeling that his own status is enhanced by his close relationship to Marse Chan. As he remembers the antebellum period he can picture it in only glowing terms: "Dem wuz good ole times, marster—de bes' Sam ever see. Dey wuz, in fac! Niggers didn' hed nothin' 't all to do—hes' hed to 'ten' to de feedin' an' cleanin' de hosses, an' doin' what de marster tell 'em to do; an' when dey wuz sick, dey had things son't 'em out de house, an' de same doctor come to see 'em whar 'ten' to de white folks when dey wez po'ly. Dyar warn' no trouble nor nothin'."

Plantation life is described in its rural splendor, a fit setting for the development of the Southern hero. What we witness in this early part of the story is the moral education of a young boy, the tender details of his *Bildungsroman*. Marse Chan not only learns formally in the school but also discovers how a Southerner must act in society. His early romance with Anne Chamberlain, the daughter of his father's political rival, is marked by a chivalric, deferential attitude; his loyalty to his body servant is unwavering; his defense of his father's honor remains constant. Chivalry, loyalty, honor, heroism: these traits equip Chan for the duel which forms the central conflict of the story.

Chan's father is a Democrat and Anne Chamberlain's a Whig; though both are loyal Southerners and eventually will join forces against the North, Chan's father—like all of Page's sympathetic characters—is opposed to secession and the extreme political measures of the Whigs. He buys slaves that Chamberlain sells, thus embittering the conservative. When a barn burns and a Negro, in trying to save the horses, is trapped in the flames, old Marse Chan rescues the Negro; but in demonstrating his instinctive loyalty and love for one who has served him, he blinds himself. This episode is made more dramatic, as Arthur Hobson Quinn notes, "because of the narrator's complete absence of comment." To the slave, "the 'marster' had a right to send his slave into danger, but that implied a duty to save him in turn, even if it cost his owner his eyesight." His son, who has now learned the code of Southern heroism and who has adopted his father's political and social beliefs, carries on the family traditions; he challenges Chamberlain's political ideas and consequently challenges the man. Insults inevitably occur, for these men are Southern firebrands, and they meet in that ancient chivalric contest—the duel.

For Chan the duel takes on religious connotations. As the Negro narrator remarks, Chan "look like he did sometimes when he come out of church." He is fighting for honor, and honor for Page always has a religious dimension. Furthermore, the duel is not so frivolous as a modern reader might believe, for it grows out of the central political conflict between Southerners in antebellum times; it reflects the tensions that will inevitably lead to the Civil War and reminds us of the divergent political views of many Southerners. Aesthetically Page is imitating Scott's *Ivanhoe,* but he is grafting onto the duel a political and historical meaning of particular significance. Chamberlain, the Whig, misses his opponent and Chan generously fires in the air. But there is no resolution to the conflict between these feuding families and, as in the story of Romeo and Juliet, the victims are the lovers, who must remain apart.

Page attempts to weld realistic and romantic elements in his legend. The war would ordinarily give an historical validity to otherwise trivial, sentimental situations; but the Civil War that Page describes seems enjoyable or at least romantic rather than onerous—it is an adventure, almost a *jeu d'esprit*. It is certainly not the Civil War described by De Forest in *Lily Ravenel's Conversion from Secession to Loyalty* or by Stephen Crane in *The Red Badge of Courage*. Marse Chan as a Southern hero is a boyhood projection, a fanciful surrogate that Page imagines for himself. "He 'peares ti like to go prowlin' around 'mon dem Yankees," the narrator says, "an' he use' to tek me wid im whenever he could. Yes, seh, he sut'n'y wuz a good sodjer! He didn' mine bullets no more 'n did mon drops o' rain. But I use' to be pow'ful skeered sometimes. It jest use 'to 'pear like fun to 'im."

Privately Chan grieves the loss of Anne Chamberlain in good chivalric fashion. His lady, like the lady of medieval legend—or of Scott's version of medieval legend—rebuffs him; the lover, though morbidly melancholy, does not question her judgment—she is, after all, a moral arbiter, an absolute spiritual criterion against which he measures his own inadequate self. Anne Chamberlain symbolizes Southern purity and innocence, qualities that are almost mystical and certainly beyond definition in Page's moral universe.

The conclusion of the story is sentimentally contrived but nevertheless poignant. Anne Chamberlain sends Chan a letter in which she confesses her love. Immediately after he has read the letter, Chan dies on the battle-field—heroically, of course—and his Negro body servant, loving him in death as well as in life, makes his coffin, places him in it, and takes him home. The Negro's love for his white master is the most moving aspect of "Marse Chan," the aspect that gives the story its verisimilitude and uniqueness. The relationship between Anne Chamberlain and Marse Chan is more artificial because Page must keep his heroine so incredibly idealistic that she is finally not human. She loves Chan in death; in death she can even dare to be erotic: "Miss Ann she tuk de coffin in her arms an' kissed it, an' kissed Marse Chan, an' call 'im by the name, an' her darlin,' an ole missis lef' her crying in dyar tell some on 'em went in, an' found her alone faint on de flo'." She dies and thus remains pristine and innocent, her abstract attributes never threatened by the practicalities of the post–Civil-War South. She and her lover are buried together—"dey's bofe in en sleep side over de ole grabeyard at home"—sexually united in death. "Marse Chan," although the intention is clearly unconscious on Page's part, is a minor example of the eroticism so many nineteenth-century American authors associated with death.

The only credible person in this story—and in those that follow—is the Negro. The other characters belong to a mythical past that cannot be realistically created because it is not real; it is Page's evocation, his "picture of a civilization which, once having sweetened the life of the South, has since then well-nigh perished from the earth." Page, as Jay B. Hubbell points out, "was among the first to see that the old life was passing away," and he is clearly responding to a deep need that he shared with other Southerners: "The later South wanted its heroes painted, not as provincial tobacco farmers but as heroes and Cavaliers. . . . There is just the difference between [Page's] Virginia and the real Virginia that one expects to find between a painting and a photograph. Certain details of the old life are dropped or barely mentioned; while others are emphasized in every possible manner."

The code of heroism reappears throughout Page's work. In "Meh Lady" he elaborates upon the desperate dignity of a Southern lady who preserves the family's plantation after her brother has died in the Civil War; in "Ole Stracted" he dramatizes the Negro's loyalty, his inability to adjust himself to a Reconstruction period in which his master no longer guides and protects him; in countless other stories—"The Burial of the Guns," "Little Darby," "Bred in the Bone," and "The Gentleman of the Black Stock"—he illustrates the various manifestations of the code and how they sustained Southern civilization; in essays like "The Old South" and "The Old Dominion" he stresses the idyllic lives of his ancestors—history becomes the sentimental memory of someone scarcely interested in facts. Page's stories and essays form one of the clearest and most forceful statements of white supremacy in nineteenth-century Southern literature.

In Page the belief in abstract virtues—as dramatized by the fusion between his private idealism and the authority of a Southern slavocracy—is crystallized to so exquisite a point that he is always on the verge of appearing ludicrous. In his most elaborate novel, *Red Rock* (1898), which is a defense of the South during Reconstruction, all the characters are stereotypes: Joseph Grease, the scalawag; Captain Middleton, a respectable Northern commander of Virginia; Steve Allen and Jacquelin Gray, the Southern heroes;

Miss Thomasina, the aging spinster who "belongs to the real where sincerity dwells and the heart still rules." Page was aware that "he had drifted into the production of a political tract," that "the real facts in the Reconstruction period were so terrible that [he] was unable to present the facts with true art," but when he measured the effects of Reconstruction at a later time—in *The Red Riders* (1924)—he was no more successful. Page was so committed to certain political and social attitudes—and to the defense of the entire Southern way of life—that he was incapable of writing realistically. The code of Southern heroism stifled his imagination. Only when the realistic facts of the Civil War barely touched upon Page's sentimental attitude could he affect the reader; when he yielded to realism completely, as in his later novels, the code was anachronistic and completely incompatible with the tensions of an industrial society.

Other Southern writers of the postbellum period found themselves paying an abject tribute to abstractions, and their fiction is also marked by facile moral polarities. So temperate a raconteur as Joel Chandler Harris, whose best work depends upon the fixed values of Southern plantation life and who created the most popular, most realistic Negro characters in nineteenth-century American fiction, could only see the insurgent Negroes in absolute moral terms—they were "egotistic" or "depraved"—and when he wrote his defense of Reconstruction, *Gabriel Tolliver* (1902), the conflict was not really between human beings but between the past and the present, between the old and the new order. Although Harris was not so committed to fixed types as Page and not so driven to create an elaborate defense of white supremacy, he inevitably invoked a code of idealized behavior to characterize the planters of the prewar period; and in *Gabriel Tolliver* he does succumb to the stereotypes. Lesser writers championed the code as they felt Southern civilization threatened by the unsympathetic Northerners and unappreciative, aggressive Negroes; and their work becomes highly ritualistic, involving as it does the same character types—the gentleman, the lady, the carpetbagger, the Negro—behaving in the same mannered way. "Look at our Southern gentleman," remarks a character in Sherwood Bonner's *Like Unto Like* (1878), "the finest product of civilization, the ornament and pride of the human race"; and other writers—Maurice Thompson in *Tallahassee Girl* (1884), and Thomas Dixon in *The Clansman* (1902)—draw gentlemen who are invariably benevolent, who treat the Negro with consideration so long as he remains a devoted servant and not an aspiring freedman, who respect the Northerner so long as he is not politically motivated, who—like the central figure of Dixon's *The Clansman,* a leader of the Ku Klux Klan—are latter-day heroes, dedicated, consecrated to the preservation of the South that their ancestors knew and cherished. The gentleman of this retrogressive fiction carries the moral burden of nineteenth-century Southern life, but there is no resemblance between fact and fiction—the gentleman loses all individuality because of the code of heroism, that elaborate fusion of idealism and authority in the name of Southern civilization, which he must demonstrate and constantly defend.

I should modify my remarks by adding that this portrait of the Southern gentleman was not exclusively Southern: it was reproduced and emulated by Northern authors of Reconstruction literature. In such works as Constance Woolson's "Rodman the Keeper" (1877) and Maude Howe's *Atlanta in the South* (1886) the gentleman was idealized. At times, as in Thomas Bailey's *My Cousin the Colonel* (1877), the excessive pride of the Southern gentleman is satirized; but this tendency was not typical, and even in Aldrich's novelette the bogus Southern "colonel" has redeeming virtues. Only in the work of John W. De Forest—in *A Union Officer in the Reconstruction* (1866) and *Miss Ravenel's Conversion from Secession to Loyalty* (1867)—and in the novels of Albion W. Tourgée—*A Royal Gentleman* (1874), *A Fool's Errand* (1879), and *Bricks Without Straw* (1880)—can we find a criticism of the type. De Forest objected to the Southerner's undue emphasis on virility, his unbearable "pugnacity," and Tourgée deplored the caste system, the assumption of white supremacy; but De Forest appreciated the self-respect and personal pride, the dignity and "high-breeding," of the "men of native intelligence," and Tourgée admired the gentleman for his social graces, for his bearing, for everything indeed but his political beliefs.

The other types of Reconstruction literature automatically assume their predetermined roles once that of the Southern gentleman has been defined. They are types before they are people, wooden figures in a vast morality play that hardly varies as it is retold by authors who bring at times a messianic dedication to their work. The lady is rarely seen in relation to her husband, and almost never in conflict with him; she is either the patient martyr to the ignominy of Reconstruction or, more commonly, the strong-minded, self-willed opponent of the carpetbaggers and scalawags. The Radical Republicans who appear in this fiction become the inevitable villains, incarnations of the seven deadly sins, cartoon caricatures who are invariably punished and traduced. Only the Negro is varied in conception; but, as Tourgée observed, he too tends to be seen in stereotypical ways, as either "the devoted slave, happy if the scene was laid in days of slavery, the guardian of his white folks if the grimmer postwar South was the period of the story, and the confused freedman who usually was rescued from semi-ludicrous predicaments by the white people to whom he once had belonged."

In the fiction of Thomas Nelson Page and Thomas Dixon these attitudes toward the Negro are most obvious, but they appear also in the stories and novels of Joel Chandler Harris, Mary Murfree, Maurice Thompson, and innumerable minor writers. In the 1880's Northern authors like Frank Stockton, Harriet Spofford, and Constance Fenimore Woolson accepted the Southern version of Reconstruction; the admirable freedman was the devoted Negro who recalled his contented existence before the war and who voluntarily remained faithful to his past masters. The favorite formula of Reconstruction authors—Northern and Southern—was one in which the Negro alleviated his ex-master's poverty. In Harris' "Aunt Fountain's Prisoner" he divided with the whites the rations he received from the Freedman's Bureau; in Jeanie Woodville's "Uncle Pompey's Christmas" he stole for his former owners; in Octave Thanet's *Half-a-Curse* (1887) he supported his previous master by fighting against a rapacious overseer. At times he maintained a pride in the disintegrating manor house, as in Virginia Boyle's *Brockenburne* (1897), Frances Baylor's *Claudia Hyde* (1894), and Paul Dunbar's "The Colonel's Awakening" (1898).* Or, if he had been affected by the radical ideas of the Republicans, he experimented with freedom—as in Harris' "Mom-Bi" (1887) and Mrs. Boyle's "A Kingdom for Micajah" (1900)—but he quickly returned to the peaceful existence of the slave.

---

* Dunbar was, of course, a Negro; but he, together with the other important black writer of the 19th century, Charles Chesnutt, adopted the standard formulae laid down by Page, Dixon, and the Southern local colorists.

More often, however, the noble Negro—like Aunt Martha of William Baker's *Mose Evans* (1874)—refused to attempt freedom under any conditions. These Reconstruction novels and stories were a lament for a tradition authors felt was being undermined; the condemnation of the freedman was largely reinforced by the reminder of better days before the war, and except for Thomas Dixon (the author of *The Leopard's Spots, The Clansman,* and *The Traitor*) postbellum writers were not bitter.

As sentimental as the fiction of Thomas Nelson Page, Joel Chandler Harris, and lesser writers may have been, it succeeded in establishing the Southern conception of Reconstruction on the national mind. The "gentlemen" were pictured as nobly enduring the indefensible and oppressive regime of Radical Republicanism, and only when the tyranny of carpetbaggers became intolerable was there reversion to such an organization as the Ku Klux Klan. The Negroes were drawn as the bewildered victims of unscrupulous carpetbagger leaders; they, as well as the whites, recalled a better time "befoah the war." In the hearts of all these Southerners there was no rebellion, no hatred, no desire for renewed strife; and their land became a welcome haven for Northerners who wished to live in an agrarian culture. So dominant was this picture of the postbellum South, so eagerly did people of the North accept it, that by the mid-1880's Northern writers were imitating these same themes of reconciliation in their own Reconstruction fiction.

The Negro needed guidance, Page knew, but he asserted repeatedly that the guidance should be given by the Southerner— the Negro, after all, was a Southern problem. And the late nineteenth-century Northern legislators, as Rayford W. Logan has pointed out in *The Negro in American Life and Thought* (1954), tended to agree with him. The authority of Southern civilization, which had been so seriously challenged in mid-century by Northern authors, controlled the imagination of late nineteenth-century writers—with obvious exceptions, like Twain, James, and Howells —and suppressed a genuine conflict between private moral values, between personal idealism and inherited cultural traditions. The obvious questions that torment Faulkner's heroes are not even suggested in Southern fiction of the nineteenth century. And one feels, at times, that the elaborate treatment of *Huckleberry Finn* by recent critics stems in part from the fact that Twain's novel is the only important work of art by a nineteenth-century Southerner which penetrates beneath the code of Southern heroism, which challenges the authority of that repressive code. Huckleberry Finn is more genuinely a hero than the other characters in the fiction I have discussed because he asserts a private ideal against a social authority which he has come to understand; his moral perception terrifies him, precisely because it has to burn through the encrustations of a life that has always been clearly defined. The concept of heroism for other nineteenth-century Southern writers is really a concept of Southern authority. The hero perceives nothing new about himself or his culture because the conclusion to his story has been told before he begins to act; and that conclusion is not the fate which lies within character but the fate of a social condition which inhibits idiosyncrasy, development, freedom.

Page published, in 1904, *The Negro: the Southerner's Problem.* Although this long essay is not so belligerent nor so vulgar as Thomas Dixon's work of the same period, Page is equally committed to Negro inferiority; his essay is the climax, the apotheosis of the reactionary attitude in which class distinctions are rigid, in which the Southern gentleman and lady and carpetbagger, scalawag and Negro represent ideas or abstractions that the writer is promulgating. In 1903 Page had written *Gordon Keith,* warning the reader that "Gordon Keith was the son of a gentleman," that "this fact . . . was his only patrimony"; he had sent his hero into the modern world armed only with the inherited code of Southern heroism, and though Gordon Keith had triumphed morally over the inequities of city life, he seemed as incongruous in the twentieth century as his father, who "knew the Past and lived in it," who "did not understand" the present, and "did not know" the future. Six years later Page published a novel of Christian Socialism—*John Marvel, the Assistant*—in which the Southern hero is a caricature of his former self; he tries to adjust his code of heroism to socialistic problems of the twentieth century, but it is clearly not relevant, and the reader senses Page's own loss of confidence, the incompatibility of his archaic attitudes with the modernity of his subject matter. In 1906, a critic of Page's collected works suggested the reasons for "the waning influence of Thomas Nelson Page": "the fact remains that the South has outgrown Mr. Page one way or the other. The spirit of the South dramatized in his books is no longer sufficiently related to this new spirit to command its interest and obeisance . . . Henceforth the novelist of Southern life must change his scene, bring it forward. And Mr. Page can no more do this than he can change his name and his genius. Both belong essentially to the past, and as part of it they command respect, admiration, even reverence, but no longer absorbing interest."

These remarks apply not only to Page's work but to all of that nineteenth-century literature predicated upon the code of Southern heroism. The tendency to evoke the past so as to justify the present; the celebration of manners, of social customs, of military accomplishments; the deification of women; the unremitting, unmodified defense of the South—all of these attitudes seem excessive now and indeed seemed excessive to Southern writers who matured in the early twentieth century. James Branch Cabell, Ellen Glasgow, Mary Johnston, and others rebuked the chauvinism of their immediate predecessors, and they began to explore the implications of the nineteenth-century obeisance to the heroic attitude. Cabell satirized Page's "Meh Lady" in *The Rivet in Grandfather's Neck* (1915), and later in his life—in his novel *Let Me Lie* (1947)—he deplored the fact that when Ellen Glasgow's early work was written "the ghost of Thomas Nelson Page still haunted everybody's conception of the South, keening in Negro dialect over the Confederacy's fallen glories." But as self-conscious as Cabell is, one feels his inevitable pride in the Southern past that he criticizes, and his work is not wholly free of sentimentality.

Ellen Glasgow also lamented the sentimentality of nineteenth-century Southern fiction, and like Cabell she had a deep attachment to her rich Virginian heritage. She is more successful than he in creating a realistic account of the Southern past, but her novels are never completely free of those limitations she censures so severely. As she writes in *A Certain Measure* (1943), she sought to create a literature with "blood and irony" that was in no way incompatible with the feeling that "the race that inherits a heroic legend must have accumulated an inexhaustible resource of joy, beauty, and tragic passion. To discard this rich inheritance in the pursuit of the standard utilitarian style is for the Southern novelist, pure folly." In *Virginia* (1913) and *Life and Gabriella* (1916) she is capable of criticizing the idealization of Southern womanhood— as Mary Johnston did in *Hagar* (1913)—without sacrificing the specific heroic qualities of specific Southern women; these and the other novels of the "Old Dominion cycle"—especially *Barren Ground* (1925) and *Vein of Iron* (1935)—implicitly reject the slavish devotion to the code of heroism without forgoing a genuine belief in the hero. Still, Ellen Glasgow's work is not wholly satisfying. She attempts to control the romantic elements that always threaten to turn sentimental in the sort of historical saga she creates; but she is, as John Edward Hardy has suggested, "in many ways, essentially a sentimentalist" who never fully realizes "her best potentialities as an artist" and whose "fondness for 'ideas' [is] always too superficial to become really involved with her feeling for character. . . . Her intellectualism *was* basically hostile to legend," and, as Hardy concludes, "the lack of a feeling for legend, particularly, is bad for a Southern novelist." Ellen Glasgow has long been a favorite of literary historians, a "transitional" figure who rejected the sentimentality of the past but never completely accepted the earthy realism so evident in the literature of the twenties and thirties; her work, however, has rarely been examined from a belletristic point of view and largely, one suspects, because it inevitably suffers under close analysis. Her characters are too often stock types, her symbolism obvious, and her situations frequently contrived. She had a sense of place and time and conveyed that sense in what is often a powerful prose style; but these qualities are not enough to give her novels permanent significance. Nevertheless, with all of its formal limitations, Ellen Glasgow's fiction—more than that of any Southern writer before Faulkner—suggests the creative possibilities inherent in a genuine examination of one's culture, of one's past.

Twentieth-Century Southern Criticism and Literature

It is not until the 1920's, when a new generation of scholars and writers have grown to maturity, that we witness the profound criticism and analysis of all those values that dominated nineteenth-century Southern fiction. Since the time of Faulkner's greatest work we have seen an implicit challenge to and reinterpretation of the code of heroism that prevented Simms, Tucker, John Esten Cooke, Page, Dixon, and scores of other writers from ever seeing the Southerner as a human being. It is always dangerous to isolate one element in a body of fiction, to claim that it is even the primary reason for a literary renaissance. But consider Quentin Compson's suicide in *The Sound and the Fury,* his tortured cry at the end of *Absalom, Absalom!,* the brooding and ultimate despair of Horace Benbow in *Sanctuary* or the revelation of Ike McCaslin in *The Bear;* turn to Robert Penn Warren's *All The King's Men,* or to Truman Capote's *Other Voices, Other Rooms,* or to Styron's *Lie Down in Darkness,* or to the gothic stories of Flannery O'Connor: all these works, and the list can clearly be extended, struggle in one form or another with the breakdown of nineteenth-century values; and their special brilliance lies in their challenge to one set of beliefs by another. Robert Penn Warren draws an illuminating parallel between New England "before the Civil War and the South after World War I to the present." He characterizes this period as a "shock, a cultural shock, to a more or less closed and static society . . . a tension that grew out of the race situation. That moral tension had always been there, but it took new and more exacerbated forms after 1920." William Styron has pointed to an attendant conflict, "the conflict between the ordered Protestant tradition, the fundamentalism based on the Old Testament, and the twentieth century—movies, cars, television. . . . It's wonderful stuff and comparatively new, too, which is perhaps why the renaissance of Southern writing coincided with these last few decades of the machine age. If Faulkner had written in the 1880s he would have written genteel novels, like those of George Washington Cable or Thomas Nelson Page."

We would now exempt Cable—the Cable of *The Grandissimes* —from this formulation. But if the sense of Styron's contention is accurate—and the pattern that I have suggested surely supports it— then the Southern writer has indeed been the victim of unconsciously prescribed attitudes toward the people and institutions of his world. The antebellum author rarely questioned the code of the gentleman or the lady; nor did he view the Negro as an intrinsically interesting human being. By the time a writer like Simms had to measure the validity of his heritage against the demands of the American society of his own time, which insisted upon a different attitude toward human nature, he was too committed to the celebration of the South ever to create significant art. Page looked backwards and created a myth that depended not on the revelation of character but on the sentimentalized memory of people who had served a heroic way of life, each in his place, each content, each fashioning for himself an ideal behavior. That heroic way of life has been challenged by Southern writers of the past thirty years; and the result has been a literary renaissance of enduring magnitude.

Southern scholarship—to return to my original contention— has been slower in releasing itself from a crippling chauvinism. Although it might be argued that *Southern Writers: Appraisals in*

Our Time—the volume which I first censured—does not represent the best scholarship in the South, it is surely a reflection of too many "appraisals" by Southerners on Southern literature. The fact is that not until the present time does one encounter genuine criticism—appreciation is far more precise a description of the writing on Southern literature. An extensive list of conservative Southern critics who approach their subjects from the historical and social point of view primarily, avoiding any real belletristic criticism, would be too long and unrewarding a task. But one can see this tendency even in the best of Southern scholars, from Edwin Mims to Jay B. Hubbell: literary history is too often invoked as a kind of screen which conceals the intrinsic mediocrity of nineteenth-century Southern literature.* Within the past few years, however, a whole generation of Southern scholars and critics—represented most recently by the newly organized Society for the Study of Southern Literature and *The Southern Literary Journal*—promises to re-examine nineteenth- and twentieth-century literature of the South from an aesthetic as well as from an historical point of view; and most of these scholars possess an intellectual freedom and a willingness to transcend chauvinism that partially stems from confidence in the significance of contemporary Southern writing.

Every student of literature owes a great debt to Edgar Allan Poe, John Crowe Ransom, Allen Tate, Robert Penn Warren, Cleanth Brooks, and other Southerners for their seminal statements

---

* Edwin Mims' relation to Thomas Nelson Page is an early example of this predilection. In the correspondence of Thomas Nelson Page at Duke University one can read a number of letters that Mims wrote to Page when Mims was still a student. They are the natural tribute to a literary figure whose work the young Mims deeply admires. As Mims develops in sophistication and as Page, in the 1890's and the early 1900's, clearly reveals his inability to develop beyond the distinctive quality of his early work, Mims forgoes any criticism of his fellow Virginian—one can feel the sense of loyalty Mims has towards Page, his unwillingness to make a distinction between Page the Virginian and Page the writer of Virginia.

In a far more elaborate and sophisticated fashion, Jay B. Hubbell expresses a similar sympathy—to Page and all the minor nineteenth-century Southern writers he considers—which prevents him from going beyond an historical and social treatment of his subject. His monumental study, *The South in American Literature,* is an invaluable source book and a real beginning for any student of Southern literature. But one does not have a keen enough sense of the aesthetic discrimination necessary in a book that deals with so many writers whose works are, after all, of little literary merit.

on the practice of literary criticism as well as for their own fiction and poetry. Now that a new group of highly imaginative Southern critics are evaluating the literature of their region, one can anticipate a scholarship as exciting and productive as contemporary Southern fiction—a scholarship liberated finally from any form of sectionalism or obvious self-defense, free finally from a parochialism that limited nineteenth-century Southern literature itself.

THREE

The Black Hero

1

The
Idealism
of
Negro
Literature

Any adequate
description of the Negro's contribution to American literature must
inevitably account for the recurrent violence that we find in so
many varied works: brooding sexuality in Jean Toomer's *Cane;*
abrasive relations between Negroes and whites of the Caribbean in
Eric Walrond's *Tropic Death;* brutal murder in Richard Wright's
Native Son; compulsive aggression in Chester Himes' *If He Hollers
Let Him Go;* a culminating race riot in Ralph Ellison's *Invisible
Man;* historical vengeance and suicide in James Baldwin's *Another
Country.* Violence is purgative in these and other books by Negro
writers; it releases hostility and announces the black man's existence
in a convulsive, unpredictable manner; and, after the long, per-
forced silence of the Negro throughout the nineteenth and early
twentieth centuries, it tears aside the historical curtain and prepares
us for a private drama of lives we can scarcely have imagined because they were only reflected in the fiction of white authors who
usually had a case to plead, a civilization to protect.

Violence is a natural and expected feature of Negro writing, **125** for in the absence of a coherent and usable literary tradition, the Negro author has remained very close to fact—his first significant artistic achievement was in the form of autobiography—and he has recorded his despair directly; but violence in itself is of little literary interest or importance, and in the case of the Negro its meaning lies in what inspired the gesture and particularly in the resulting works of art—measured not for their "historical" or "sociological" significance, as so often they tend to be, but for their intrinsic aesthetic value. Inspiration varies, but the accomplished art of Negro authors is characterized by a pervasive idealism that seems paradoxical when one considers the frustration out of which it grows. Yet the one American who is most qualified to view the world as absurd refuses to do so; the one American who might most understandably resort to "black humor" rejects that aesthetic —and ultimately moral—point of view; the one American who should inform his work with rejection seeks to find modes of acceptance. Behind the violence, sometimes indistinguishable from it, lies an idealism that is peculiarly and historically American, in at least one strain of our literature, and that suggests the reason for a great flowering of Negro literature in our own time.

2

THE   *Booker T.*

TWO   *Washington*

TRADITIONS   *and*

W. E. B.

Du Bois

One way
of beginning to understand the different forms that this idealism
has assumed is by considering briefly two books which inaugurate
important Negro writing in America: Booker T. Washington's *Up
From Slavery* (1901) and W. E. B. Du Bois' *The Souls of Black
Folk* (1903). Washington's work is the most famous slave narrative
in our literature. Earlier autobiographies—notably Frederick Douglass' powerful indictment of slavery, *My Bondage and My Freedom*
(1855)—illuminate the Negro's attitude toward white supremacy
in the nineteenth century, but *Up From Slavery* comes at a moment in American history which affords Washington a special
opportunity to write a public document as well as a personal
memoir—*Up from Slavery* is, at all times, directed to its white
audience.

"I was born a slave on a plantation in Franklin County, Virginia," Washington records; "my life had its beginnings in the   **127**

midst of the most miserable, desolate, and discouraging surround-
ings." With this straightforward, unpretentious opening, one is
prepared for a faithful depiction of Negro life on the plantation—
from the inside, as it were, and not through the benevolent, paternalistic eyes of Thomas Nelson Page or Joel Chandler Harris; one
is prepared for an iconoclastic autobiography of real historic, if not
aesthetic, value. But except for several descriptions of the impoverished condition of Washington's family, the early pages of *Up
From Slavery* presents a picture of slavery no different essentially—
no more human, or inhuman, as the case may warrant—from that
of Page or Harris, and, moreover, one that is continually conditioned by Washington's optimism and religious faith:

> Then, when we rid ourselves of prejudice, or racial feeling, and
> look facts in the face, we must acknowledge that, notwithstand-
> ing the cruelty and moral wrong of slavery, the ten million
> Negroes inhabiting this country, who themselves or whose ances-
> tors went through the school of American slavery, are in a
> stronger and more hopeful condition, materially, intellectually,
> morally, and religiously, than is true of an equal number of
> black people in any other portion of the globe. This is so to such
> an extent that Negroes in this country, who themselves or whose
> forefathers went through the school of slavery, are constantly
> returning to Africa as missionaries to enlighten those who re-
> mained in the fatherland. This I say, not to justify slavery—on
> the other hand, I condemn it as an institution, as we all know that
> in America it was established for selfish and financial reasons,
> and not from a missionary motive—but to call attention to a fact,
> and to show how Providence so often uses men and institutions
> to accomplish a purpose.

The title of Washington's narrative suggests his inexorable
optimism: he is interested in the Negro's movement away from
slavery, up rather than through, a movement that in Washington's
own case was effected by his "struggle for an education." He based
his personal confrontation with white America, although at times
it scarcely seems to be a confrontation, on the belief that "every
persecuted individual and race should get much consolation out of
the great human law, which is universal and eternal, that merit,
no matter under what skin found, is in the long run, recognized
and rewarded"; and the tension that exists in *Up From Slavery* is

between Washington's unwavering self-belief, his tenacious self-reliance and idealism, and the society that excluded him. By accepting without question *laissez-faire* capitalism and by adopting those puritanic virtues—hard work, cleanliness, earnestness, and thrift—of the American culture which had suppressed the development of his race, he knew that he must succeed.

And from all practical points of view he did succeed. His life story is a lesson for persecuted people, a kind of primer on how to succeed in spite of your background.* "As I now look back over my life," he reminds us, "I do not recall that I ever became discouraged over anything that I set out to accomplish." This unwillingness to be dismayed is reflected in his comments upon racial conditions in America: conditions are improving, movement is upward and away from slavery, the Negro simply has to improve himself to improve his situation. He speaks of the ruthlessness of the Ku Klux Klan, but he assures the reader that he has "referred to this unpleasant part of the history of the South simply for the purpose of calling attention to the great change that has taken place since the days of the 'Ku Klux.' Today there are no such organizations in the South, and the fact that such ever existed is almost forgotten by both races. There are few places in the South now where public sentiment would permit such organizations to exist." The Negro ministry, he admits, was at times corrupt, but "the 'calls' to preach, I am glad to say, are not nearly so numerous now as they were formerly, and the calls to some industrial occupation are growing more numerous. The improvement that has taken place in the character of the teachers is even more marked than in the case of the ministers." He describes the poverty of Negroes in the surrounding area of Tuskegee "mainly for the reason that later I want to emphasize the encouraging changes that have taken

---

* The editors of *The Negro Caravan* (New York, 1941) suggest, in their introduction to the section on Biography, that autobiographies like Washington's or Kelly Miller's *Out of The House of Bondage* (1914), Robert Russa Moton's *Finding a Way Out* (1920), William Pickens' *Bursting Bonds* (1923), James Corrother's *In Spite of Handicap* (1916), Benjamin Brawley's *The Lower Rungs Of The Ladder* (1925), and A. Clayton Powell's *Against The Tide* (1939) are "American success stories," written by men who had risen "over such obstacles as prejudice, poverty, and lack of privilege"; and they point out "that the tradition whose motto is *ad astra per aspera* is not genuinely autobiographical. These books served for race edification and encouragement; they serve less as revelations of personalities."

place in the communities, not wholly by the work of the Tuskegee school but by that of other institutions as well." Improvement is the keynote that is struck in *Up From Slavery,* an improvement that results from honest labor—"nothing ever comes to one, that is worth having, except as a result of hard work"—and Washington presents his simple lesson simply, earnestly, entirely unconscious of what seem to us platitudes, employing a bare, unpretentious, utilitarian prose that suits his practical ideas. His autobiography is characterized by the sentimental idealism of a good man—particularly of a good American—whose every line is poised deliberately between teaching and preaching.

One reads *Up From Slavery* as one reads a moral tract and not a work of literature, for it is infused with how life could be if only one were as virtuous, as selfless, as determined, as self-confident as Booker T. Washington himself. The book lies heavily in one's hands, for it lacks the essential ingredient of literature— the ingredient that Richard Wright's *Black Boy,* with all its obvious blemishes, possesses—that is necessary for enduring autobiography: the complexity of the inner life. Toward the end of his autobiography, Washington confesses that "fiction I care little for. Frequently I have to almost force myself to read a novel that is on every one's lips. The kind of reading that I have the greatest fondness for is biography. I like to be sure that I am reading about a real man or a real thing." Although this is the natural bias of that kind of American who traditionally has considered fiction frivolous, it nevertheless suggests the imaginative dimension that is lacking in *Up From Slavery;* and one concludes that Washington succeeded in life, if not in literature, precisely because he did not permit himself to explore the complex results of slavery on the Negro's sensibility in the late nineteenth century.

Booker T. Washington's stiff moral position—his acceptance of American culture and his desire to be assimilated into it—represents one aspect of the idealism present in Negro writing. One can find its imaginative counterpart in the work of his two contemporaries, Charles W. Chestnutt and Paul Dunbar, who avoided the tensions of the Negro mind and who created dialect stories and poems similar to those of white authors who had commented upon Negro life in the 1880's and 1890's. Chestnutt and Dunbar reflected "the styles popular at the time," as Ralph Ellison has recently pointed out, "styles uninterested in the human complexity of Ne-

groes. These were the styles of dialect humor transfused into literature from the *white* stereotype of the Negro minstrel tradition."

From still another point of view, one can discover a later and
more sophisticated instance of Booker T. Washington's compromising attitude in the literary criticism of William S. Braithwaite, the
most influential Negro critic of the 1920's. Braithwaite, in an essay,
"The Negro in American Literature," is careful not to censure
Thomas Nelson Page, Joel Chandler Harris, or George Washington
Cable too severely for their characterization of the Negro. When
he turns to the work of Negro writers, he readily admits that "all
that was accomplished between Phyllis Wheatley and Paul Laurence
Dunbar, considered by critical standards, is negligible, and of
historical interest only." And the chief reason, he believes, that the
literary energy of many able Negro writers "has been dissipated
is the great attention of Negroes to polemical issues." Like Booker
T. Washington, Braithwaite is disturbed by the Negro who is contentious, and he cites as his example, Claude McKay, author of
the book of poems, *Harlem Shadows* (1922), and the later novels,
Home to Harlem (1928), *Banjo* (1929), and *Banana Bottom*
(1933). "Claude McKay, the poet who leads his generation, is a
genius meshed in this dilemma. His work is caught between the
currents of the poetry of protest and the poetry of expression; he is
in turn the violent and strident propagandist, using his poetic
gifts to clothe arrogant and defiant thoughts, and then the pure
lyric dreamer, contemplating life and nature with a wistful sympathetic passion. . . . Negro poetic expression hovers, for the moment, pardonably perhaps, over the race problem, but its highest
allegiance is to Poetry—it must soar."

Later critics were also censorious of Negro writers who, they
felt, were either too bitterly polemical or who seemed to describe
only the Dionysian aspects of Negro life. In 1927 Benjamin Brawley
claimed that the writers of the Negro Renaissance—particularly
those who wrote of Harlem—portrayed only prostitutes, gamblers,
and other marginal figures; George Morse also criticized this portrayal as one which presented what he called "the fictitious" Negro;
and Dubois, Sterling Brown, and others found fault with those
Negro writers who exaggerated the aspects of violence and "licentiousness" in Negro life. There is little question that these critics
were justified, but they express a certain embarrassment at this
revelation of a very real element in Negro life of the twenties and

thirties—they speak more as sociological than as literary critics, for the limitations of McKay and others are the limitations of perception and understanding, of talent, as it were; later writers like Wright, Ellison, and Baldwin also depict the violence in Harlem, Chicago, and elsewhere, but they succeed in strengthening their work with a greater intellectual authority, a deeper creative vision. Although Benjamin Brawley, Sterling Brown, and James Weldon Johnson—another critic who censured the Renaissance writers for their description of "the picturesque and exotic"—are far more sophisticated than Booker T. Washington, they resemble their predecessor in their desire to have Negro literature reflect life as it ought to be rather than as it was—or, at least, as it seemed to be to the creative artists—and there is a sentimental idealism that colors much of their writing.

Braithwaite is more extreme than these later critics; whereas they want Negro writers to record the "workaday" facets of black people, the sociologically relevant facts of Negro life, Braithwaite urges the Negro to be as little Negro as possible. His chief praise is accorded that literature which "emerges from the color line and is incorporated into the body of general and universal art." It is only "a mere accident," he claims, "that birth or association" has caused Jean Toomer to write of Negro life; and the highest achievement of Du Bois' *The Souls of Black Folk,* it would seem, is the way in which is suggests the Negro's assimilation into American life: "It is only through the intense, passionate idealism of such substance as makes *The Souls of Black Folk* such a quivering rhapsody of wrongs endured and hopes to be fulfilled [that] the poets of the race with compelling artistry can lift the Negro into the only full and complete nationalism he knows—that of the American democracy. No other book has more clearly revealed to the nation at large the true idealism and high aspiration of the American Negro."

There is no question that *The Souls of Black Folk* is grounded in idealism, but it is a very different idealism from that expressed by Booker T. Washington, Chesnutt, Dunbar, and Braithwaite himself—Dubois' book initiates, in fact, the central, most vital and permanent themes of Negro writing in America. Washington's concern with the social welfare of the Negro was naturally at odds with the creative temperament, and his idealism, on the practical level, did not sufficiently account for the white man's resistance to genuine civil rights—he represented, as Du Bois pointed out in *The*

Souls of Black Folk, "the old attitude of adjustment and submission." A tough-minded sociologist who was interested in the facts of Negro life in America, Du Bois also concerned himself with the "souls of black folk," with their inner lives as well as with the host of social wrongs inflicted upon them; his book and much of his later writing served as a liberating influence on the imagination of Negro artists.*

In the first essay of *The Souls of Black Folk,* "Of Our Spiritual Strivings," Du Bois characterizes in bold terms the race prejudice that then existed in the United States:

> But before that nameless prejudice that leaps beyond all this he stands helpless, dismayed, and well-nigh speechless; before that personal disrespect and mockery, the ridicule and systematic humiliation, the distortion of fact and wanton license of fancy, the cynical ignoring of the better and the boisterous welcoming of the worse, the all-pervading desire to inculcate disdain for everything black, from Toussaint to the devil,—before this there rises a sickening despair that would disarm and discourage any nation save that black host to whom "discouragement" is an unwritten word.

The subsequent essays are statements of the despair under which Negroes have lived and still live in America. What seemed militant in 1903—and indeed was militant—in comparison to Washington's conciliatory point of view now appears to be merely objective observation. "The problem of the twentieth century," as

---

* It is rather ironic that later in the century Du Bois was sharply critical of some of the fiction written during the Negro Renaissance. He attacked, for example, Claude McKay's *Home to Harlem* for pandering to "that prurient demand on the part of white folks for a portrayal of Negroes of that utter licentiousness which conventional civilization holds white folks back from enjoying." Having urged a full examination of Negro life, Du Bois, as well as those critics mentioned above, found the unsavory aspects of such an examination distasteful. But this has been the obvious dilemma of Negro critics and artists throughout the century: how does a writer, deeply conscious of social evils that have beset him and his people, explore in a disinterested way the qualities of human nature—regardless of their consequences, regardless of their possible pejorative effects on the politics of his race. The difficulties in attempting to resolve this tension within the mind of the sensitive Negro writer go far in explaining the dearth of significant Negro fiction and poetry as opposed to the interesting criticism and sociological literature in which the problem is fully explored.

Du Bois states in his essay on the Freedmen's Bureau, "is the problem of the color line,—the relation of the darker to the lighter races of men in Asia and Africa, in America and the islands of the sea." And his essays on Booker T. Washington, the training of black men, the black belt, and on the relationship between "the sons of man and master"—the finest essay in *The Souls of Black Folk*—have proven so accurate that we never question Dubois' self-conscious confession:

> I have sought to paint an average picture of real relations between the sons of master and man in the South. I have not glossed over matters for policy's sake, for I fear we have already gone too far in that sort of thing. On the other hand, I have sincerely sought to let no unfair exaggerations creep in. I do not doubt that in some Southern communities conditions are better than those I have indicated; while I am no less certain that in other communities they are far worse.

The hope, the muted idealism, that emerges from Du Bois' recognition of the tensions between the races and the evils inflicted upon the Negro is far more persuasive than the compromising optimism of Booker T. Washington. As James Weldon Johnson suggests in *The Autobiography of an Ex-Coloured Man,* Du Bois made a beginning for "the future Negro novelist and poet" who wished "to give the country something new and unknown, in depicting the life, the ambitions, the struggles, and the passions of those of their race who are striving to break the narrow limits of traditions."

The Autobiography of an Ex-Colored Man, as Johnson himself admits, was a natural result of Du Bois' early achievement. Published anonymously in 1912, it did not receive wide popularity until 1927 when Carl Van Vechten praised it highly, claiming that the book "reads like a composite autobiography of the Negro race in the United States in modern times." Van Vechten's judgment seems justified, for Johnson's book has the verisimilitude of an autobiography: one is so persuaded by *The Autobiography of an Ex-Coloured Man* that he never suspects it is the fictitious creation of a man who was also a song writer, a poet, and a political activist for the NAACP. Johnson achieves his effect through his unpretentious style, his intimate point of view, his natural attitude toward the Negro and white worlds in which he travels; and the simplicity of his presentation makes the bewildered state of his light-skinned

Negro convincing and compelling. *The Autobiography of an Ex-Coloured Man* is concerned with a man's renunciation of his racial heritage and the guilt that results from his self-betrayal. By limiting his point of view to the mind of his hero and by almost completely avoiding a moral commentary of his own, Johnson impresses upon us the confused state of a growing boy who does not know if he is colored or white, who has only a dim sense of his parentage, and who searches for a role he can assume in American society.

The nameless hero traces his moments in a "little town of Georgia a few years after the close of the Civil War," through his youth in Connecticut; his adulthood in Jacksonville, New York, and Paris; and his marriage to a white woman in New York. His entire life is rendered ambivalent because of his white skin and his realization that his mother is of mixed blood. Johnson wisely avoids the sensational aspects of his theme: the boy's mother is clearly in love with the gentle white father, a dim but very real presence in the novel, and the parents have agreed—at what emotional cost we can only surmise—to separate. The boy's departure from Connecticut, after he has learned of his Negro background and after his mother has died; his life among Negroes in Florida; his introduction as a musician to the nightlife of New York; his experiences as a valet for a wealthy white man in Europe—all of his adventures lead to his first instinctive and idealistic decision to return to the United States so that he can voice, as a composer, "all the joys and sorrows, the hopes and ambitions, of the American Negro, in classic musical form." But his idealism is quickly stifled by the authority of American bigotry. After witnessing the lynching and burning of a Negro by white Southerners, he decides to abandon the Negro race because of "shame, unbearable shame. Shame at being identified with a people that could with impunity be treated worse than animals. For certainly the law would restrain and punish the malicious burning alive of animals." Although these decisions are not strongly enough motivated, the book concludes properly with the narrator's acquiescence to the white culture, his unheroic but humanly convincing surrender to the course of action that makes the fewest demands on him and on his children.

James Weldon Johnson's work is transitional in the history of Negro literature in America. It recalls the social acquiescence toward whites that one finds in Chesnutt, Dunbar, and Booker T. Washington, but it also suggests the open criticism of Dubois and the more direct commentaries soon to be made by the writers of the Negro Renaissance. The central ambivalence of Johnson's novel—the white-skinned boy who discovers that he has Negro blood but then decides to reject his Negro image so that he can prosper practically—can be explained by Johnson's specific aims in *An Autobiography of an Ex-Coloured Man,* but the historical moment in which it was written greatly modified the tone, the point of view, and the theme of his novel. A few years later Negroes burst upon the literary scene in an attempt to present the diversity of Negro life in Panama, Haiti, Georgia, Washington, Chicago—and, of course, in the center of American Negro life, Harlem.*

* Johnson's changing attitude toward the writers of the Negro Renaissance illuminates the delicate balance in the minds of so many Negro artists and critics of this period. As an artist, Johnson admired Carl Van Vechten's *Nigger Heaven* for not viewing "the Negro as a type"; but as a critic (in his autobiography, *Along This Way,* 1937) he deplored the emphasis of Renaissance writers on the "picturesque and exotic" aspects of life in Harlem.

3

THE   *Langston*

NEGRO   *Hughes,*

AWAKENING   *Jean*

Toomer,

Rudolph

Fisher,

and

Others

The Negro Renaissance

produced the first important body of literature by American Negroes. In 1925, Alain Locke, a formative and sophisticated Negro scholar, published an anthology of contemporary writing by Negroes that attempted "to register the transformations of the inner and outer life of the Negro in America that have so significantly taken place in the last few years"; and he called his volume, *The New Negro, An Interpretation*. The Negro was undergoing a metamorphosis, Locke maintained, in which he was shedding the old chrysalis of the Negro problem and "achieving something like   137 a spiritual emancipation." Whereas the old Negro had always been a type in the fiction of white authors and had consequently seen himself in "the distorted perspective of a social problem," the New Negro was "shaking off the psychology of imitation and implied inferiority" and creating a literature concerned with the human behavior of individuals in their private lives. "The American mind," Locke concluded, "must reckon with a fundamentally changed Negro."

The metamorphosis that characterizes the writing of Negroes in the 1920's is represented, in Locke's volume, by such prose writers as Rudolph Fisher, Eric Walrond, and Jean Toomer; by the poets Claude McKay, James Weldon Johnson, Countee Cullen, and Langston Hughes; and by essayists and social thinkers like Kelly Miller, E. Franklin Frazier, Charles S. Johnson, Walter White, and W. E. B. Dubois. These are some of the important writers of the Negro Renaissance—or Awakening, to use a more accurate term—and their contribution to American literature, minor in its intrinsic aesthetic significance, is an interesting footnote to the important literature of the 1920's. Caught up in the post-war mood of disillusionment they were too self-conscious, as Ralph Ellison has recently noted, of the despair that informed so much of the work of white authors in this period. But if their themes were typical of the "lost generation," their techniques resembled those of the local color writers who preceded them by fifty years, many of whom—Thomas Nelson Page, Joel Chandler Harris, George Washington Cable, and others— were responsible for the image of the Negro that dominated America literature until the 1920's. Like the local colorists, these Negro writers celebrate folkways and note the significance of place —British Guiana, Panama, Harlem, Chicago, or Georgia—in the lives of their characters; they make extensive use of dialect and are fond of the exotic; and their work tends to be sentimental and impressionistic, avoiding the close or penetrating analysis of human character. We see a new Negro emerge in the 1920's—a fully human Negro and not a refraction of the white author's sensibility, a character rather than a caricature—but we do not yet see deeply into his mind.

When we search for the particular forces that lie behind the changing Negro character of the 1920's, we are impressed by the way in which the comic, essentially idealistic Negro of nineteenth-century literature has become frenetic, pugnacious, curious, and at times violent. Rudolph Fisher's work, which appeared in the twenties and thirties, may serve as an example. In short stories such as "The City of Refuge," "Vestiges," and "Miss Cynthie," and his novels, *The Walls of Jericho* (1928) and *The Conjure-Man Dies* (1932), Fisher presents a basically satirical, often ambivalent point of view. In the stories, which constitute his most effective writing, a similar situation recurs: an adult whose character has been formed in the South arrives in Harlem, discovers that "the city of refuge" is in fact a "city of Satan" where deceit, disloyalty, and avarice have come to dominate the lives of many Negroes. Fisher is particularly effective in evoking the saturnalian quality of Harlem life in the 1920's, but he attempts more than mere local color; he humanizes the corrupt as well as the innocent figures in his stories, and he suggests the great influence of place in the morality of his characters. The ambivalence of his point of view is suggested by the recurrent idealism that is beneath the surface of his fiction and that emerges as the conclusion to so much of his work.

Fisher's finest story, "Miss Cynthie" (*Story,* 1933), describes the arrival of a religious Southern Negro woman whose grandson is a tap-dancer and singer, a recognizable, indeed almost mythical hero in Harlem. Although the seventy-year-old woman finds it difficult to accept the role of this boy whom she had always thought of as a doctor, a dentist, or, as she reminds herself rather whimsically, at least an undertaker, she comes to realize that he has developed organically and honestly, on his own terms—and that, to an extent, his terms were hers too, for she had first sung to him, she had first given him her joy and her own love of music. She finds herself, at the end of her grandson's performance in a cabaret, tapping time to the orchestra's jazz recessional, recognizing that her early advice to the boy—"Son, do like a church steeple—aim high and go straight"—has been achieved.

Fisher's work recreates the general ambience of Harlem—its music, its humor, its frenetic tempo, its violence and its affirmation of life. Influenced by Carl Van Vechten's *Nigger Heaven* (1926), Fisher and other Negro writers celebrated or, in some instances, censured what was characterized as the Dionysian nightlife of Harlem in the twenties. Claude McKay, who had established himself with the collection of vigorous protest poems entitled *Harlem*

Shadows (1922), made his minor contribution to the Renaissance with *Home to Harlem* (1928), a novel that concentrates upon the sexual mores of certain Negroes in Harlem, particularly those "sweetmen" who are kept by women—in Harlem and in the richer Negro section of Brooklyn—and who seek to free themselves of sexual bondage. McKay tries to recreate the violent morality of prostitutes, club owners, and longshoremen, although too often his book is little more than a report of what one might have heard in a part of Harlem in that postwar period. There is a self-consciousness about McKay's treatment which reveals that he is writing for a white audience and perhaps exaggerating for special effects, in a way that is not too dissimilar to a minstrel show—now, of course, a pugnacious, often defiant minstrel show that refuses to be conciliatory; but, in refusing to conform to the white man's stereotype, McKay simply creates a different type who has not yet become a human being. "Simple, raw emotions and real," he concludes, removing his mask and talking directly to his white reader. "They may frighten and repel refined souls [that is, white souls], because they are too intensely real, just as a simple savage stands dismayed before nice emotions that he instantly perceives are false."

Langston Hughes' *The Ways of White Folks* (1934) presents the conflict between whites and Negroes more openly. Rather than examine the mores of Negro life intrinsically, privately, and thus refute the image that the white man has of the Negro, Hughes describes the ways of white folks in relation to the Negro; and he adopts a cynical point of view—he is neither the Negro nor the white man but ostensibly the disinterested, skeptical observer—and he creates a mocking tone that suggests how little white folks know Negroes. The ways of white folks in Hughes' stories are violent ways: abortion (in "Cora Unabashed"), lynching (in "Home"), lust (in "A Good Job Done"), paternal irresponsibility (in "Red Head's Baby"). Negroes are either the victims or the helpless observers of these vices, and in the stories they embody Hughes' belief in the animated life. Whites have sacrificed the spontaneous life for the idea. In a typical story, "The Blues I'm Playing," a wealthy white woman takes on a Negro girl pianist as her protégée, but the woman has no understanding of Harlem or of jazz, and when the girl wants to marry a Negro student the woman cannot appreciate why the talented pianist wishes to sacrifice her talent for an actual life with the man she loves. "Why did white folks think you could live on nothing but art?" the girl broods, knowing that the woman cannot conceive of Negroes as she conceives of white people. Hughes' idea of depicting the fantasies that white Americans have of Negroes is sound and at times well-executed, but it leads to its own distortions, for the white people are now merely vapid aristocrats or hardened creatures seeking to molest Negroes. Hughes was only slightly more successful in his other work—in the poetry of *The Weary Blues* and *A New Song*; in his semi-autobiographical novel, *Not Without Laughter*; and in his various volumes that center upon the satirical character of Simple—by adopting a more controlled ironic attitude toward his material; he was never, however, able to produce a single volume of permanent interest.*

The limitation of *The Ways of White Folks*—and this can be said of most of the fiction and poetry of the Negro Awakening— is the lack of subtlety and complexity, the inability to admit the gradations of feeling, the facile tendency to create types—grotesque types. Like the local color fiction of the 1880's and 1890's, it is too often written to formulae and creates its own panorama of expected figures: the Negro as primitive; the Negro as victim; the white man as supercilious or vulgar or violent. There were some writers who escaped the charged atmosphere that seemed to encourage the polarization of character. Countee Cullen created some protest poetry, as in "The Black Christ," and racial verse, as in "Heritage," but his most successful achievement was in the form of lyrics that

---

* The reader may wonder at this rather perfunctory treatment of Hughes in so elaborate an essay, for Langston Hughes seems to be ever present when one discusses any aspect of Negro letters since the Negro Renaissance; but as I imply, my estimation of Hughes' writing is not especially high. Although I agree with David Littlejohn (in his brief critique of Negro literature, *White on Black*) that Hughes had the fullest and most sustained career of any Negro writer in America, I do not find any one volume of his particularly rich in ideas or rewarding in artistic achievement; his verse is scarcely more textured than popular songs, although individual lyrics like "I've Seen Rivers" and "Evenin' Air Blues" have a distinct poignancy; his fiction is superficial in terms of almost every traditional standard; and the irony that he has made his special trademark, especially in the Simple anecdotes, seems to me obvious and not very tough-minded. Hughes' career has been comprehensive, invaluable in its service to Negro writers in general—one thinks particularly of his early emphasis on the folk materials of Negroes—but his own work does not bear scrutiny. It is rather symptomatic that in his later years he became an anthologist and a journalist.

were consciously influenced by Keats. Poems like "To John Keats," "Harlem Wine," and "She of the Dancing Feet Sings" are carefully structured, musically informed, and moving—but moving in a distinctly minor way. James Weldon Johnson also wrote lyrical verse, collected in a series of volumes that explore, for the most part, his experiences as a Negro in America; but Johnson never quite escaped his early, rather facile success in musical comedy, and his verse does not have the tensions of significant poetry. Sterling Brown attempted dialect poems in *Southern Road* (1932); Anne Spencer, Angelina Grimke, Georgia Douglas, William S. Braithwaite, and others wrote reflectively and lyrically of subjects other than race, but none of them ever became more than a poetaster. The one writer of the Negro Awakening, however, who possessed talent of significance and who was able to concentrate his many natural gifts into one remarkable volume was Jean Toomer: *Cane,* a potpourri of stories, and poems, is Toomer's only full-length work, and it is the most impressive achievement of the Negro Awakening.

The available facts of Jean Toomer's life touch upon only the inner pattern of his mind. Born on December 26, 1894, in Washington, D.C., he was educated in the public schools of Washington, the University of Wisconsin (1914), where he went to study law, and for another short period in the City College of New York. He taught in the schools of Sparta, Georgia, and much of the background to *Cane* stems from that experience. Toomer was a restless man; in the twenties and thirties he settled at various times in New York, Chicago, and Carmel, California. His most intense, really his only period of literary activity, was in the twenties when his stories, essays, and poems appeared in *The Double Dealer, Broom, Opportunity, Crisis, The Little Review, Secession,* and other experimental and short-lived magazines. Although Toomer, a near-white Negro, was always self-conscious about his racial heritage—at the time of his second marriage to a white woman he remarked that he "would consider it libelous for anyone to refer to [him] as a colored man," that he really did not "know whether there is any colored blood in [him] or not"—and though he sought to identify himself with a certain brand of mysticism then popular, he focused his best work on racial issues, seen, however, in human rather than political or sociological terms. Each of the significant stories in *Cane* is strengthened by racial consciousness; the short novel, "York Beach," included in *The New American Caravan* in 1929, suggests the tensions that stem from racial differences; a long essay, "Race Problems and Modern Society" (1934), discusses the Negro's role in a predominantly white culture; and *Essentials,* a book of private meditations, recognizes the fact that "races are real; but, to men, races are prejudices."

Essentials was published in 1931 and defines Toomer's attempt to transcend the specific problems of race. He had come to feel that "Walt Whitman's average man has turned out to be Babbitt," that his generation had "two emblems, namely, the machine-gun and the contraceptive." Toomer wished to "reject compromises which give you nothing because they give you less than you want" and to insist upon the significance of man's conscience. In spite of his disillusionment with a country in which materialism was of paramount importance, Toomer continued to feel that "conscience, the heart of the human world, still beats feebly in our sense of decency."

Toomer ceased to write extensively after 1931. "The Flavor of Man," an address delivered to a group of Quakers at Philadelphia in 1949, suggests his allegiance to the Society of Friends, his concentration on man's spiritual condition, his persistent idealism, and his deep faith in God; but the address is little more than a loosely conceived transcendental tract. Toomer's achievement as an artist is represented by *Cane,* a classic of Negro literature, *sui generis,* which succeeds in capturing the quality of youthful striving and the frustrations that attend the transition from adolescence to maturity.

Cane is a miscellany of Toomer's early work, containing fictional portraits and poems of life in the villages of Georgia and in Washington, D.C. The language is impressionistic and richly textured. As a consequence, the poetry included in the volume is burdened by incremental repetitions and tends to blur before the eye; but the fiction—particularly short stories such as "Becky," "Fern," "Esther," "Blood Burning Moon," and "Avey"—is a vivid depiction of young people at moments of intense and often primitive passion. Usually the conflict is racial; usually the victim has mixed blood; and frequently he or she is left disillusioned, like the figures in Sherwood Anderson's *Winesburg, Ohio*—a book that doubtless had its influence on *Cane*—as ideals or dreams are destroyed by the sudden awareness of reality. In "Becky," a white woman who has two Negro sons becomes a pariah to both Negroes and whites; in "Fern" the girl, whose name is Fernie May Rosen, is doubly scarred by being the daughter of a Jewish father and a Negro mother; in "Blood Burning Moon," a Negro field hand kills the white lover and owner of the colored cook whom he loves himself and is burned alive by the community.

These poignant stories are, for the most part, elaborate character sketches, a gallery of portraits of life in Georgia and in Washington, D.C. The situations and events that Toomer presents are realistic in all their details, and most of them, when recounted, are filled with violence, murder, and human misery; but they are not depressing or morbid because of the author's sympathetic attitude toward his characters and because of his graceful, tender style. Toomer never judges his characters; in describing their most debased behavior, he always reminds us of their humanity, and he brings a respect to them that inevitably elicits our respect as well as our compassion and pity. The facts are realistically and honestly rendered; but they are given the romantic coloring of Toomer's moral imagination—and the contours of Toomer's imagination tend always toward the idealistic. At his best, Toomer does not view the vague desires and failures of his characters as pathetic. The frustrated lovers of "Theater" and "Box Seat"; "Robert," the man with rickets; "Carma," the unfaithful wife; "Karintha," the prostitute—all these figures are fallible human beings rather than victims.

Two of Toomer's finest stories, "Esther" and "Avey," may illustrate the author's special talents and his understanding of those people who do not have the strength to overcome their limitations. "Esther," written in a highly imagistic prose that mirrors the fantasies of a near-white girl, describes the disillusionment which results when Esther discovers that her self-created hero has become a drunken, dissolute man. She has sacrificed her life for King Barlo—for the "King" that she has privately imagined him to be—and in a last attempt she seeks to save him from those who threaten to degrade him; but when she sees Barlo "the thought comes suddenly that conception with a drunken man must be a mighty sin." The humiliation that she experiences, as Barlo and his friends mock her, is the humiliation of her dream and of her belief in an ideal that has given meaning to her constricted life. Toomer is especially effective in evoking the sexual fantasies of the fair-colored girl for the "clear-muscled, magnificent, black-skinned Negro," described as an ivory God, who is possessed of a vision that he is the risen man whom Jesus has announced, a fabulous figure who leaves town and becomes the personal myth that sustains Esther in her loneliness and her estrangement from both the Negro and the white communities. In the years of Barlo's absence, Esther grows to conceive of herself as his protectress, for "the thought comes to her that those purposeless, easy-going men [surrounding Barlo] will possess him, if she doesn't"—Toomer subtly employs an imagery of fire and darkness that suggests the hell to which Esther innocently advances, half in fear, half in sexual desire, and he forgoes any moral comment on the disillusionment that Esther experiences when "jeers and hoots pelter bluntly upon her back." King Barlo has surrendered his role as a God to his role as Satan, and for the innocent young woman redemption of this fallen figure is no longer possible.

Disillusionment is also the controlling theme of "Avey," a more personal, intimately written story in which the idealist is a boy and his adversary, the girl Avey. Focusing upon the period of sexual awareness, Toomer draws a picture of an adolescent who cannot persuade the girl he loves to be as ambitious, as "serious," as he; but his impatience with her laziness stems really from his impatience with himself and after "the business of hunting a job or something" has bruised his "vanity" so that he can recognize it, he is able to tolerate her weakness. For a moment he tries to resurrect her from a life as a prostitute—he asks "her to hope, and build up an inner life against the coming of that day"—but she falls asleep in his arms and his passion dies. The narrator's final description of Avey as an "orphan-woman" suggests the absence of human communication between the two figures, despite their understanding of each other; and Avey's isolation becomes a fact that the narrator has learned to accept. Toomer creates a poignant contrast between the young man's idealism and the girl's lethargy, her weariness, her fundamental indifference—an indifference that is more haunting than death, for it is in effect a denial of life. "I talked," the narrator concludes, "about an art that would be born, an art that would open the way for women the likes of her. I asked her to hope, and build up an inner life against the coming of that day." But the girl is asleep in his arms, a creature out of his youth, someone whom he no longer knows and who can have no place in his present, changing life.

The traditional analytic approach to a writer like Toomer

must always be less than satisfactory, for much of his effect depends upon the fantasies created through his poetic prose; his style is suggestive, elusive, and impressionistic rather than strictly denotative, a style that respects the mysteries of the people it describes. These people are made lonely by their submission to an environment which in their weakness they cannot remake. Toomer concerns himself with prostitution (in "Karintha," "Avey," and "Box Seat"), infidelity (in "Carma"), miscegenation (in "Becky"), physical disease (in "Rhobert"), and passion and violence (in "Blood Burning Moon," "Theater," and other stories); but in his awareness of the various ways human beings manage to destroy themselves and in his sense of their inward complexity, he renders the figures of *Cane* as more than merely victims, more than simply pariahs.

Implicit in *Cane* is Jean Toomer's faith in man, the idealism present in even his bleakest stories. "I am of no particular race," he was to write in a book of definitions and aphorisms called *Essentials* (1931). "I am of the human race, a man at large in the human world, preparing a new race." The poets whom Toomer admired were visionaries—Dante and Blake as well as Emerson, Whitman, and the transcendentalists; and he believed that "we do not have states of being; we have states of dreaming." Toomer persistently attempted to transcend the limitations of race and to concentrate on what he termed his "first values: Understanding, Conscience, and Ability." He scarcely developed artistically after the publication of *Cane;* he became instead increasingly introspective, increasingly concerned with the mind rather than with the world of experience. *Essentials* (1931) is a volume of definitions and aphorisms that reads like a mystic's handbook; his last published work, *The Flavor of Man* (1949) is a consecration to the life of the spirit, in which he attempts to convince us that "the alternatives of life are starkly these: transcendence or extinction." These works are ultimately private meditations, private affairs; *Cane* is Toomer's enduring work of art, in which youthful idealism is crippled by the authority of experience.

Cane is the only volume written during the Negro Awakening that one can consider a significant contribution to our literature; it is a minor American classic, similar in tone, style, and theme to Sherwood Anderson's *Winesburg, Ohio.* The violence that one finds in the work of Eric Walrond, Rudolph Fisher, Langston

Hughes, and Claude McKay is too often unfocused, explosive, or diffuse, incoherent protests or analyses of Negro and American life that are never truly profound or memorable. These writers—along with white authors like Dubose Heyward (in *Porgy,* 1924) and Carl Van Vechten (in *Nigger Heaven,* 1926), who celebrated the instinctual life of the Negro even more forcefully than their Negro counterparts—were ultimately censured, as we have seen, by such critics as W. E. B. Du Bois, James Weldon Johnson, and Sterling Brown who felt, as Brown wrote, that "the drama of the workaday life, the struggles, the conflicts [were] missing" in much of the Renaissance literature. But this criticism seems only partially true: the same reservations, after all, may be made of Hemingway, Fitzgerald, Anderson, and other genuine artists who, unlike the social writers of the thirties, avoided the "workaday life" of their characters. Negro authors of the 1920's were interested in demonstrating their humanity, in altering images of themselves that they knew were not accurate, and if, as Benjamin Brawley warned in 1927, they offered "new stereotypes, hardly better than the old," much of the reason lies in the absence of an intrinsic literary tradition from which they could develop. It would be inaccurate, furthermore, to group these writers together, as if they were united in their literary goals, as if they wrote in accordance with some mutually understood manifesto. Each of them had his own distinctive voice, his own particular point of view, and their limitations are artistic limitations. Whatever their shortcomings, however, they did examine the mores of black America in an honest and daring manner, and they opened areas of experience which later, more discriminating writers explored with greater subtlety—they were the first writers to describe the private lives of Negroes in America and their work suffers from the excesses that so often attend early work in any literary tradition. The Negro Renaissance was not really a rebirth since there had scarcely been the creation of imaginative Negro writing before the 1920's; it was rather a troublesome, suggestive, exhilarating awakening. The true Renaissance was to develop in the next generation and in the form of three distinguished, sharply individual writers—Richard Wright, Ralph Ellison, and James Baldwin.

4

THE   *Richard*

MAJOR   *Wright,*

AUTHORS   *Ralph Ellison,*

James Baldwin

Of these three
major Negro authors, Wright is least sophisticated and most direct
—his work is burdened by the violence and frustration, the alienation and subjugation present in Negro life, and his mood is
misanthropic, dour, as bleak as the world he describes. Ellison is
most self-conscious and literary, and though his early stories, written
in the late thirties and the forties, take full account of the economic
and social misery of the Negro, his writing has increasingly tended
toward the idealistic—he has become, so far as the contemporary
world permits him to be, the Emerson of American Negro writing.
Baldwin penetrates into all the aspects of violence in Negro life
but controls his awareness of this violence by a fundamentally
idealistic view of the individual—no matter how bitter he may be,
abstractly or concretely, Baldwin's central theme is the possibility
of *caritas* between whites and blacks in America. This kind of
dialectic among the three writers would, of course, be ultimately
unfair to each of them, particularly to Ellison and Baldwin whose
148   work is far more complex than I have suggested, and we should

not insist upon the formulation too rigidly; but it is not an altogether invidious or arbitrary formulation because the authors have responded to each other's writing quite overtly and dramatically, almost dialectically, in terms of rejection or acceptance or modification, and they have interpreted Negro life in America from different points of view that are illuminating. The violence and idealism of Negro literature in America resonate most richly and intricately in the work of these three interesting writers.

Each of these authors creates a Negro hero who will not truckle or seek assimilation into the white world—they feel no identification with the sentimental idealism of Booker T. Washington. Indeed Washington becomes, in Ellison's *Invisible Man* most notably, the Negro's Benjamin Franklin, full of pieties and rigidities and fears that can only inhibit manliness and the growth of genuine heroism. Violence is central to the work of Wright, Baldwin, and Ellison; but the violence serves as a moral indictment of American authority and inevitably assumes an idealistic aspect. These younger Negro authors possess the moral and therefore literary advantage of having been socially, economically, and ethically oppressed—or, if not privately oppressed, as in Ellison's case, bound to the suffering of other Negroes through the existential fact of color. Their violent criticism of the white power structure is clear—that is the passion that infuses their work and leads to moral perceptions not so sharply defined, when defined at all, by white authors. Passion and perception have a clear purpose, too, in the writing of American Negroes: the creation of complex human beings with whom the race can identify—the creation, ultimately, of literary heroes. *"Negroes want to be treated like men,"* runs Baldwin's famous lyric cry. "The idea seems to threaten profound, barely conscious assumptions." In the work of Wright, Ellison, and Baldwin, we witness for the first time the intricate creation of men, of Negro heroes whose idealism challenges the authority of American society that has too long kept them, in Baldwin's words once again, "either a ward or a victim." The sudden shift from victimization to heroism —or at least a heroism *in potentia*—helps to explain much of the peremptory violence in Negro literature and many of the ideological polarities, the extreme claims, the bitter denunciation of whites in Negro life; violence is the creative act itself, the creation of the self in defiance of a society that has been historically antagonistic to Negro manliness. Nowhere is this shift or rupture more dramatically and nakedly expressed than in the writing of Richard Wright.

Wright was concerned with the sources of power in America and the quixotic, violent reactions of the Negro as he tries to adjust himself to a hostile, alienating white society. His autobiography, *Black Boy* (1945), traces the first seventeen years of his life, his rejection of the religion of his grandmother and aunt, to whom his paralytic mother had sent him, his distrust of all people, his loneliness, his discontent with the poverty of his family, his impatience with that image of white authority that controlled him. As Wright matured, he defined his life almost completely in terms of adjustment to those individual white people whom he served. Unwilling to be humble before his employers, unwilling to acknowledge a condition of inferiority which he did not feel, he reacted unpredictably and violently.

Violence became the dominant characteristic of Wright's life and work. *Black Boy* defines how Wright attempted to suppress his tendency toward extreme behavior, how he had to dissemble before those white Southerners who expected him to be submissive. When he discovered the imaginative possibilities of literature, his own discontent and need for personal freedom found itself mirrored in the violence of fictional characters in twentieth-century American literature. "I vowed that as soon as I was old enough I would buy all the novels there were and read them to feed that thirst for violence that was in me, for intrigue, for plotting, for secrecy, for bloody murders."

Soon he was able to borrow if not buy fiction from the library by pretending that the note he presented to the librarian had been written by his employer: "Dear Madam: Will you please let this nigger boy have some books by H. L. Mencken?" Mencken, the editor of *The American Mercury* and the iconoclastic figure many young writers admired for his repeated criticisms of parochial values in America, impressed Wright because of his courage in attacking prejudice. "He was using words as a weapon," Wright recalls in *Black Boy,* "using them as one would a club." Inspired by Mencken's candor, Wright turned to Sinclair Lewis, Theodore Dreiser, and other social novelists and found their indictments of American materialism corroborated by his own experiences; in time he sensed that he must live in the North where he hoped that "life could be lived with dignity."

Wright came to Chicago in 1927, but he found little dignity in the way Negroes were treated. Because of his disillusionment with American democracy, he was attracted to the Communist Party, and in one of his earliest essays, "Blueprint for Negro Writing," he urged the Negro writer to adopt the Marxist point of view. Wright began publishing poems and essays in various radical journals: *Left Front, New Masses, Midland, The Daily Worker,* and *International.* He joined the John Reed Club, but when he refused to abandon his writing for a more political role in Communist activities, he decided to resign from the Club. In the following years, Wright was director of the Federal Negro Theater and a member of the Federal Writers Project, a subdivision of the WPA which sought work for unemployed authors. Throughout this period he found himself resisting the authority of the Communist Party, although he remained in sympathy with its principles. "I knew in my heart," he wrote later, "that I should never be able to write that way again, should never be able to feel with that simple sharpness about life, should never again make so total a commitment of faith."

Wright's first important work was *Uncle Tom's Children* (1938), a collection of long stories that emphasize the alienation and frustration of Negro sharecroppers in the rural South and the violence that occurs when these individuals contend with the restrictions of the white world—none of the young Negro figures in these tales accepts the legacy bequeathed by Uncle Tom, the emasculated slave in Harriet Beecher Stowe's novel. The stories themselves have little artistic merit—they are gracelessly written, awkwardly structured, and thematically obvious; but they have the raw power that stems from Wright's wrath at a white world which humiliates the Negro by denying his humanity—form and content are consistently organic, organic through their very imperfections.

"The Ethics of Jim Crow," the autobiographical sketch that introduces the volume, sets the mood of awakening rebellion: after Wright has been gashed by a white gang, his mother reprimands him, warning him never to fight with white boys, disillusioning him in her attempt to form still another child of "Uncle Tom." In "Big Boy Leaves Home," Negro boys, romping nakedly and quite innocently in a swimming hole, are discovered by a terrified white woman who imagines that they intend to rape her; Wright depicts the deep anxiety—an anxiety so profound it must be culturally conditioned—that grips the boys as they flee lynching mobs and travel to unknown places. In "Down by the Riverside" the antipathy of whites toward blacks is expressed as a Negro's wife loses her child because white people prevent her and her husband from reaching a hospital in time; the husband has stolen a boat and killed the owner of the boat, desperate acts necessary to his wife's survival, but his wife dies and he himself is murdered. In "Long Black Song," a white man rapes a Negro woman when her husband is gone, and the humiliated husband tries to retaliate by shooting the seducer and some of the white mob that pursues him—the story ends with the Negro waiting defiantly to be burned with his home. In "Fire and Cloud," Negroes march in protest of the white community, when the welfare board refuses to supply enough food to Negro families after a crop failure; the Negro Reverend, who has vacillated in his support of the Negroes, is molested by whites who feel that he has not succeeded in suppressing the passions of his people, and ultimately, in despair, he turns to the Communist Party and to the conclusion that "Freedom belongs to the strong!" The final story, "Bright and Morning Star," is the best known and most successful of those included in *Uncle Tom's Children,* although it is burdened by Wright's persistent didacticism. The conflict is between a Negro family—a mother and two children—involved with the Communist Party and the white community that wishes to subdue its influence. The mother kills a Negro who informs on her son, and she is shot in turn by the white mob; but she dies with the sense that she has preserved her dream of equality among all races. Wright's point of view is clear: the mother has converted her Christian values into the idealistic promise of Communism; unlike Wright's mother, in "The Ethics of Jim Crow," she has gladly surrendered her old ideas for this new ideology—there is no conflict between the old and the new generations.

Thus we have come full circle in *Uncle Tom's Children:* from individual, frustrating rebellion we have turned toward collective, hopeful action; from individual violence we have moved to the violence that stems from a new, measured idealism. Sociologically this conversion is understandable: Wright's bitterness over the Negro's individual impotence naturally pointed to some kind of collective action, and the Communist Party, growing in importance in the 1930's, offered a natural way of formalizing his frustrations, of providing a program for his tendency toward violence, and of suggesting a solution to the Negro's problem. But from an aesthetic point of view, the movement away from the individual and his personal condition is lamentable, for the stories become increasingly tendentious and obvious, as the Negro confronts his environment more often than he confronts himself—words have indeed become weapons, but awkward and ephemeral and abstract weapons because the people who use them have no inner life.

The tendentious aspect of Wright's fiction caused him to see his central figures as types in a huge social drama. The most celebrated example is, of course, Bigger Thomas of *Native Son,* in whom message entirely supplants the idiosyncrasies of human nature. Wright was dissatisfied with *Uncle Tom's Children,* though not because of any sense of aesthetic failure; he felt that he "had written a book which even banker's daughters could read and weep over and feel good about." He was determined to create a novel which "would be so hard and deep that they [the white readers] would have to face it without the consolation of tears." *Native Son* is indeed hard, but it is not very deep; and if the reader does not weep, it is not because he has experienced those thoughts that go beyond tears, it is because he has ceased to believe in Wright's hero, Bigger Thomas, and, as a consequence, ceased to care.

As Wright himself confessed, in "How Bigger Was Born," he sought to make *Native Son* into a symbolic novel. "For a long time," he notes, "I toyed with the idea of writing a novel in which a Negro, Bigger Thomas, would loom as a symbolic figure of American life; a figure who would hold within him the prophecy of our future." As one reads *Native Son,* one is continually reminded that Wright is manipulating his characters for the purposes of his message. From Bigger's point of view the Daltons—that white family for whom he works—symbolize *noblesse oblige;* from the point of view of young, liberal Mary Dalton and her boy friend, Jan, Bigger symbolizes the deprived Negro who can be used to satisfy and forward their own progressive notions. The trip that Bigger takes with this young couple through the Black Belt of Chicago is a parody of the white liberal's voyeuristic interest in Negro life, as Jan and Mary force Bigger to show them the "real" life—that is, the promiscuous life—of the Negroes.

Native Son functions almost totally on this symbolic level and is severely limited because of its didactic intentions; but in those moments when Wright describes Bigger's compulsive behavior, the boy's attempt to tear himself loose from external controls, he is indeed impressive. Bigger's behavior is characterized almost completely by fear and violence: while planning to rob Blum's grocery store he grows frightened and childlike—momentarily human—but at the same time his resistance is so violent that he nearly kills his friend; when he is surprised by Mrs. Dalton in Mary's room, he cannot control his fear and commits the central act of the novel—the murder of Mary Dalton. Although the newspapers cannot conceive of this murder as the work of a "simple Negro mind" and assume that Bigger is a dupe of the Communist Party, Wright underscores the fact that "it was the first full act of his life; it was the most meaningful, exciting and stirring thing that had ever happened to him. He accepted it because it made him free, gave him the possibility of choice, of action, the opportunity to act and to feel that his action carried weight." But, of course, the pathos implicit in Bigger's act of freedom is its failure, paradoxically, to liberate him.

Caught in the tension of desiring freedom and of never achieving it, except in momentary acts of violence, Bigger strikes one as not the character of a naturalistic novel but as the projected figure in an expressionistic drama, as an extreme version of the dehumanized Negro whose very denial of humanity disturbs us—we are reminded of Marlow's haunting comment in *Heart of Darkness* that the Africans "were not inhuman. . . . That was the worse of it—this suspicion of their not being inhuman"; and he functions in a kind of dreamlike state that is scarcely real but that establishes a dream logic in the book which takes him from one fragmented and hallucinatory act to the next, a compulsive movement that frightens and fascinates us even if it never convinces us of its novelistic credibility, that taunts and provokes the dark dread lodging in white people in America. And in the degree to which Bigger is an extreme projection of the novelist's imagination, the white people become distorted images that a Negro of Bigger's limitations, experiencing Bigger's despair, might create or even invent.

The violence that dominates the first two sections of *Native Son*—"Fear" and "Flight"—cannot sustain itself, not even in Wright's tortured imagination; it needs definition and meaning, and of course it is given a special kind of meaning in the third section, "Fate," in which idealism asserts itself in the form of communism. Wright is not content to articulate the meaning of his hero's tragedy but feels compelled to shape that meaning in generally idealistic terms that suggest the solution to the Negro's dilemma in America. James Baldwin, in "Many Thousands Gone," the most perceptive analysis of this novel that has yet been written, has indicated the falsity of Wright's idealism by suggesting that *"Native Son* finds itself at length so trapped by the American image of Negro life and by the American necessity to find the ray of hope that it cannot pursue its own implications. This is why Bigger must be at the last redeemed to be received, if only by rhetoric, into that community of phantoms which is our tenaciously held ideal of the happy social life. . . ."

Robert Bone points out, in *The Negro Novel in America,* that "for Richard Wright, Marxism became a way of ordering his experiences; it became in literary terms, his unifying mythos. It provided him with an intellectual framework for understanding his life as a Negro." But after the publication of *Native Son,* that framework crumbled and Wright was left with no ideological design for his protest; in 1941 he officially resigned from the Communist Party. Wright was a man of great passion but of few ideas; throughout his life he responded intellectually to current movements—to whatever was culturally *de rigueur*—and just as he had begun his career by subscribing to communism and by creating fiction similar to that of Theodore Dreiser—the influence of *The American Tragedy* on *Native Son* is too obvious to pursue—he was soon greatly affected by the existentialist movement that was developing in Europe in the 1940's. "The break from the United States was more than a geographical change," he reflected at the time. "It was a break with my former attitudes as a Negro and as a Communist—and an attempt to think over and redefine my thinking. I was trying to grapple with the big problem, the problem and meaning of Western civilization as a whole." As an outsider —religiously, politically, artistically, and racially—to America, Wright embraced existentialist thought and used it as the philosophical framework of his next novel, *The Outsider* (1953), in which he creates an ambiguous man, Cross Damon, who attempts to achieve noble ends through brutal deeds, who is a cross between Christ and the Devil, and who seeks, at all costs, absolute personal freedom. Although Cross Damon is responsible for four deaths, the deaths have been the consequence of his rebellion against a hostile society, and he dies in innocence, his purpose accomplished. Although, as one critic notes, the novel "completely negates the fundamentally optimistic American idealism," Wright assumes a hopeful attitude toward the future: "The myth men are going," he concludes. "The real men, the last men are coming. . . . Somebody must prepare the way for them." But this kind of abstract idealism is blurred completely by the violent and nihilistic behavior of Wright's central figure.

Without the ideological support of communism and existentialism, Wright's work lost its pseudo-intellectualism, the possibility for any kind of idealism, and became what it really always was— a raging indictment of America. His last three works of fiction are nightmare visions of his rejected country: *The Long Dream* (1957) traces a Negro boy's attempt to escape Southern white domination, which is expressed largely in sexual terms; *Eight Men* (1961), a collection of stories that had been written during Wright's entire career, suggests the emasculation so many Negro men feel, as they confront arrogant white adversaries; and, in *Lawd Today* (1963), a Negro lives through a typical day, seeking escape from his dismal existence and announcing his hatred of white society in the most violent terms: " 'Lawd, if I had my way I'd tear the building down.' If only there was something he could do to pay the white folks back for all they had ever done! Even if he lost his own life in doing it!"

Thus Wright's voice has become a kind of irrational bellow, howled at the country that has betrayed him and filled him with disgust. In the last years of his life he grew interested in the developing independence of the African nations; but after traveling into Ghana and along the Gold Coast, he knew that Africans "were black men and so was I, but . . . they would know one for a stranger." His last writings reiterate his sense of alienation—an alienation as self-willed as it had once been forced upon him: "I am a rootless man," he remarks in *White Man Listen!* (1957), "but I'm neither psychologically distraught nor in any way disturbed because of it. Personally I do not hanker after, and seem not to need as many emotional attachments, sustaining roots, or idealistic allegiances as most people. I declare unabashedly that I even cherish the state of abandonment, of aloneness . . . I welcome it." But this is the statement—a public statement, as it were—of a man who has come to accept the fate imposed upon him. All of Wright's work suggests his desire to enter into the white western world and his frustration at being excluded: that collision and all the consequent anxieties that torment the characters in his fiction lead to the inevitable violence which finds no satisfying or perdurable solution in communism or negritude or self-considered alienation but leaves the Wright victim simply alone and misanthropic.

This victim never quite becomes the hero—he dies or is destroyed in the creation of his self-hood, and his pathos lies in his arrested heroism. The strength of Wright's work is in the tragedy that strikes a boy who possesses all of the qualities of the hero— prowess, courage, intelligence, and idealism—but who can never realize them because of the authority of white society. Wright's fiction—consider only the titles of his first three books, *Uncle Tom's Children, Native Son,* and *Black Boy*—concentrates on the idealism of youth as it confronts this social authority; the tension between idealism and authority can not be resolved within the character of the incipient hero and the boy perishes or grows misanthropic, his potential heroism sacrificed to a power he cannot appropriate himself.

One does not encounter misanthropy in the work of Ralph Ellison. Although Ellison is deeply conscious of the Negro's history of humiliation, the suffering which Wright expresses so nakedly, he views the Negro in terms of possibility and transcendence. His essay on *Black Boy,* "Richard Wright's Blues," suggests his affirmative point of view; for in defining the blues as "an impulse to keep the painful details and episodes of a brutal experience alive in one's aching consciousness, to finger its jagged grain, and to transcend it, not by the consolation of philosophy but by squeezing from it a near-tragic, near-comic lyricism" and in characterizing Wright's autobiography as a book conditioned by these transcending qualities of the Negro blues, Ellison suggests those aspects of Wright's life that were humanizing. "And while it is true that *Black Boy* presents an almost unrelieved picture of a personality corrupted by brutal environment," he reminds us, "it also presents those fresh, human responses brought to its world by the sensitive child." Ellison is not blind to the bleakness of Wright's youth—no American writer of our time is more aware of the realities of American history —but he concentrates on all the humanizing forces within the boy's character so that the bleakness is blurred; and he generalizes about

the Negro's complexity until our attention is focused on the possibilities of the Negro's life rather than on its present constrictions
—the reader is forced to conclude that he is not viewing Richard
Wright so much as he is sharing Ralph Ellison's version of Wright,
distorted to fit the younger writer's attitude toward human nature.
Wright's achievement, Ellison concludes in his essay, is that "he
has converted the American Negro impulse toward self-annihila-
tion and 'going-underground' into a will to confront the world,
to evaluate his experience honestly and throw his findings un-
ashamedly into the guilty conscience of America."

Ellison himself never needed to be converted: his own confrontation with the world was far less violent than Wright's and
that of many other twentieth-century Negroes, largely because his
youth was significantly different from theirs. Although he recognized the limitations inflicted upon him in Oklahoma City, Oklahoma, where he was born in 1914 and where he grew up, Ellison
"thought those limitations were unjust"; as he notes in *Shadow
and Act* (1964), a collection of his criticism, "I felt no innate sense
of inferiority which would keep me from getting those things I
desired out of life." Oklahoma had been a state only seven years
at the time of his birth; "thus it had no tradition of slavery, and
while it was segregated, relationships between the races were more
fluid and thus more human than in the old slave states." Ellison
was compelled to attend the usual segregated schools, but he was
able to develop his interest in jazz and then in classical music
because of the excellent programs that his teachers offered. "Inter-
estingly enough," he has remarked, "by early adolescence the idea
of Renaissance Man had drifted down to about six of us [students],
and we discussed mastering ourselves and everything in sight as
though no such thing as racial discrimination existed."

Ellison wanted to be a composer of symphonic music, and from
1933 to 1936 he attended Tuskegee Institute. During his junior
year he went to New York to study sculpture; but he lost interest
in the art form and resumed his study of musical composition. In
New York he met Wright, who had just published *Uncle Tom's
Children,* and in 1937 Ellison wrote a review for *New Challenge,*
the magazine which Wright was editing. Soon Ellison was publishing regularly in *The New Masses* and *The Negro Quarterly,*
clarifying many of his ideas in regard to race, politics, and literature. Like Wright—like almost all Negro writers of the 1930's—

Ellison was attracted to political radicalism, and some of his early work—"The Birthmark" (*The New Masses,* 1940); "Recent Negro Fiction" (*The New Masses,* 1941); and "The Way It Is" (*The New Masses,* 1942)—expresses his interests in left-wing politics.

Ellison's artistic sense, however, was far more developed than Wright's—he never conceived of his own fiction as a device for exclusively expressing social protest, although protest mars some of his early work. After 1943 he ceased to concern himself primarily with politics and turned to the theme that dominates all of his later work: the need of white Americans to recognize Negro identity in all of its diversity. "Mister Toussan" (1941), a short story published in *The New Masses,* had already explored that idea, and later stories approached it from various points of view. Within a few years he had published several stories: "That I Had the Wings" (reprinted as "Mr. Toussaint"), "In a Strange Country" (1944), "Flying Home" (1944), and "King of the Bingo Game" (1944). These stories, together with "A Coupla Scalped Indians" (1956), have not yet been collected, but they indicate that Ellison is an impressive short story writer as well as a novelist and essayist.

"Flying Home" and "King of the Bingo Game" are Ellison's finest stories, and they reflect his thinking about racial issues in the period that immediately precedes the writing of *Invisible Man.* In "Flying Home," which was published in *Cross Section* in 1944, Ellison underscores the difficulty that a young Negro has in knowing his place in contemporary white society and his own complex relationship to his racial heritage. "Son, how come you want to fly way up there in the air?" the old, officious Negro asks the hero, who has been on a training mission and has crashed into a plantation in Alabama; and the flyer thinks, "Because it's the most meaningful act in the world . . . because it makes me less like you." Feeling cut off from this Negro fieldhand "by age, by understanding, by sensibility, by technology, and by his need to measure himself against the mirror of other men's appreciation," the flyer, who is waiting for a plane from the nearby airbase, seeks admiration in the eyes of his white superiors; but assimilation is impossible, whether he wants it or not—too much of the white world, as represented by the plantation owner who tries to have the flyer put in a strait jacket, will not permit it. Ellison is particularly successful in suggesting the hero's unwilling realization that part of him is represented by the old, unattractive Negro—the fieldhand is the one who saves him finally from the white man—and his pathetic attempt to be as white as the white world will permit him to be. In a recent interview, published in *Harper's* (March, 1967), Ellison sums up the feeling that runs through this story and all of his subsequent work:

> If I cannot look at the most brutalized Negro on the street, even when he irritates me and makes me want to bash his head in because he's goofing off, I must still say within myself, 'Well, that's you too, Ellison.' And I'm not talking about guilt, but of an identification which goes beyond race.

"King of the Bingo Game," published in *Tomorrow* in November, 1944, pursues a similar theme and technically is even closer to *Invisible Man* in its use of Gothicism and macabre humor. It tells of a Southern Negro who sits in a movie house in the North and watches the same movie repeatedly, tirelessly playing the bingo game during the intermission and believing that by winning the game he will save his wife from some fatal illness and himself from poverty. For the desperate man, close to psychological breakdown, the game is life—all that is left of a life that has continually cheated him and that now finds him unemployed because he has no birth certificate. He holds five cards, illegally, and wins the prize of $36.90, but in order to take the jackpot he must press the button just long enough to stop the spinning wheel between the "double-zero"; and as he stands before the audience in the darkened theatre, he suddenly realizes "that as long as he pressed the button, he could control the jackpot. He and only he could determine whether or not it was to be his." The audience howls at him, but he has ceased to care: "Let them yell. All the Negroes down there were just ashamed because he was black like them. He smiled inwardly, knowing how it was. Most of the time he was ashamed of what Negroes did himself. . . . Didn't they know that although he controlled the wheel, it also controlled him, and unless he pressed the button forever and forever and ever it would stop, leaving him high and dry, dry and high on this hard high slippery hill and Laura [his wife] dead?" He has come to realize that "For as long as he pressed the button he was the-man-who-pressed-the-button-who-held-the-prize-who-was-the-King-of-Bingo." When he is finally taken away and his hand is released from the wheel, it stops at double-zero, but he senses that "his luck [has] run out on the stage" and that he has been stricken by men who represent a society that will never permit him to win, no matter how many cards he holds, no matter how carefully he studies the rules of the game, no matter how willful or obstinate he is. For him the wheel is God, as he cries, but God is part of the illusion in the movie house that has nothing to do with the man's actual life.

"King of the Bingo Game" is a hard gem of a story, written at that point in an author's career when he has come to realize his full creative powers, poised delicately between the grotesque and the realistic, between the illusory and the actual, between madness and seeming sanity; the movie house is the perfect American setting for Negroes and whites to create their fantasies; and the bingo game, as America's particular wheel of fortune, is compelling —and frightening when Ellison reminds us of who in fact operates the game.

The same kind of juxtapositions control the form of *Invisible Man*. In the many scenes of the novel—the battle royal; the incidents in the Southern Negro college and the paint factory; and the various adventures in Harlem—Ellison confronts an idealistic boy with the absurdities and horrors of America and traces his movement toward what he claims is a more informed and chastened social idealism—although, in fact, "the end is in the beginning," and these words, which come before the epilogue, constitute the true conclusion to the novel. At the outset, "in those pre-invisible days," the boy visualizes himself "as a potential Booker T. Washington"; and he listens with respect to the white philanthropist, Norton, as he exhorts the boy to study Ralph Waldo Emerson, "for he was important to your people. He had a hand in your destiny." He promises the older man to read Emerson and the man is pleased: "Very good. Self-reliance is a most worthy virtue. I shall look forward with the greatest of interest to learning your contribution to my fate." That contribution lies in the lesson which the boy learns, a lesson that denies the central doctrines of Emerson in a manner similar to that of Melville in *The Confidence-Man:* like the barber at the end of Melville's novel, the protagonist of *Invisible Man* does not trust the world that wants to dupe him; he becomes "ill of affirmation, of saying 'yes' against the nay-saying of [his] stomach—not to mention [his] brain," and "after years of trying to adopt the opinion of others [he] finally rebels. [He is] an invisible man."

As an autobiographical odyssey from the provinces to the city, from boyhood to manhood, from innocence to an apprehension of evil, *Invisible Man* is a satire on the myth of self-reliance, self-improvement, and the heroic ideal. It is couched in the form of an autobiography, like so much American literature, and reminds us of the rich tradition of personal confession in Negro writing itself, from the slave narratives and *Up From Slavery* to *Out of the House of Bondage* (1914), *Finding a Way Out* (1920), and *Against the Tide* (1939). Like Cervantes' *Don Quixote* and Jane Austen's *Northanger Abbey, Invisible Man* satirizes a tradition and, at the same time, becomes the exemplary work within that tradition. The Negro boy is imbued with ideals, and he wants to be a hero in the image of Emerson and Booker T. Washington; he too has a gift for oratory and leadership. But the authority of American society constantly mocks the hero's ideals, mocks indeed their very visibility, and the Invisible Man becomes a figure like Melville's Israel Potter or, in his more bitter moments, the Confidence Man.

Having fought through his illusions of American society and the illusions others have foisted upon him, the Invisible Man has come to a perception of his absurd condition as a Negro; but whereas Melville's last scene in *The Confidence-Man* is properly nihilistic, Ellison feels it necessary to offer an epilogue of idealism that belies the actual events of the novel—he speaks like Emerson the essayist whereas he has written, with all the modifications of a twentieth-century sensibility, like Melville the satirical novelist. In the epilogue he claims to understand his grandfather's deathbed advice, offered five years before: "I want you to overcome 'em with yesses, undermine 'em with grins, agree 'em to death and destruction, let 'em swoller you till they vomit or bust wide open."

> Perhaps he hid his meaning deeper than I thought, perhaps his anger threw me off—I can't decide. Could he have meant—hell, he *must* have meant the principle, that we are to affirm the principle on which the country was built and not the men, or at least not the men who did the violence. Did he mean say "yes" because he knew that the principle was greater than the men, greater than the numbers and vicious power and all the methods used to corrupt its name? Did he mean to affirm the principle, which they themselves had dreamed into being out of the chaos and darkness of the feudal past, and which they had violated and compromised to the point of absurdity even in their

own corrupt minds? Or did he mean that we have to take the responsibiliy for all of it, for the men as well as the principle, because we were the heirs who must use the principle because no other fitted our needs? Not for the power or for vindication, but because we, with the given circumstance of our origin, could only thus find transcendence?

And in the same epilogue he promulgates the doctrine of Emersonian self-reliance, framed now in ostensibly personal terms:

> My world has become one of infinite possibilities. What a phrase—still it's a good phrase and a good view of life, and a man shouldn't accept any other; that much I've learned underground. . . . I've come a long way from those days when, full of illusion, I lived a public life and attempted to function under the assumption that the world was solid and all the relationships therein. Now I know men are different and that all life is divided and that only in division is there true health. . . . Whence all this passion toward conformity anyway?—diversity is the word . . . Life is to be lived, not controlled; and humanity is won by continuing to play in face of certain defeat. Our fate is to become one, and yet many—This is not prophecy, but description.

But to a great extent it is prophecy—in the sense that Thoreau's *Walden,* Emerson's early essays, and Whitman's "Song of Myself" are prophecy—abstractly persuasive but, as the novel itself has shown, actually impossible in a contemporary America that, in all of its authority, forces the Negro victim into a cellar where his former idealism can only be seen in the most ironic and despairing terms. The power of the novel lies in its full dramatic realization of the external violence that forbids personal growth; thus the conclusions in the epilogue strike one as gratuitous, given the novel that precedes it—an afterthought, as it were. Although *Invisible Man* is beyond question the finest single fiction in the history of Negro literature and one of the most impressive American novels since the Second World War, it fails to achieve its high aesthetic aim, in a fundamental way it fails. It never really resolves the disparity between the Negro's experiences and what the Negro says about his experiences; it does not offer us much hope for the groping Negro hero—and this hopelessness is true, this bewilderment amidst violence provides the great strength and truth of the novel

—but the novelist, speaking overtly in his own voice, asks us to hope. As Marcus Klein, in a fine essay on Ellison in *After Alienation,* points out, "The novel, apparently, owes much to *Notes from the Underground* and not least an ending that it does not clearly earn."

Ellison's criticism, most of which follows the publication of *Invisible Man* and has been included in the volume entitled *Shadow and Act* (1964), develops the affirmative conclusion of the novel. From the writing of "Richard Wright's Blues" (1945), through the subsequent essays—his interview in the *Paris Review* (1955); the essays on music; "That Same Pain, That Same Pleasure: An Interview" (1961); "The World and the Jug" (1963, 1964), which is an exchange with Irving Howe; and "Hidden Name and Complex Fate" (1964)—Ellison has formulated perhaps the most cogent statement of idealism in contemporary American literature—a statement that, in the abstract form it has assumed, lies in the tradition of Emerson. "I have no desire to write propaganda," he notes in the interview of 1961. "Instead I felt it important to explore the full range of American Negro humanity and to affirm those qualities which are of value beyond any question of segregation, economics or previous condition of servitude. The obligation was always there and there is much to affirm. . . . Our strength is that with the total society saying to us, 'No, No, No, No,' we continue to move toward our goal. So when I came to write I felt moved to affirm and to explore all this—not as a social mission but as the stuff of literature and as an expression of the better part of my own sense of life." In his most recent interview, in *Harper's Magazine* (March, 1967), Ellison has clarified his position even more completely:

> I mean that it's futile to argue our humanity with those who willfully refuse to recognize it, when art can reveal on its own terms more truth while providing pleasure, insight, and for Negro readers at least, affirmation and a sense of direction. We must assert our sense of values, beginning with the given and irrevocable, with the question of heroism and slavery.
>
> Contrary to some, I feel that our experience as a people involves a great deal of heroism. From one perspective, slavery was horrible and brutalizing. It is said that "Those Africans were enslaved, they died in the 'middle passage,' they were abused, their families were separated, they were whipped, they were raped,

ravaged, and emasculated." And the Negro writer is tempted to agree. "Yes! God damn, wasn't that a horrible thing!" And he sometimes agrees to the next step, which holds that slaves had very little humanity because slavery destroyed it for them and their descendants. That's what the Stanley M. Elkins "Sambo" argument implies. But despite the historical past and the injustices of the present, there is from *my* perspective something further to say. I have to *affirm* my forefathers and I *must* affirm my parents or be reduced in my own mind to a white man's inadequate—even if unprejudiced—conception of human complexity. Yes, and I must affirm those unknown people who sacrificed for me. I'm speaking of those Negro Americans who never knew that a Ralph Ellison might exist, but who by living their own lives and refusing to be destroyed by social injustice and white supremacy, real or illusory, made it possible for me to live my own life with meaning. I am forced to look at these people and upon the history of the U. S. and conclude that there is another reality behind the appearance of reality which they would force upon us as truth.

Any people who could endure all of that brutalization and keep together, who could undergo such dismemberment and resuscitate itself, and endure until it could take the initiative in achieving its own freedom is obviously more than the sum of its brutalization. Seen in this perspective, theirs has been one of the great human experiences and one of the great triumphs of the human spirit in modern times. In fact, in the history of the world.

Thus Ellison takes his position, quite self-consciously, in the tradition of American idealism. He is certainly one of the most widely cultured of our present writers and, as he has remarked so often, his influences range from Dostoevsky to Malraux; but the Americans have had a great impact upon his imagination as well. The two writers with whom he has curiously identified himself—apart from T. S. Eliot and Hemingway, who was his "true father-as-artist"—are Emerson and James. In "Hidden Name and Complex Fate," he notes that his father named him after Emerson, "and much later, after [he] began to write and work with words, [he] came to suspect that [his father] was aware of the suggestive power of names and of the magic involved in naming. . . . I did not destroy that troublesome middle name [Waldo] of mine, I only suppressed it. Sometimes it reminds me of my obligations to the man who named me. . . . I could suppress the name of my namesake out of respect for the achievements of its original bearer but I cannot escape the obligation of attempting to achieve some of the things which he asked of the American writer. As Henry James suggested, being an American is an arduous task, and for most of us, I suspect, the difficulty begins with the name."

The difficulty of being an American novelist, one should add, who has now committed himself to a position of idealism and affirmation, is to render that idealistic position into convincing novelistic terms. Ellison has not yet given us the dramatic correlative to his abstract formulations. The burden of his short stories and of *Invisible Man* is their ironic despair; but so many of his remarks since *Invisible Man* have been concerned with diversity, the possibility of Negro life, that he seems to be preparing his audience for a major novel that will go beyond the stereotypes that have so long limited our literature about the Negro.

James Baldwin has made a career of analyzing the stereotypes of Negro life that have constricted the American imagination and rendered both whites and blacks impoverished through the denial of human complexity. His achievement has been remarkable, for he has dramatically asserted a way of life that is only vaguely felt and understood by most people; he has created the Negro for his white audience just as Hawthorne, a century earlier, created and defined the Puritan world for his audience. But Baldwin has, in the sixties, gone beyond recording and illuminating the lives of black people, beyond exposing white myths about a white America; he has created a mythology of his own in which whites and blacks have been liberated from old stereotypes only to be imprisoned in new ones.

"Negroes want to be treated like men," Baldwin protests in his essay "Fifth Avenue, Uptown"— like men and not like wards or victims. But only a few years later, in *The Fire Next Time,* the simple demand that white Americans confront the reality of Negro humanity assumes an aggressive character—blacks are beautiful and whites occupy a house the Negro man may not even want to enter; in *Another Country,* whites are pale, effete, and inadequate when juxtaposed beside the heroic Negroes Rufus Scott and his sister Ida; in *Tell Me How Long the Train's Been Gone,* the black boy asks his older brother, "Are white people—*people?* People like us?"— and we realize that we have come full circle to what is one of the most curious distortions of human nature ever conceived by an important American writer. Norman Mailer may seem to exaggerate when he says that the militant Negro "does not want equality any longer, he wants superiority, and wants it because he feels he is in fact superior"; but the record of Baldwin's writing—as one sensitive index to what has happened in American Negro life during the past twenty years—would seem to corroborate and intensify Mailer's perception. The fragile figures of Baldwin's early work become the pugnacious heroes of his most recent fiction. The author wants to create mythical black creatures—genuine Romantic heroes out of another age—but his sense of realism pulls him away from myth or symbology, forms more suited to his essentially religious temperament. Herein lies Baldwin's central problem as an artist: beginning his career with realistic essays and fiction, which describe Negroes as victims and then as men, he seeks in his work of the sixties to create preternatural heroes who are always black; working within the realistic forms of the essay and the novel, he is emotionally drawn to the apocalyptic sermon and romantic fable which polarizes human beings until they are dangerously close to becoming only types, symbols, ideas—sinners and gods, oppressors and victims, whites and blacks, evil and good. The increasing militancy of Baldwin's political and social posture has affected his writing in the most fundamental way—words are now weapons as they once were with Richard Wright. In Baldwin's writing, more than in that of any other contemporary black author, we can measure the history of Negro protest in America during the last generation—its protest and its violence, its struggle to make a legitimate moral criticism of American authority and create new heroes more natural, powerful, and idealistic than those heroes it refuses to inherit from the white world.

Baldwin's account of race relations, as painfully recorded in *Go Tell It On The Mountain* and the two collections of essays, *Notes of a Native Son* and *Nobody Knows My Name,* is dominated by dehumanization. It includes life in the Harlem Ghetto, where Negroes live because "white people do not think they are good enough to live anywhere else"; it includes segregated schools in which a Negro boy "decides, that if all this studying is going to prepare him only to be a porter or an elevator boy—or his teacher —well, then the hell with it"; it includes persecution of black people, on every social and political level, when "it is only too clear that even with the most malevolent will in the world Negroes can never manage to achieve one-tenth of the harm which we fear." One of Baldwin's virtues in his early work is perhaps the most obvious: he brings to a white person the Negro point of view with an intense honesty; and he implicates the reader by forcing him to share that point of view; "it is a terrible, an inexorable law, that one cannot deny the humanity of another without diminishing one's own: in the face of one's victim, one sees oneself. Walk through the streets of Harlem and see what we, this nation, have become."

Baldwin's early essays—"Everbody's Protest Novel," "Many Thousands Gone," "Notes of a Native Son," "Fifth Avenue, Up-town," and "Nobody Knows My Name"—are among the finest polemical pieces written since the Second World War; they seem already part of the permanent record of racial relations in this country, definitive of a certain way of being even as we now read them. Personally they speak of Baldwin's youth, a youth that culminated in the death of his father (so movingly described in "Notes of a Native Son") when he discovered the legacy that had been given him: "Nothing," his father had said, "is ever escaped."

Baldwin was just nineteen years old when his father died, and this legacy, which for his father meant God's justice and eternal judgment, and other eschatological certainties, became for the boy, ineluctably and terribly, existentialist. *Nothing is ever escaped—* neither color nor one's sexual reality nor death. His early work is an attempt to assert that fact: *Go Tell It On The Mountain* records the fanaticism of his father and the boy's emergence into a Godless world; the essays reject white abstractions such as "equality" and "freedom" and "wealth." Like Frederic Henry in *A Farewell to Arms,* Baldwin finds abstract words obscene and empty beside the individual heroic acts committed, the specific results achieved. "I am very often tempted to believe," he has said, "that this illusion [that our state is a state to be envied by other people because we are powerful, and we are rich] is all that is left of the great dream that was to have become America; whether this is so or not, this illusion certainly prevents us from making America what we say we want it to be."

The process of rejection and negation, which has occupied Baldwin until the present day, suggests his special contribution to the thought of our time: he rejects the abstractions, the promises, the white man's vague projections of hope for the Negro—he denies all but the very tangible. He has concerned himself with the history of his own suffering as a Negro, and much of his writing has been of a remarkable caliber. But Baldwin is one of the most impressive essayists of the twentieth century and the most important Negro essayist in our literature precisely because he is not only autobiographical, not only a Negro—he is a self-appointed conscience of the nation, scrutinizing moral behavior, demanding that the idealistic become the actual, probing insistently in ways that are at times carefully controlled and rational, at times exaggerated or hysterical or hortatory or wrathful but that are always revelatory. Apart from his clear vision of how complex a fate it is for a black man to be an American, Baldwin achieves his effects through suggestive, formal juxtapositions: the omniscient "I" of his essays represents America and thus the point of view constitutes an implicit self-indictment of the country; the form of his best essays is firm and tightly controlled, in contrast to the fluid and chaotic materials described; the tone is cool and moderate, in the early essays at least, as opposed to the inherent violence of the subject; and the style is sophisticated, intricate, thickly textured, highly metaphorical, and above all literary, as it protests all those forces of American life that have tried to prevent James Baldwin and that have succeeded in preventing so many less tenacious, less gifted Negroes from ever achieving a complete cultural life.

Yet a significant shift in Baldwin's tone occurs in the early sixties, one which suggests that though the author has a clear view of the black man's complex fate in America, he does not perceive the white man's. After dedicating his early career to an exposure of white myths about black men, he now creates black distortions about white men. Every critic has noticed the rough texture of Baldwin's prose, his new belligerency, the use of a militant posture that Baldwin once censured in Richard Wright, and most critics have suggested that this new tone signals the death of Baldwin as an artist. Perhaps. But prognosis does not begin to explain the complexity of this talented man and the meaning of his fate as an author in contemporary America. In his early work Baldwin asserted his idealism against the authority of America and dedicated his writing to a banishment of the gods, the shibboleths, the lies of American history and contemporary American life. But in his writing of the sixties—particularly in *Another Country* and *Tell*

Me How Long the Train's Been Gone—he substitutes new gods, new shibboleths, new lies, although now they are black and now they survive only because of the social militancy which encourages them and which they in turn reflect. The white sentimentality Baldwin attacked surrenders to black sentimentality. Although *Another Country* (1962) and *Tell Me How Long The Train's Been Gone* (1968) suggest a widening scope of his vision, a struggling toward new modes of expression, they polarize the concepts of idealism and authority, of love and power in the most extreme, often elementary, and intellectually embarrassing fashion. Passion does duty for thought. False white heroes, whom Baldwin once criticized so cogently, surrender to equally false black heroes, and the inability of white people to recognize the black man's complexity becomes Baldwin's unwillingness if not inability to admit diversity among those whites who do not sympathize absolutely with black people.

In *Another Country* Baldwin tries to demonstrate all of his obsessive concerns: racial distinctions and inequalities, sexual awareness, and the question of national, American identity. The only element missing is the religious quarrel with himself: there is no God in the novel, no Christianity, no religion of any kind, and from one point of view the book is a celebration of the senses, an attempt to show how far the sensual can carry one into an understanding of oneself. Viewed in this way, the title of the novel suggests not only the other country that is France (from which the young innocent, the inverse Jamesian hero, emigrates), nor the other country that is Harlem (which no white man in the book, not even Vivaldo the novelist, can ever understand), nor the land in which homosexuality is as common and proper as any form of sexual behavior: *Another Country* is fundamentally that place where middle class values —sponsored by white people—are abhorrent, where an adoption of them leads (as in the case of one character, a commercially successful novelist with two children) to inevitable spiritual destruction. "Hope?" the novelist's wife says to her lover, as she bitterly reflects upon her husband's hollow success. "No, I don't think there's any hope [in America]. We're too empty here. . . . This isn't a country at all, it's a collection of football players and Eagle Scouts. Cowards. We think we're happy. We're not. We're doomed."

We are asked, through the tone of this passage and in the thematic thrust of the entire book, to take this thought as Baldwin's; we are asked to assent to its essential truth; we are expected to take it seriously. Now, judged in terms of its intrinsic value as an idea, this indictment of America is nonsense—and dangerous nonsense. If one of Baldwin's essential demands is that we cease to adhere to the white myths of America then it is only fair to demand that he not substitute other myths. America is neither a collection of football players and Eagle scouts, nor is it a country of cowards—the complexity of this country is too great for that kind of facile, glib accusation, an accusation and a caricature as false as the white myth of happy Negro slaves or Negro sexuality. Nor is the country doomed—one tires of hearing Baldwin sound like the political version of an attenuated Jonathan Edwards. When *The Fire Next Time*—an essay that also speaks ominously of impending tragedy and doom—reaches a wider, more literate, sympathetic and liberally disposed audience than any single essay by a Negro or white man in American history, the country is not yet doomed. Baldwin's statement as well as many others like it in his recent work is simply sentimental nihilism. Saul Bellow makes the point most cogently: "Frightful things have happened; but is the apocalyptic interpretation true? The terminations did not fully terminate. Civilization is still here. The prophecies have not been borne out. Novelists are wrong to put an interpretation of history at the base of artistic creation—to speak the last word. It is better that the novelist should trust his own sense of life. Less ambitious. More likely to tell the truth."

The closest we come to visualizing the actual despair of any character is the beginning of the novel, when a Negro drummer, Rufus Scott, emerges as a lost, alienated creature, "entirely alone, and dying of it," a part "of an unprecedented multitude." This character, who seems to be a further development of another, younger drummer in the story "Sonny's Blues," has grown deeply disillusioned and now directs his hatred and bitterness almost exclusively toward the white world. After playing in a nightclub, he picks up a Southern white girl, takes her to a party and has intercourse with her on the terrace; but this act is hardly erotic, for it is charged with wild aggression. *"I told you,* he moaned, *I'd give you something to cry about,* and, at once, he felt himself struggling to explode or die. A moan and a curse tore through him while he beat her with all the strength he had and felt the venom shoot out of of him, enough for a hundred black-and-white babies."* Rufus

Scott's relationship with Leona, the white girl, is Baldwin's method of expressing the racial tension in this country. He does this in sexual terms because he feels, as he tells us in *The Fire Next Time,* that the white man—especially the liberal white man—wants and needs the Negro's love. Rufus, however, offers his sympathetic mistress not love but lust, not friendship but only bitterness, not genuine heroism but a kind of sentimental, even sensational bravura. Yet she, who has traveled north seeking refuge from the terrors of the South, forgives him his brutality. "He's just lost," she explains, "and he beats me because he can't find nothing else to hit."

The bitterness of Rufus Scott is Baldwin at his most effective; certainly the novel loses its intensity and violent point of view after Rufus has committed suicide. But Baldwin expects his reader to have too great an awareness of the environmental conditions of his Negroes, to bring unreasoned sympathy to them, regardless of their cruelty. He asks his reader to assume the background that makes Rufus so hostile, he depends on the world outside the novel for the effects he achieves within the novel. Why does Rufus commit suicide? the reader asks. Why is he driven to such despair? In a novel so rooted in actual experience, the Negro's suicide has to grow out of his own despair, his own disillusionment, and if we are never given even the suggestion of why this particular human being has reached an irrevocable attitude of hatred toward the world and toward himself, then his suicide is finally no more than a melodramatic act of defiance.

Baldwin's limitations here are regrettable, for he almost realizes dramatically the provocative ideas of his essays. And Rufus Scott is his most mature creation of the assertive Negro who is ultimately beaten by the society surrounding and oppressing him—he is the Negro *in extremis,* and Baldwin's unwillingness to pursue his moral, social, and sexual problems is a betrayal of his intentions in the book. The root of Baldwin's inability to draw Rufus as a character rather than a concept lies in his misguided view of Rufus' heroism. Rufus is a hero like no other Negro in Baldwin's previous fiction—or indeed in his early essays. He is stronger, more talented, more natural, more sensual, more attractive than anyone else in *Another Country*—he is superior to the other characters. No victim, *he* victimizes; and his suicide is a sociological abstraction which the reality of the novel does not support. He must die because he is a myth of the black hero struck down by a white society that will not grant his superiority. We see him only in terms of his natural-istic despair; his heroism is remembered, clouded over in a series of retrospective passages. If he lived on in the novel and we saw him at close range, he could only become preposterous, given Baldwin's attempt to portray him as a black hero no one else—least of all the white characters—can approximate.

When Baldwin transfers Rufus's vision of the white world to his sister Ida and has her develop a relationship with Rufus's closest white friend, Vivaldo, he loses firm control of his material. Vivaldo is seeking the reality of the Negro, but Ida frustrates "any attempt on his part to strike deeper into that incredible country"; and we are left to conclude that the whites in this novel—even those who are as sympathetic as Vivaldo—are incapable of understanding and communicating with the Negro. They are inferior in every respect to the blacks, victims of the novelist's distorted vision, divided simplistically between wounded creatures (most of whom are homosexual) and insensitive middle-class sell-outs. The sexual en-counters and the arguments between Vivaldo and Ida are meant to provide a clear idea of Baldwin's meaning: these two people, black and white, have thrown off family and religion and race and country, and, alienated from all the institutions surrounding them, depending exclusively on themselves, they seek the reality of each other. They fail, as the others in the novel fail: homosexuals who find themselves seducing white and black heterosexuals; homo-sexuals who have heterosexual affairs. The sexual as well as the racial barriers are down and Baldwin demands that we understand and accept these other worlds of the Negro and the homosexual. But his description of them is too private and suggestive, never fully developed: whenever the characters meet one another the confrontation is violent, and they inevitably are left desperately alone, reliant on their own inadequate resources. None of them—with the exception of Rufus—approaches the heroic mode because, we are almost compelled to believe, they are not black or lovers of blacks; all are unable to survive in America, and they exercise an inordinate self-pity, seeing themselves too easily as wounded victims of larger, undefined cultural forces.

At the end of the novel a young French homosexual comes to America to be with his friend, a rising actor who has had abortive sexual relations with Americans. In a curious reversal of the James pattern, this innocent boy, whose name significantly is Yves, travels to America on a journey that Baldwin calls "toward Bethlehem." Now, after the violence of their experiences, perhaps the Americans will see this *ingénu* from another country as the promise of the future, perhaps they will be resurrected through him to a new and total understanding of themselves. Baldwin reduces the people of his novel to a spiritual nudity, makes them strip away the illusions of themselves until they are left in an existential self-awareness, cognizant of the significance of death (Rufus's death), and of race (Ida's blackness), and of their own individual essence. Yves comes into the new world, as the Jamesian heroine went into the old—although he has none of the toughness of James's girls, he has fear and hope and little else. He leaves his Eden, like Eve, to meet his mate, who lives in the other country that is reality, in the place "which the people from heaven [have] made their home." In a country terrorized by blackness and sex and death, by any attempt to realize in concrete terms those proclamations it professes; in a country so dedicated to timeworn abstractions, to "all that jazz about the land of the free and the home of the brave," there is only one possible way of life for anyone who wishes to transcend the illusion of personal safety: that of the existentialist.

The vision of *Another Country* is more convincing than its dramatic rendition; Baldwin has yet to discover his fictional correlatives, the existential quality of the existential life he recommends—abstractly. Few would argue that the sentimental pieties of freedom and bravery and courage should be attacked—Hemingway wrote their epitaph generations ago. Few would dispute those sections of *Another Country* that call into question—as Baldwin's essays once genuinely questioned—the myths by which *many* white Americans live. But insofar as the book cannot create the human complexity which it claims that whites have denied blacks, it fails; it contradicts intrinsically its own terms. Baldwin's early essays succeed because they analyze white power and its denial of Negro complexity; his early essays and the novel *Go Tell It On The Mountain* are impressive because they dramatize and reveal that Negro complexity. But Baldwin cannot describe white people with anything like complexity, he cannot accomplish the *sine qua non* of all major authors: the humanization of the antagonist, the man who *appears* inhuman.

The Fire Next Time succeeds as an essay because it combines Baldwin's two favorite subjects—the description of youth in Harlem and the criticism of white America. It is specific in terms of Negro life and conceptual in regard to white America, reminiscent of Baldwin's early work in the first section and homiletic, angry, and extreme in the second part. In *The Fire Next Time,* Baldwin brings into focus the polarities that lie at the center of contemporary American life, at least as envisaged by our writers: power and love, authority and idealism; and his desire is to persuade the individual to a sense of personal power and authority that will permit him to realize ideals that have thus far been only illusions. In this essay Baldwin reaches back to that point in adolescence when he first felt that God and safety were perhaps not synonymous, when he became "afraid of the evil within me and afraid of the evil without." Baldwin focuses now on the moment of sexual and social awareness, on the moment when he became aware of what it meant to be black. When he was thirteen years old he crossed Fifth Avenue on his way to the 42nd Street Library and "the cop in the middle of the street muttered as I passed him, 'Why don't you niggers stay uptown where you belong?'" This time for him, as one feels deeply while reading of his early experiences, was one of "dreadful speculations and discoveries"; and the chief discovery, the most frightening discovery, in the process of becoming an American was that white people "had the judges, the juries, the shotguns, the law—in a word, power. . . . This world is white and they are black. White people hold the power, which means that they are superior to blacks (intrinsically, that is: God decreed it so), and the world has innumerable ways of making this difference known and felt and feared. Long before the Negro child perceives this difference, and even longer before he understands it he has begun to react to it, he has begun to be controlled by it."

Baldwin shows us that a sensitive Negro boy faces the grim choice which awaits the impassioned individual: he can become either demonic or saintly. Growing up in Harlem, he "certainly could not discover any principled reason for not becoming a criminal"; what he knew he had to discover was "a gimmick, to lift him out, to start him on the way." And the gimmick he used was "his career in the church." The key to Baldwin's present attitude is evident here at the very outset of his essay; it sets the mood and tone of what he is to say: religion is a gimmick, a way out, an abstraction one uses for very concrete ends. "To be born, in a white country, an Anglo-Teutonic, anti-sexual country, black" is to realize the great necessity for some, for any gimmick—even if it is the religion of one's ancestors, borrowed from the white world. This religion, of course, has been enormously influential on Baldwin's writing, but it is the music of the religion, the drama of the religion, the fire and excitement that have lingered, and not the essence. Even as a boy, when he taught Sunday school, he felt that he "was committing a crime in talking about the gentle Jesus, in telling them [the children] to reconcile themselves to their misery on earth in order to gain the crown of eternal life. Were only Negroes to gain this crown? Was Heaven, then, to be merely another ghetto?"

The process of growing up was a throwing off of inherited superstitions, inherited religious attitudes which did not convince the boy that he could achieve the freedom and the love he sought in life. He turned, in time, to the more sensual aspects of the life immediately around him; these seemed more liberating, for, as he has grown to feel, "to respect and rejoice in the force of life, of life itself, is to be *present* in all that one does, from the effort of love to the breaking of bread." It now seems to Baldwin that "if the concept of God has any validity or any use, it can only be to make us larger, freer, and more loving. If God cannot do this, then it is time we got rid of Him."

The white Christian church has failed the Negro and this is surely one of the reasons Baldwin can begin to sympathize with the Muslim group and with the power that the Muslim group manifests. The obsessive subject of *The Fire Next Time* is power—the power of a Christianity which "has operated with an unmitigated arrogance and cruelty" towards all those people in the world it has wished to convert; the power of the police in Harlem; and the opposing "sanctification of power" that has been advocated by the Muslims. Baldwin creates a kind of Manichean drama in *The Fire Next Time,* pitting the white power structure against the black, indicating that the use of power itself is evil as it suppresses the goodness and love that are inherent in people. Most dangerously that power now resides within the individual himself—our technological achievements have outstripped our moral ability to handle them. "We human beings now have the power to exterminate ourselves; this seems to be the entire sum of our achievement. We have taken this journey and arrived at this place in God's name. This, then, is the best that God (the white God) can do. If that is so, then it is time to replace Him—replace Him with what? And this void, this despair, this torment is felt everywhere in the West, from the streets of Stockholm to the churches of New Orleans and the sidewalks of Harlem." Unable to believe in the white God, Baldwin finds it impossible to accept the black; and when Elijah Muhammed asks him, during his visit to the Chicago headquarters of the Muslim group, " 'And what are you now?' " Baldwin knows that he really can not say "that he [is] Christian." He answers, " 'I? Now? Nothing. . . . I'm a writer. I like doing things alone. . . . I don't, anyway, think about it a great deal.' "

What he has become, in this essay at least, is the existential hero who searches beneath the facade of abstractions and generalities for a solution to survival in America. Part of the answer is the glorification—one is tempted to say the deification—of the senses; another part is a constant awareness of death"; but the most significant aspect is the reaffirmation of love within people. "I knew the tension in me between love and power, between pain and rage, and the curious, the grinding way I remained extended between these poles—perpetually attempting to choose the better rather than the worse."

That tension between love and power, between idealism and authority, is the very essence of Baldwin's art. His examination of the power structure in America and the way it has stolen the human dignity and self-respect of Negroes has been the burden of the essays in *Notes of a Native Son* and *Nobody Knows My Name;* the search for love informs his novels—*Go Tell It On The Mountain, Giovanni's Room, Another Country,* and *Tell Me How Long The Train's Been Gone*—and constitutes the conclusion of *The Fire Next Time:*

> Love takes off the masks that we fear we cannot live without and know we cannot live within. I use the word "love" here not merely in the personal sense but as a state of being, or a state of grace—not in the infantile American sense of being made happy but in the tough and universal sense of quest and daring and growth. And I submit, then, that the racial tensions that menace Americans today have little to do with real antipathy—on the contrary, indeed—and are involved only symbolically with color. . . . That man who is forced each day to snatch his manhood, his identity, out of the fire of human cruelty that rages to destroy it knows, if he survives his effort, and even if he does not survive

it, something about himself and human life that no school on earth—and, indeed, no church—can teach. He achieves his own authority, and that is unshakable. This is because, in order to save his life, he is forced to look beneath appearances, to take nothing for granted, to hear the meaning behind the words.

By recognizing power, whether white or black, for what it is; by perceiving the imminence of death; by reexamining "everything white Americans think they believe in" and rejecting the myths of heroism and freedom and purity that have so long deluded us and been our refuge; by asserting the inner power that lies in our common humanity, "we can end the racial nightmare, and achieve our country, and change the history of the world." The idealistic conclusion of the essay is purposeful: "I know that what I am asking is impossible. But in our time, as in every time, the impossible is the least that one can demand—and one is, after all, emboldened by the spectacle of human history in general, and American Negro history in particular, for it testifies to nothing less than the perpetual achievement of the impossible."

The tension between idealism and authority, between love and power, in *The Fire Next Time* is stretched to the breaking point. One respects the arguments of the essay and admires the apocalyptic prose with which they are conveyed—even though one feels a little like a sinner in the hands of an angry god—but one knows that this tension must snap and the argument assume a reality that reflects more concretely the existential character of our lives. Baldwin fails in *Another Country* and *Tell Me How Long The Train's Been Gone*—fails in a deeper and more troubling way than the aesthetic. These last two novels deify blacks and castigate whites in morally simplistic terms; they offer illusions to replace the illusions Baldwin has undermined. Perhaps this is the ugly law of cultural compensation—William Styron cannot write a good book on Nat Turner without being attacked far beyond legitimate literary terms. Criticism of black literature is so often banal because it is so chauvinistic—blacks praise blacks and whites are afraid to use the criteria they would naturally apply to other literature. It has become almost impossible to speak or write honestly about black life and literature in this country—one must be conscious of almost everything but the sense of one's statement. That is indeed a dangerous state for literary criticism, not to speak of politics, and Baldwin has contributed to the confusion. Baldwin's achievement was very great indeed in the forties and fifties: he had to work and wedge his feet downward, in Thoreau's words, "through the mud and slush of opinion, and prejudice, and tradition, and delusion, and appearance, that alluvion which covers the globe . . . till [he came] to a hard bottom and rocks in place, which [he could] call reality, and say, This is, and no mistake." Like Thoreau, Baldwin told us again and again, "Be it life or death, we crave only reality." But in his last two books he gives us sentimental rhetoric, easy accusation, all that he once scorned.

"I want to be an honest man and a good writer," Baldwin wrote in the introduction to *Notes of a Native Son*. He was fully aware that his virtuous wish—one is inclined to say his naïve hope—is no easy task for any author at any time in any country. It has proven too great a burden for him to bear: *Another Country* and *Tell Me How Long The Train's Been Gone* are neither honest nor good. In denying the complex humanity of white people, Baldwin has diminished that of blacks. No, not of blacks alone. Of all Americans.

One of Baldwin's many achievements has been the clarification of all those problems that confront Negro artists. As Richard Wright opened the door for Baldwin, so Baldwin has performed that function for younger Negro writers. The central conflict in his career—that tension between realistic analysis and romantic chauvinism—suggests one of the disturbing paradoxes in the literature and criticism of black Americans today. We are witnessing a remarkable renaissance in Negro writing itself, one that is characterized by diversity and complexity and the unpredictable; at the same time there is a narrow chauvinism and parochialism in Negro literary criticism that is too often little more than propaganda—indeed at times the criticism seems to be a branch of militant Negro politics. But my purpose here is not to quarrel with a criticism that is excessively self-conscious.* I want to conclude this account of the idealism that runs inexorably through Negro literature by viewing it as a peculiarly American phenomenon, by seeing it finally where it ought to be seen—in the larger context of American literature.

* I do quarrel with this criticism, however, in an essay, "Our Mutual Estate: The Literature of the American Negro," which appears in *The Antioch Review*, XXVIII (Fall, 1968), 293-303.

5

Contemporary
Negro
Literature

The history of the American Negro, to borrow Richard Wright's image, is the mirror of American history—the Negro is indeed "America's metaphor." And the intricate ways that violence and idealism have figured in the writing of Negroes suggests the reasons for the Negro Renaissance that we are now witnessing. This Renaissance derives its strength and diversity from sources that are curiously similar to those that characterized the literary Renaissance of mid-nineteenth-century New England. Like the transcendentalists and their circle, Negroes use the church—and specifically the Protestant church—as a moral touchstone; and equally significant for both groups of authors is the deep impact of oratory on the written language. But in our age, when words and expressions like "soul" or "moral reality" or "self-reliance" or "Universal Being" or "truth" are always carefully placed within quotation marks, to indicate their archaic or special use, the religious feeling of the Negro undergoes many different manifestations and outward appearances—although it is symptomatic that the word "soul" should in no way seem naïve or archaic in the idiom of Negro life; it is an absolutely honorific term. The use of ecclesiastical elements expresses itself in music—note, for example, the significance of jazz in Negro funeral processions—or in drama

—consider Baldwin's *Blues for Mr. Charlie,* which has strong similarities to the morality play—or in so many other plays, novels and stories: William Demby's *Beetlecreek* (1950), Owen Dodson's *Boy At the Window* (1951), and Loften Mitchell's *Tell Pharaoh* (1967). Most notably, however, this theological reality—its outward trappings, at least—quickly surrenders to the political and social reality of the young Negro's world, and the tensions that develop from that adjustment or repudiation produce a distinctively original, highly imaginative literature, as they produced a renaissance among the transcendentalists in the mid-nineteenth century, or, more recently, among Southern writers in the 1930's and 1940's, or among Jewish authors of the forties and fifties: the abrasive collision of the old and new ideologies, whether they be theological or philosophical or political, result, in each case, in remarkable works of art.

This idealism stems organically from the most realistic treatment of Negro life in America. The awful tensions that develop between ghetto life and the idealism of a sensitive Negro boy; between the abstract language of the white world and the specific speech of Negroes; between the American dream of whites and the American nightmare of blacks; between the traditional fate imposed upon the black boy and his hidden feeling that he might finally achieve the freedom he instinctually craves—these tensions define the black renaissance and lend its bitter-sweet idealism a verisimilitude rare in American literature today. Like the transcendentalists, the Southern writers, and the Jewish authors, these black artists challenge the American image imposed upon them. They will not be defined historically or linguistically or morally. They defy the authority of the country (in this case the bigotry and moral rigidity of white society) and the tension between the idealism and authority of America, when it is drawn through the realistic description of a suffering people whose suffering the author condemns implicitly, leads to literature that unsettles the complacent imagination. "Grant me that I am human," cries Gwendolyn Brooks in her eloquent, personal poetry about the heroic ideals of ordinary Negroes:

> Grant me that I am human, that I hurt
> That I can cry.
> Not that I now ask alms, in shame gone hollow.
> Nor cringe outside the loud and sumptuous gate.
> Admit me to our mutual estate.

Other analogues with the New England Renaissance suggest themselves and illuminate the present character of Negro literature. The Negro author of today is intensely aware of the political background and history of his particular dilemma—which is the dilemma of American history—and much of his literary authority develops from an intimate knowledge of his past. His reading of American history is not merely an academic exercise—as it is with most students who are unconscious, as Ralph Ellison has pointed out, of events before their own time, who have no real sense of historical continuity—but a way of calculating his losses, of measuring why he lives the way he does. History is crucial to a definition of himself, and it is no accident that the first Negro intellectuals were historians. Now that the artists are beginning to take account of their place in history we can expect an aesthetic criticism of American beliefs and ideologies that we have rarely experienced before. Dubois' trilogy *The Black Flame* (running from 1957 to 1961) and Chester Himes's *The Third Generation* (1954) represent broad accounts of the Negro in American history by two older writers; but young authors like William Melvin Kelley in *A Different Drummer* (1962), Ronald Fair in *Many Thousands Gone* (1965), and Ernest Gaines in *Of Love and Dust* (1967) are equally sensitive to the burden of slavery, and they tend to see the past in terms of the current moment.

Baldwin and Ellison—as well as authors like John A. Williams, Paule Marshall, Ernest Gaines, LeRoi Jones, and Eldridge Cleaver —are forever scrutinizing themselves as Americans: they are as self-conscious about their social and literary role in this country as Emerson was of America's position in the tradition of European culture. "What does American society *mean* when regarded out of my *own* eyes," Ellison asks in the introduction to *Shadow and Act*, "when informed by my *own* sense of the past and viewed by my *own* complex sense of the present?" In their protestations that nobody knows their name and that they are invisible, Baldwin, Ellison, Williams, and Kelley assert themselves as virulently as the transcendentalists of a century before, they too confront a cultural tradition with their own humanity and offer works of art that are truly indigenous. "The Negro writer," Kelley has said, "must use his art . . . to help repair the damage done to the soul of the Negro in the past three centuries." Our early writers responded angrily to Sydney Smith's question, "In the four quarters of the globe, who reads an American book?" and produced a literature that made that question seem only ephemerally true if not indeed ill-informed. These Negro authors are equally self-conscious of Negro life and art, they too are defensive; and like the New Englanders they are creating a distinctively American literature.

In their examination of America, Negro authors reveal a complexity in American society that is not readily discovered in the work of white writers. We begin to sense this complexity in the blues, which, as Ellison has suggested, are our closest approximation to tragedy and "fall short of tragedy only in that they provide no solution, offer no scapegoat but the self." The writer of the blues has suffered but he has come to understand his suffering, and he expresses "the possibility of conquering it through sheer toughness of spirit." This specific art form now finds its formal expression in the writing of Negroes who have been given a more traditional, more academic training: witness Williams' *Night Song* (1961), Kelley's *A Drop of Patience* (1965), and some of the poetry of Melvin Tolson and LeRoi Jones. It seems evident that Negro writers, because of the conditions of their life and the memories of their ancestors' lives, will continue in the Gothic tradition that has produced our greatest literature and that historically has proved to be a vehicle for the tragic vision. Negroes may want, in Baldwin's words, to be treated like men, but the fact is that Negro authors have not yet created men, they have projected types; and though this tendency, which has crippled all American writing about Negroes, is a distinct artistic limitation in the work of Richard Wright, it is not in the writing of the present generation, as novels like *Go Tell It On The Mountain* and *Invisible Man* clearly indicate. The enlargement of an individual by some idea or passion—far beyond his literal credibility as an individual—can produce great romantic literature, as Hawthorne and Melville, to cite only American authors, have demonstrated; and when writers, emerging from a history of suppression and enforced silence, measure the society from their unique point of view, the results promise to be reawakening, disturbing, even threatening. Baldwin himself has failed to go beyond *Go Tell It On the Mountain,* to convert his passionate protest into great romantic or Gothic fiction in *Another Country* or *Tell Me How Long The Train's Been Gone*—these later books are sentimental, not romantic, torn unsatisfactorily between naturalism and apocalypse. But some of the younger writers have employed romantic techniques with great success and variety: one thinks of the stories in Paule Marshall's *Soul Clap Hands and Sing* (1961) and William Melvin Kelley's *Dancers on the Shore* (1964).

The reasons for the creation of types—moral types, usually— are religious as well as political; and, once again, reference back to the nineteenth century is enlightening. Our earlier writers produced moral fables and allegories because they were tyrannized by a Calvinist tradition which ignored the individual and his fallible humanity. "Never to be sure where one stands with God," Edmund Wilson suggests, "makes life extremely uncomfortable, and the constant obsession with infinite power makes it difficult to be interested in one's neighbor." Emerson, Thoreau, Alcott, and their disciples are, as scholars have frequently noted, interested in Man, not men, and their reservations about prose fiction are predictable; Hawthorne and Melville deal with people who have some fabulous or allegorical significance, and when they are most novelistic, as in *The Blithedale Romance* or *Redburn,* they are least effective. One can not draw so neat and narrow a formulation only in terms of American history—clearly Hawthorne and Melville were encouraged by European romanticism and by some of the great English poets; but native traditions and ideologies did operate strongly upon the imagination of our finest nineteenth-century authors.

Negro writing has instinctively adopted the Gothic tradition of American literature and given its more supernatural and surrealistic characteristics a realistic basis, founded on actual lives often lived in the Gothic manner, that is indeed terrifying: the nightmare world of Poe or Hawthorne has become the Monday morning of the Negro author, as we have seen in our discussion of Toomer's *Cane,* of Wright's *Uncle Tom's Children* and *Native Son,* of Ellison's *Invisible Man,* and Baldwin's *Another Country.*

The examination and often rejection of the religious and political past, as expressed in romantic and Gothic works of art, is given unique authority through the language of the Negro author. Just as Emerson called for a natural language that would reflect the reality of "the meal in the firkin, the milk in the pan, the ballad in the street," the Negro artist seeks to make his experience organic by using a language that is the natural expression of the people: words in his fiction are the signs of natural facts. It is difficult to analyze completely or precisely the various character-istics of this language, although Norman Mailer offers a perceptive beginning in "The White Negro," and it is even more difficult to predict the uses to which the language will be put—one can only sense its fruitful and intricate possibilities in Albert Murray's views of what is called the "Black Aesthetic," Williams' *Sissie* (1963), Kelley's *Dem* (1967), and a story such as Murray's "Train Whistle Guitar." The language has an intensity and vigor that are absent from much of our contemporary prose, and because of its specific quality, it makes the persistent, ever emerging strain of idealism less theoretical, less abstract: in contemporary Negro writing, ideal-ism has developed from suffering, from the hard facts of existence. The Negro was the man, he suffered, he was there; and now his suffering has been translated into a literature of diversity and com-plexity, of the unspoken and the unpredictable, of all the beauty and the terror that inform a literary renaissance.

There is no artistic legacy that the transcendentalists have bequeathed to Negro authors; nor is there any substantive influ-ence, with the possible exception of Emerson's relation to Ellison, of transcendental thought upon that of the Negro. Too much has oc-curred in literature and life in the intervening century for writers to have the same response to Nature or to speak of self-reliance or God or the goodness present in the Universe so affirmatively and so dogmatically. And if American Negroes are deeply conscious of their national past, we must remember that they are also aware of cultural traditions in Europe: Jean Toomer has clearly absorbed many of the techniques of Joyce; Ellison owes as much to Dostoev-sky as he does to the Gothic writers of American literature; Bald-win has literary obligations to French and English writers; and Eldridge Cleaver has been influenced by Jean Genêt, Bakunin, and Nechayev.

But if there is no direct literary influence, there is a parallel phenomenon that suggests the meaning of current Negro writing and that reminds us of a significant trend in American literature. The "blackness of black," that Melville so admired in Hawthorne's work, does indeed inform the work of some of our greatest authors, from Poe through Hawthorne and Twain and Faulkner; but there is an idealism that also characterizes the writings of Emerson and Thoreau, Whitman and James, Hemingway (the later Heming-way), Faulkner (the later Faulkner), and Salinger (the later

Salinger). In Negro writing the two strands—the Gothic and the idealistic—are fused. Often the Gothic, as in the work of Richard Wright, seems to be a solitary feature, but upon closer inspection it is really a technique for conveying the author's idealism: out of all that darkness appears some light, however tentative it may be.

When we reconsider transcendentalism, not as a singular literary or religious movement in mid-nineteenth-century America but as a recurrent manifestation of idealism that is a dominant aspect of American culture, we recognize that many of its characteristics—the religious fervor, the sense of history, the Romantic point of view, the deep concern with language—are precisely those characteristics that are helping to create what we can consider to be the genuine Negro renaissance in American literature.

In much of American writing since the Second World War there is a lack of clear purpose, an idealism that is convincing only so long as it remains tentative, uncertain, potential. As we shall see in the chapters on Mailer, Salinger, and Bellow, effects are blurred, and the one figure who emerges more frequently than any other is the comic hero—Mailer himself, Seymour Glass, and Herzog—whose idealism is not quite wholly crushed before the authority of modern society but who can contend with that authority only in a comic fashion. That tentative idealism becomes vigorous affirmation in Negro literature, as it has become in Negro life generally—indeed the one aspect of American life that forces all Americans to reexamine their humanity or inhumanity is the racial problem. The dark voice of America cries "No, in thunder!" and refuses to lie or let us lie to ourselves; it threatens all that we thought we knew about American history and life; it speaks of black heroes who through their idealistic convictions feel they cannot only reform the forces of authority in America but also reassert that idealism which has always been the redemptive figure in the complex texture of American life.

In society Martin Luther King and Malcolm X evoked that idealism and struggled and finally died to realize it; their affirmation lay not only in what they said but in their knowledge that a wide audience heard them speak and read their books in absolute accord—the hero and his followers were one.

In social criticism, Eldridge Cleaver links the idealistic fervor of black youths and white students—groups, we should remember,

who will dominate American life in the next decades—and finds
in them the only hope in America today:

> The foundations of authority have been blasted to bits in America
> because the whole society has been indicted, tried, and convicted
> of injustice. To the youth, the elders are ugly Americans; to the
> elders, the youth have gone mad. . . . The young whites know
> that the colored people of the world, Afro-Americans included,
> do not seek revenge for their suffering. They seek the same things
> the white rebel wants: an end to war and exploitation. Black and
> white, the young rebels are free people, free in a way that Ameri-
> cans have never been before in the history of their country. And
> they are outraged.

In the literature of the black renaissance, more persuasively
than anywhere else, writers expose all forms of social abuse and
assert an idealism that is compelling because it comes from the
man who is, in fact, most justified in scorning idealism. Baldwin's
The Fire Next Time; Ellison's essays and interviews; William
Melvin Kelley's early fiction—*A Different Drummer* (1962),
Dancers on the Shore (1964), and *Drop of Patience* (1965); Paul
Marshall's *Brown Girl, Brownstones* (1959) and *Soul Clap Hands*
(1961); John A. Williams' *Night Song* (1961) and *Sissie* (1963)—
these and many other works suggest the diversity of the black
renaissance in America. In Paule Marshall's work one reads of the
difficult transition from Barbados to Brooklyn, as seen by a sensitive Negro girl; in John A. Williams' early books the jazz world
and Negro matriarchy are explored; in LeRoi Jones's best poetry
one feels that this world is "a place where you/cant go anywhere
without the awareness of the hurt/the white man has put on the
people"; in the poetry of Gwendolyn Brooks, one feels a simplicity
and terseness, an anger that is all the more powerful for being
tense and controlled:

> People who have no children can be hard:
> Attain a mail of ice and insolence:
> Need not pause in the fire, and in no sense
> Hesitate in the hurricane to guard.
> . . . While through a throttlng dark we others hear
> The little lifting helplessness, the queer
> Whimper-whine; whose unridiculous

Lost softness softly makes a trap for us.
And makes a curse. And makes a sugar of
The malocclusions, the inconditions of love.

This idealism is tough. It has nothing to do with the sentimental pieties that have always plagued so much popular writing
in America but resembles the practical idealism of other rebirths
in American literature. Emerson and Thoreau were idealists, but
they were also Yankees; Faulkner spoke of "the eternal verities of
the heart," but in his best work his characters look back into a
dark past that drives many of them to suicide or madness or impotence; the Jewish writers of the forties and fifties measured their
rich heritage against the dull assimilation of American life. Significantly it was Malcolm X, in his autobiography, who criticized the
Jews for intermarrying and, in the process, losing their profound
and idiosyncratic culture.

Malcolm X's criticism was intended as a warning to black
people in America; his autobiography is an idealistic testament to
the need for racial pride and manliness. Malcolm X called himself
"the angriest black man in America," but his book concludes on
a note of accommodation—accommodation to the belief that not all
white people are devils. And through Malcolm X's final perception
we can measure the dangerous artistic tendency that has always
been the burden of the Negro writer and that is the special problem
of many highly gifted writers of the contemporary renaissance in
America.

The idealism of black writers is powerful so long as it is
centered on the diverse humanity of individual Negroes, so long
as it challenges the authority of a society that denies the human
differences of black people. However justified the rage of black
men may be, it cannot exist alone, directed at whites, directed finally
at people who have become no more than stereotypes. The failure
of Claude McKay's novels and of Richard Wright's conclusion to
Native Son; of Baldwin's *Another Country* and *Tell Me How
Long The Train's Been Gone;* of Kelley's *Dem,* Williams' *The
Man Who Cried I Am,* and LeRoi Jones's plays is largely due to
their simplification of white people. The achievement of black
authors in this generation has been very great indeed, the fusion
of daring language and historical sensitivity, the use of Gothic
terror in the most realistic settings, the moral bewilderment that

stems from the Negro's instinctual idealism and the bigotry of a white society. That achievement has resulted in a most significant branch of American literature today. It has been wrought, moreover, at the greatest personal expense and projected with a frightening honesty. But implicit in this achievement is the great danger of surrendering to sentimental rhetoric, easy accusation, the creation of white instead of black stereotypes, of yielding to all the myths that the Negro writer once scorned.

No one dares to be morally lethargic in the face of the Negro dilemma, the America dilemma—no one, any longer. The Negro author himself has gained the courage necessary for significant art from his dynamic place in a culture which, sooner or later, must realize that color, as Baldwin has reminded us, is only symbolic. *Symbolic*—for black people as well as for white.

FOUR

The
Disenchanted
Hero

INTRODUCTORY *The*

Twentieth

Century

For the
twentieth-century American, idealism has been eclipsed by the
violence of war and by the authority with which organizations of
huge and frightening proportions have dwarfed the human personality. No significant writer in modern American literature has
avoided the central conflict between human possibility and institutional power, between hope and violence, between idealism and
authority. Self-reliance assumes the practical function of self-sur-
vival. Dogmatic, nihilistic answers turn into uncertainties, tentative
explorations of the self; the figure in the carpet becomes a question
mark, and the ceaseless inquiries into the reality of twentieth-century man take on a desperate character: How does one survive war
and its effects without remaining so bitter that life loses meaning?
How does one carve out a life of self-regard in the face of collective power and authority? How can one live without absurdity
when one considers life philosophically absurd? How can one care
about a private idealism when public authority becomes overwhelming? How does one believe in one's self? How does one
believe in the hero if one can no longer believe in heroism?

In the work of Hemingway and Fitzgerald inherited idealism **193** collides with the forces of war and class distinctions: Hemingway's heroes may forsake their country and the war, but Europe and the separate peace afford little permanent solace; Gatsby may change his name, as he modernizes his manners, but it leads only to death. There is a finality in the finest fiction of Hemingway and Fitzgerald, as they write a farewell to the heroic ideal, that one does not feel in literature after the Second World War. The conclusions of *The Great Gatsby* or *Tender is the Night,* of *A Farewell to Arms* or "The Snows of Kilimanjaro" speak "the last word" with an emphasis and a force that is incompatible with the writing of Salinger, Bellow, and Mailer. Salinger's first important story may end with the suicide of his central figure, but the stories that follow form an elaborate explanation of that suicide—a movement away from suicide to experiences of joy. Mailer's *The Naked and the Dead* is true to its title, but his subsequent work is open-ended, as he gropes for a hero in the modern world, as he talks and talks and still talks, unwilling to put a terminal point to his thought. Compare Hemingway's terseness with Mailer's prolixity: the style of certitude, the style of amplification. Mailer always wants the additional clause that will clarify, modify, keep the monologue going—the monologue must be kept going; and his verbosity is shared by Salinger, Bellow, and other contemporary writers.

Thematically the work of contemporary writers is critically different from that of Hemingway and Fitzgerald. In Salinger's fiction the hero is initially a feeble boy or boyish man who protests the phoniness of a world that does not understand him; but this realistic boy soon becomes a poet, a saint, a hero so committed to idealism that the authority of the world seems less awesome because it is less real. In Saul Bellow's writing the awkward hero seeks freedom from a purposeless suffering in his desire to achieve human dignity, a measure of affirmation. As Bellow has said of himself, "I seem to have asked in my books, How can one resist the controls of this vast society *without* turning into a nihilist, avoiding the absurdity of empty rebellion? I have asked, Are there other, more good-natured forms of resistance and free choice?" Finally, in Norman Mailer's fiction and essays the need for idiosyncratic growth, for individual power, becomes desperate and despairing— Mailer feels it in retreat everywhere, even in himself, and much of his work is consequently fragmented, unfinished, the shredded patchwork of an heroic vision.

More than any contemporary American author, Mailer reflects the difficulty of maintaining the heroic ideal when the authority of America is seen in all its ugly manifestations, when one possesses a piercing vision that in a different time—less journalistic, less dominated by mass media and anti-poetic forms of communication—would have been turned to the steady creation of novel after novel; Mailer's career suggests the difficulty of retaining belief of some sort without giving way to utter cynicism. This conflict is well-stated in "Superman Comes to the Supermarket," an essay which illuminates all of Mailer's work and which may serve as a perceptive summary of the conflict between idealism and authority that lies at the center of twentieth-century American literature.

Since the First World War Americans have been leading a double life, and our history has moved on two rivers, one visible, the other underground; there has been the history of politics which is concrete, factual, practical and unbelievably dull if not for the consequences of the actions of some of these men; and there is a subterranean river of untapped, ferocious, lonely and romantic desires, that concentration of ecstasy and violence which is the dream life of the nation.

The twentieth century may yet be seen as that era when civilized man and underprivileged man were melted together into mass man, the iron and steel of the nineteenth century giving way to electronic circuits which communicated their messages into men. . . . This loss of personality was a catastrophe to the future of the imagination, but billions of people might first benefit from it by having enough to eat—one did not know—and there remained citadels of resistance in Europe where the culture was deep and roots were visible in the architecture of the past.

Nowhere, as in America, however, was this fall from individual man to mass man felt so acutely, for America was at once the first and most prolific creator of mass communications, and the most rootless of countries, since almost no American could lay claim to the line of a family which had not once at least severed its roots by migrating here. But, if rootless, it was then the most vulnerable of countries to its own homogenization. Yet America was also the country in which the dynamic myth of the Renaissance—that every man was potentially extraordinary—knew its most passionate persistence. America was the land where people still believed in heroes: George Washington; Billy the Kid; Lincoln, Jefferson, Mark Twain, Jack London, Hemingway; Joe

Louis, Dempsey, Gentleman Jim; America believed in athletes, rum-runners, aviators; even lovers, by the time Valentino died. It was a country which had grown by the leap of one hero past another —is there a county in all of our ground which does not have its legendary figure? And when the West was filled, the expansion turned inward, became part of an agitated, overexcited, superheated dream life. The film studios threw up their search lights as the frontier was finally sealed, and the romantic possibilities of the old conquest of land turned into a vertical myth, trapped within the skull, of a new kind of heroic life, each choosing his own archetype of a neo-renaissance man, be it Barrymore, Cagney, Flynn, Bogart, Brando, or Sinatra, but it was almost as if there were no peace unless one could fight well, kill well (if always with honor), love well and love many, be cool, be daring, be dashing, be wild, be wily, be resourceful, be a brave gun. And this myth, that each of us was born to be free, to wander, to have adventure and to grow on the waves of the violent, the perfumed, and the unexpected, had a force which could not be tamed no matter how the nation's regulators—politicians, medicos, policemen, professors, priests, rabbis, ministers, ideologues, psychoanalysts, builders, executives and endless communicators—would brick-in the modern life with hygiene upon sanity, and middle-brow homily over platitude; the myth would not die. Indeed a quarter of the nation's business must have depended upon its existence. But it stayed alive for more than that—it was as if the message in the labyrinth of the genes would insist that violence was locked wth creativity, and adventure was the secret of love.

Mailer's general formulations are an introduction to his specific belief that John F. Kennedy might become the hero of our time, the extraordinary man who could elicit the creative spirit of the nation—"Superman Comes to the Supermarket" is, as Mailer himself later confesses, ultimately a propaganda piece, more wish than fact, more hope than actuality; but in the passages I have quoted Mailer defines precisely the dual pattern of American life and literature which our writers have pursued in their desire to tap that "subterranean river of untapped, ferocious, lonely and romantic desires, that concentration of ecstasy and violence which is the dream life of the nation."

In this last section I have chosen to discuss five prose artists who are not only among our most accomplished authors but who have cogently dramatized the central issue in twentieth-century American literature: the conflict between idealism and authority as it lodges within the man who seeks to be a traditional hero. *Within the man.* The tension between idealism and authority is largely external for the Emersonian hero and the violent figure who recurs in Negro literature—they fight their battles in the open arena where good and evil, the present and the past, freedom and oppression, love and power, are unambiguously opposed to one another. The lack of tension between the Southern Gentleman and his society is equally external, equally public—until at least the time of Faulkner. In the twentieth-century literature of white Americans, however, the hero assumes the private, internal burden of this conflict—he must resolve it within himself because it is "trapped within the skull." He may finally reject the *concept* of heroism, like Hemingway, or record its tragic decline, like Fitzgerald; he may struggle to make it real, like Bellow, Salinger, and Mailer. But for each of these writers heroism becomes a matter of ultimate and final concern, one that is bound to the perpetuation of self-belief, of self-esteem—of the singular, solitary self in conflict with a society that threatens its growth and full realization.

ERNEST   *The*

HEMINGWAY   *Renunciation*

of

America

The profound
influence of Hemingway on contemporary American writing extends far beyond matters of technique. It may be true that authors like Ralph Ellison have read him "to learn his sentence structure and how to organize a story"; but most current writers respond to the antagonistic relationship that Hemingway assumed toward the platitudes of the past, his renunciation of "abstract words such as glory, honor, courage, or hallow," of the abstraction of heroism itself. Hemingway's view is limited, as critics always say, but it is neither evasive nor shallow; it suggests a clear and often painful understanding of absurdity, marked by a disembarrassment of past American myths. If "all modern American literature comes from one book by Mark Twain called *Huckleberry Finn,*" as Hemingway has asserted, then American writing since the Second World War, in terms of its denial of inherited abstractions, derives from Hemingway's best work—his work is indeed the starting point for any discussion of heroism in twentieth-century American
198   literature. After Hemingway, certain words, certain modes of

thought no longer have dignity: they are obscene beside the concrete facts of our existence. In place of the concept of heroism
Hemingway creates a personal code for the hero that celebrates two
persistent American virtues—work and love—which lead inevitably
to self-respect, survival, and human dignity.

The special contours of Hemingway's thought are apparent at
the outset of his career—there is none of the typical groping of
the young writer, none of the intellectual posturing or uncertainty
that attends the search for a distinct point of view. The author of
In Our Time seems full-grown, his attitudes those of someone
who has suffered and come to understand his suffering. "You and
me we've made a separate peace," Nick Adams tells his friend
Rinaldi. "We're not patriots." Renunciation, death, and individual courage—Hemingway's pervasive themes—characterize the
wounded man; he knows what he denies, although he does not
yet know what to accept. The vignettes are charged with the violence of war whereas the stories, most of them set in the time of
peace, have the mood of terror and despair: the boy witnesses the
Indian husband committing suicide because he can't "stand things";
he loses faith in his mother because of her idealism; he sacrifices
his girl because she threatens to domesticate him; he learns, in "The
Battler," that "you got to be tough to survive"; he returns from
war, determined not "to tell any more lies, to live along without
consequences"; he knows, as a married man, that "there isn't any
good in promising" to repeat the pleasant things in life; and, in
"The Big Two-Hearted River," he knows that nothing can touch
him because he is "in the good place . . . in his home where he
[has] made it" and where, so long as he does not "rush his sensa-
tions any" and thinks only of the present, he can suppress the
anxiety that threatens to defeat him.

Hemingway's first book is a remarkable achievement, and the
most remarkable aspect of its achievement is an unrelieved despair
that seems unnatural in so young a man. Hemingway has matured
in a way that is rare for Americans and that, because of his clear
understanding of the worst that life can offer, constantly mocks the
values of the country he renounces. *In Our Time* is a diptych in
which Americans and Europeans regard each other through the
eyes of remembered youth. Although the vignettes are filled with
the horror of war and the stories that follow take place in nature
and in peace, the same themes recur—the imminence of death, the

absurdity of idealism, the need to renounce the authority of the world—as if the war that the writer has experienced conditions the view of his earlier life and gives it a tragic sense and a despair it may not in fact have had.

For Hemingway America most clearly represents the authority which has undermined his idealism; and he concentrates, throughout *In Our Time,* upon the vapidity of life in America. In the story "Cross Country Snow" Nick Adams tells his friend that his wife is going to have a baby and that they will return to the States; but neither he nor his wife anticipates the trip. We are not told why, but we sense that America holds no significance for him any more; it is a place of the past to which youth, sensitive youth, is no longer attracted. Earlier in the volume, Hemingway has already suggested the absence of vitality in the country he has rejected. America smells of death and decay; it is old and rigid in its unawareness of a changing world; and it assumes the unnatural, morbid qualities of a dying that arrives early in life. "The End of Something" is concerned primarily with the end of a love affair, but the vagueness of the title and especially the opening paragraphs imply the simultaneous ruination of America—death occurs on the private and the public level. "In the old days Hortons Bay was a lumbering town," Hemingway writes, but now the last departing schooner is loaded with "circular saws and all the rollers, wheels, belts and iron . . . carrying with it everything that had made the mill a mill and Hortons Bay a town." Marjorie, the girl whom Nick will soon leave, makes the observation that is more ominous than she realizes—"There's our old ruin, Nick"—and she connects the end of her affair with the end of a natural innocence in America. In the following story, "The Three Day Blow," Nick's friend tells him that Marjorie can now "Marry somebody of her own sort and settle down and be happy"; the dread of "going to Sunday dinners" at the house of Marjorie's parents "and having them over to dinner and [the mother] telling Marge what to do and how to act," suggests that Nick has refused to accept the middle-class routine of American life. The new world has lost its natural innocence, and in its place is that dullness which is a form of death and which militates against the growth of the romantic hero. For this young man the authority of a mechanized society has devoured the idealism that was its finest quality. In another time —before the war—the Hemingway hero would have found release for his idealism; but in his own time idealism dies before it can be born.

The renunciation of America dominates the stories of *In Our Time*. In "The Battler," Nick meets a mad ex-prizefighter and a vagrant Negro, both of them destroyed and perverted by American society, both traveling purposelessly across a country in which, as Nick now realizes, "You got to be tough"; in "A Very Short Story," which anticipates in part the subject of *A Farewell to Arms*, the young hero loses his girl to an Italian officer, returns to America where he does "not want to see his friends or anyone," and contracts "gonorrhea from a sales girl in a loop department store while riding in a taxicab through Lincoln Park." The story is part of Chapter VI, which is introduced by the vignette that describes Nick's wound and his decision to make "a separate peace," to abandon patriotism; the juxtaposition of Nick's renunciation and the veteran's debasement in Lincoln Park reinforce the deterioration that Hemingway associates with American life.

These elements—sometimes oblique, sometimes direct, like the varied modulations of a persistent, ever-present leitmotiv—are given clear focus in Chapter VII. The prefatory sketch describes the combat soldier's desperate need of Jesus, his willingness to "do anything" Jesus wants if only he will keep him "from getting killed"; but the next night he does not tell the prostitute "about Jesus. And he never [tells] anybody." This loss of belief is repeated in the climax of the story that follows, "Soldier's Home," when Krebs, who went to war "from a Methodist College," tells his mother that "he cannot pray"; and its significance is further magnified by its position in a context of general renunciation. "By the time Krebs returned to his hometown in Oklahoma the greeting of heroes was over. He came back much too late." Although he is "still a hero to his two young sisters," he is disoriented in America, at odds with his parents and the girls whom he is expected to court—"the world they are in was not the world he was in." He refuses to inherit the moral legacy of his grandfather, who fought in the Civil War; and when his mother tells him that "God has some work for everyone to do. . . . There can be no idle hands in His Kingdom," Kreb answers simply, "I'm not in His Kingdom." The mother insists that "All work is honorable as he [the father of Krebs] says," but Krebs has renounced the Puritan ethos of his ancestors: morality has become, as Hemingway states in *Death in the Afternoon,* whatever you feel good after and immorality whatever you feel bad after. "He did not want any consequences. He did not want any consequences ever again. He wanted to live along without consequences." The story is blunt and hard and suitably nihilistic; the rejection of God, of country, of family, of work as salvation is in accord with the reality that the boy has discovered—away from America. But it is paradoxical—and the paradox becomes increasingly painful and penetrating as we trace the development of Hemingway's fiction—that in fact work *is* salvation for Hemingway; it is all that bears any true and lasting meaning, the only kind of idealism in which he can believe; it is all, in those final, tormented years of his life, that holds any value for him at all.

The subsequent stories of *In Our Time* emphasize the decline of American vitality from various points of view: "Mr. and Mrs. Elliot" are incapable of having a child—Mrs. Elliot is "sick as Southern women are sick. That is women from the Southern part of the United States"; and her disintegration begins with her departure from America. She is incapable of confronting the difficulties of the outside world whereas her husband writes long poems and lives on "an income of nearly ten thousand dollars a year," combining fantasy and materialism in a peculiarly American way. In "Cat in the Rain" an American woman tells her husband that she wants "to eat at a table with my own silver. . . . I want candles. And I want it to be spring and I want to brush my hair out in front of a mirror and I want a kitty and I want some new clothes." Nick Adams, in "Cross Country Snow," thinks of America as a place where he does not want to return, not even briefly. And in "The Big Two-Hearted River," when he does return to Seney, he finds "no town, nothing but rails and the burned-over country." Nature, in the form of the river, is there, divine in contrast to the civilization that has decayed, and rejuvenating to the young, tense man; but its juxtaposition to the corrupting industrialism of the country reduces its redemptive power. The volume ends properly with the vignette entitled "l'envoi," a satiric portrait of the king and queen of Greece—"like all Greeks he wanted to go to America." But no American wants to return to America, and these stories of *In Our Time* suggest why. Like Joyce's *Dubliners,* Hemingway's first book renounces the country and the church and the parents of the author's youth.

A shadow has fallen between the hero and his youth, the shadow of the war. These early stories are about youth, but they do not have the feeling of youth; they are stories of initiation, but there is a hardness in the style, the point of view, that cuts quickly across the innocence of the hero and creates a reservoir of feeling beneath the language: the dignity of the language is that seven-eighths of it remains unspoken. The unmistakable tension that one feels in the prose has its source in Hemingway's war experiences. The spontaneity of youth and the aesthetic control of maturity; the experiences of a boy and the craft of an adult; the youthful events and the knowledge of adulthood as it recreates the events—these opposites fuse and produce a tension whose roots are in the conflict between the natural idealism of youth and the ugly authority of war.

The stories are not organic in the sense that *Huckleberry Finn*, for example, is organic: insight does not flow from the sensibility of the boy himself, who speaks in his own voice with the innocence he must have possessed when he was young. But the stories are organic in another sense that is equally effective, particularly in terms of the rhythms of twentieth-century life which Hemingway wishes to reflect; insight flows from the collision of idealism and authority—idealism has been traduced by the horror of war—and is conveyed in the voice of a disenchanted, hardened hero who must now rely upon himself alone and not upon an inherited set of beliefs. After the war, when the disillusioned veteran returns to the country where he first learned the code of the hero, he associates America with the authority of a bellicose and regimented twentieth century in which the old virtues, the traditional moral abstractions, are without meaning. All he can do is create a private code which will sustain him in an absurd world.

The renunciation of America is expressed in broader, more definite terms in *The Sun Also Rises* as the sentimental, boyish Robert Cohen encounters those genuine, embittered expatriates who have forgone the kind of life that America represents to them. Cohen is a man who is "fairly happy," Hemingway tells us, "except that, like many Americans he would rather have been in America"; he returns from his visit to the States with a completed novel, "more enthusiastic about America than ever," a man apparently more certain of himself but also incurably sentimental. He has been reading *The Purple Land* by W. H. Hudson: "for a man to take it at thirty-four as a guide book to what life holds is about as safe as it would be for a man of the same age to enter Wall Street direct from a French convent, equipped with a complete set of the more practical Alger books."

Cohen's youthful idealism, linked as it is to the naïve optimism, innocence, and unreality of Horatio Alger—that archetype of sentimental American heroism—is especially ludicrous in the European setting of the book. And his banality is reinforced by other characters and incidents that form a kind of American shadow to the sharp and vivid scenes throughout the narrative. Robert Prentiss, "a rising new novelist," is "from New York" by way of Chicago, and is characterized as "still only a child" who elicits Jake Barnes's contempt because of his garrulous, offensive nature. When Jake returns to his room he reads a wedding announcement that has been sent to him from his home town—"Mr. and Mrs. Aloysius Kirby announce the marriage of their daughter Katherine"—but he knows "neither the girl nor the man she [is] marrying"; America is scarcely a memory, and this kind of marriage promises a continuity and an order, the appearance of a reality, that he has forsaken. On the trip to Burguete, Bill Gorton and Jake are recognized as Americans by a fellow countryman who, as his wife reminds him, "could have come over [to Europe] ten years ago" but who always said, "See America first"—the other American tourists are condemned by Bill as "Pilgrims, Goddamn Puritans" and considered with contempt. Later Bill and Jake meet a Basque who tells them he was in America forty years ago, but his recollections are clearly of a country that neither Bill nor Jake recognizes—the shadow behind their own shadowed America. Then, before they fish, Bill baits Jake and brings into focus the renunciation of America and the significance of work, even as it is mocked, in the lives of these two expatriates. "You're an expatriate. You've lost touch with the soil. You get precious. Fake European standards have ruined you. You drink yourself to death. You become obsessed by sex. You spend all your time talking, not working. You are an expatriate, see? You hang around cafés." Jake answers, "It sounds like a swell life. . . . When do I work?" And Bill tells him, "You don't work. One group claims women support you. Another group claims you're impotent."

Impotence refers literally to Jake but metaphorically to those Americans who have accused him of being impotent, who would accuse the two men of being homosexuals if they had heard Bill say that he was "fonder of [Jake] than anybody on earth." Bill concludes his harangue on Americans in a mood of high absurdity, but the objects of his scorn are nevertheless significant: "That was what the Civil War was about. Abraham Lincoln was a faggot. He was in love with General Grant. So was Jefferson Davis. Lincoln just freed the slaves on a bet. The Dred Scott case was framed by the Anti-Saloon League. Sex explains it all. The Colonel's Lady and Judy O'Grady are Lesbians under their skin." Whether in a farcical or a serious mood, Hemingway's sympathetic characters see America fundamentally as a place of decay or death. Jake tells Bill that W. J. Byran is dead and shortly afterwards Bill satirizes "the Great Commoner," Mencken and Frankie Fritsch, Bishop Manning and Wayne B. Wheeler; he then turns to Ford, President Coolidge, Rockefeller, Jo Davidson, and, in mockery of the American dream he urges Jake to dream— "All our biggest business men have been dreamers." The ideal of work has been debased by the authority of commercial success; the American dream has become a sentimentality, a crudity, no longer the unattainable yet very real concept which lures the hero into an attempt to overreach himself.

The distinctions between these expatriates and other Americans are explicitly drawn when Jake and Bill come to the Hotel Montoya in Pamplona, a place where only aficionados stay. As lovers of the bullfight, the residents of the Hotel Montoya form a kind of elite, artistic fraternity, and they are amused that Jake "should be an American. Somehow it was taken for granted that an American could not have afición. He might simulate it or confuse it with excitement, but he could not really have it." Later Montoya, the owner of the hotel, consults Jake about the wisdom of sending Pedro Romero to have coffee at the Grand Hotel with the American ambassador; when Jake suggests that he not give Romero the message, Montoya is relieved and confides that Americans can have an injurious effect on bullfighters: "People take a boy like that. They don't know what he's worth. They don't know what he means. Any foreigner can flatter him. They start this Grand Hotel business, and in one year they're through." Jake agrees: "There's one American woman down here now that collects bullfighters."

The bullfight, in the last pages of the book, represents art (or

Hemingway's form of work) and heroism, an exquisite type of tragedy which measures the reactions of the various characters and reveals their fundamental worth. It is appropriate that Cohen should be the only member of the group who cannot understand or appreciate the Spanish sport, who is "not worried how [he'll] stand it. [He's] only afraid [he] may be bored." Throughout these scenes there is the implicit contrast between Romero's athletic perfection, his artistry as a bullfighter, and Cohen's romantic attitude toward boxing and football. We remember Cohen's earlier childlike desire to be a boxer, "now that he knows something of handling himself"; Cohen is the eternal amateur, unable to handle himself at all, whereas Romero is the professional whose self-discipline is integrally related to a tragic and noble vision of life that is particularly Spanish. The American is the barbarian, without discipline and without humility, whereas the Spaniard is the hero who represents the control of a highly civilized artist: he has merged the ideal of his work with the authority of a culture that sanctions his work. For Hemingway, Romero is the purest representative of his own idealism; and he is placed in obvious contrast to all those who have sacrificed idealism, who have no work that lends significance to their lives.

Cohen never really likes the bullfight and, as Mike repeatedly reminds him, he does not belong among these people; nevertheless, he seems to enjoy the persistent criticism of the others, "the childish, drunken heroics of it," as Jake comments. When he fights with Jake he further alienates himself and reminds us of his insufferable immaturity. Jake finds him crying at the hotel, lying on the bed in the same kind of "polo shirt" that he used to wear at Princeton, an adolescent whose mind is filled with fantasies about heroism but who is himself a mockery of the hero. After Cohen has left Pamplona, Hemingway contrasts his artlessness and fundamental cowardice with the artistry and heroism of Romero, an artistry which even the Americans eventually come to recognize and admire: "Romero did always smoothly, calmly, and beautifully, what he, Belmonte [an ex-bullfighter], could only bring himself to do now sometimes. The crowd felt it, even the people from Biarritz, even the American ambassador saw it, finally."

The last section of the novel begins at the Hotel Montana in Madrid, a fitting place for Hemingway's ideas to be overtly expressed. Brett assures Jake that Romero has "wiped out that damned

Cohen" and as they leave the hotel, eat supper, and drive around the town—much as they aimlessly drove around Paris earlier in the novel—there is the sense that America, as represented by the visitors to Paris, by the wealthy tourists, and especially by Cohen himself, has been completely renounced.

Renunciation is the theme of *A Farewell to Arms,* too, but in this more lyrical work, Hemingway enlarges his meaning to include all forms of romantic beliefs. The name of the central figure is scarcely mentioned by his lover and only several times by Hemingway himself; like Stephen Crane, whose hero also bears the suppressed and withheld name of Henry, Hemingway wishes to suggest attitudes that are more than merely personal, more than nationalistic; but unlike Crane, Hemingway is bidding farewell to all badges of courage—not to courage itself but to the artificial names it has been given.

America is part of the prehistory of the novel, a distant place that has nothing to do with reality. "It was a long time since I had written to the States," Frederic Henry remarks, "and I knew I should write but I had let it go so long that it was almost impossible to write now. There was nothing to write about. I sent a couple of army Zona di Guerra post-cards, crossing out everything except, I am well. That should handle them. Those post-cards would be very fine in America; strange and mysterious." Thus the hero, whose eager enlistment in the war represented a belief in the possibilities of heroism, renounces the America that shaped his earlier romantic notions and assumes some of the characteristics of the people among whom he lives. Rinaldi exaggerates when he asserts that "You are really an Italian. All fire and smoke and nothing inside. You only pretend to be an American." But it is true that Frederic Henry has consciously shed those American traits he finds so distasteful. America does not really exist for anyone in the novel, and when Catherine Barkley expresses a desire to go to America with him—to Niagara Falls and San Francisco—it is clear that they never will, that America has become in effect a fantasy.

This act of renunciation leads to Frederic Henry's still larger decision to bid a farewell to arms and thus a farewell to the false names that heroism assumes. Hemingway prepares the reader by having Rinaldi assure Frederic Henry that if he can prove he "did an heroic act" he will get the silver star. "Did you do an heroic act?" he asks Henry and the lieutenant answers, "No. . . . I was blown up while we were eating cheese." Later Henry characterizes an Italian from San Francisco as a man who has been in the Italian army, who wants to join the American army so that he can earn more money, and who is obsessed with the medals he has won. "He was a legitimate hero," Henry concludes, "who bored every one he met. Catherine could not stand him." When Henry returns to the war, he finds himself unable to believe in the abstractions so easily uttered by patriots—all forms of patriots, from all countries—and expresses his disgust in the famous passage that serves really as the thematic climax of the novel:

> I was always embarrassed by the words sacred, glorious, and sacrifice and the expression in vain. We had heard them, sometimes standing in the rain almost out of earshot, so that only the shouted words came through, and had read them, on proclamations that were slapped up by billposters over other proclamations, now for a long time, and I had seen nothing sacred, and the things that were glorious had no glory and the sacrifices were like the stockyards at Chicago if nothing was done with the meat except to bury it. There were many words that you could not stand to hear and finally only the names of places had dignity. Certain numbers were all you could say and have them mean anything. Abstract words such as glory, honor, courage, or hallow were obscene beside the concrete names of villages, the numbers of roads, the names of rivers, the numbers of regiments and the dates.

The renunciation of abstractions is so absolute and final that it creates a tone more depressing than that of any other novel by Hemingway—with perhaps the exception of *Across the River and Into the Trees*. In *The Sun Also Rises, For Whom the Bell Tolls,* and *The Old Man and the Sea*, the accomplished work of the Hemingway hero—Romero, Robert Jordan, Santiago—defies the absurdity of the life which people lead and relieves the books of complete despair; but in *A Farewell to Arms* the only force that can counteract the denial of heroism is Frederic Henry's love for Catherine Barkley and that love tends to be as abstract as the heroism renounced—it is, as Edmund Wilson remarks, "the abstraction of a lyric emotion." In any event, Catherine dies, love dies, and the hero confronts his future with neither work nor love to sustain him.

Most of Hemingway's important fiction in the twenties and early thirties expresses this attitude of absolute denial. "In Another Country," like *A Farewell to Arms,* rejects those abstractions that obscure genuine heroism. The narrator realizes that he has "been given the medals because" he is "an American," that in fact he could not have performed the heroic acts of those Italians wounded in the hospital with him, that he is "very much afraid to die"; and his innocence, distinctly American as seen "in another country," is contrasted with the bitterness and sophistication and enviable dignity of the Italian major whose young wife has unexpectedly died. "A Way You'll Never Be" mocks the innocence of Americans more directly. The wounded Nick Adams assures the adjutant of the arrival of several million Americans, "twice as large as myself, healthy, with clean hearts, sleep at night, never been wounded, never been blown up, never had their heads caved in, never been scared, don't drink, faithful to the girls they left behind them, many of them never had crabs, wonderful chaps." Because of Nick's own shell-shocked condition the usual suppression of emotion is absent and the denunciation of war and its tendency to foster mock-heroism is direct—Nick Adams has only "the ribbons and the papers" of heroism but "the medals come later" and in any case he knows that "You can purchase others in Milan." He remembers his own innocence in volunteering to fight in this war —the idealism that so innocently and easily challenged the authority of a military enemy—and how that innocence turned to cynicism. "At one time I was under the age limit," he remarks, "but now I am reformed out of the war."

There is a terror that follows the farewell to abstractions, which broods over *A Farewell to Arms* and these stories, the terror in which the safety of illusions has been forsaken and the hero is alone, with only himself to believe in and without the courage to manifest self-belief. This sense of dread is particularly embodied by the Americans. In "Hills Like White Elephants" the American's desire to have his lover undergo an unwanted abortion compels her to recognize his egoism and cowardice—the world isn't theirs any more, she knows, and "once they take it away, you never get it back." In "A Canary for One" an American lady, who is a little deaf, insists that "American men make the best husbands"—she has separated her daughter from a Swiss man—and the woman, "wholesome and middle-aged and American," is beset by fears of various kinds: she is afraid of the French night train that travels so fast, afraid that she will be in a wreck, afraid that she will not depart on time; and, as an act of compensation, she is bringing her daughter a canary, as fragile as herself. In "Now I Lay Me" the wounded and insomniac soldier listens to his American roommate recommend that he marry "some nice Italian girl with plenty of money"; the roommate is returning to America, "very certain about marriage," knowing that it will "fix up everything," but the soldier lives with the hard reality of all that he has renounced. These victims experience the kind of despair that leads inevitably to a denial of all traditional values—as expressed so absolutely in the parody of the Twenty-third Psalm which concludes "A Clean Well-Lighted Place."

Variations on the general theme of renunciation are more formally stated in a later story, "Fathers and Sons." America—especially Victorian America—is not the country of Nick Adams any more and his rejection is particularly vivid because he has returned, at the age of thirty-eight, for his father's funeral—the burial of the father and of the country become fused in his and in the reader's mind. He cannot transmit the experiences of his youth to his own son: "Could you say she [the Indian girl Trudy] did first what no one has ever done better and mention plump brown legs, flat belly, hard little breasts, well holding arms, quick searching tongue, the flat eyes, the good taste of mouth. . . . Long time ago good. Now no good." But nevertheless the boy has a persistent curiosity about his grandfather—"What was my grandfather like?" he asks. "I can't remember him except that he gave me an air rifle and an American flag when I came over from France that time. What was he like?" Nick is reluctant to remember, for he is trying to accept the manner of his father's death; he does not want to visit the tomb, but he realizes that he must acquiesce to the natural desire of the boy: " 'We'll have to go,' Nick said. 'I can see we'll have to go.' " Their visit, however, will be to a tomb, generalized now into at least two meanings: Nick has sacrificed both his father and America, and the death of his father suggests the larger spiritual death of his country, a self-desecration that fills him with remorse. The death of heroism in America has been in fact suicidal. Later, in *The Green Hills of Africa,* when Hemingway speaks of his rejection of America, it will be in still more bitter terms; and in *For Whom The Bell Tolls,* when he specifies the death of Robert Jordan's father—the father in both the story and the novel is clearly Hemingway's own father—he remembers that it was suicide and he is filled with disgust.

When the American experiences life intensely and heroically it is always in another country, it is always brief—a short happy life, as in the story of Francis Macomber. Wilson, the Englishman, is the professional hunter—one might call him the professional hero—and Macomber, the American, with a "face that would stay adolescent until it became middle-aged," is his student, an amateur engaged in an initiation into manhood and a conversion from the American to the European attitude toward life. Wilson, who brings the wisdom and the discipline of the European father, watches his surrogate son fight the fear that has caused him to be a perpetual boy and a cuckold: "he had seen men come of age before and it always moved him. It was not a matter of their twenty-first birthday. . . . It's that some of them stay little boys so long, Wilson thought. Some all their lives. Their figures stay boyish when they're fifty. The great American boy-men. Damned strange people. . . . Beggar had probably been afraid all his life. Don't know what started it. But over now. . . . Fear gone like an operation. Something else grew in its place. Main thing a man had. Made him into a man. Women knew it too. No bloody fear."

By accepting Wilson's code Macomber has acted heroically—in Africa, a "new" continent where man has not been crippled by the kind of civilization that Margot Macomber represents, where the hills are still green and an individual can realize his possibilities by truly confronting them. At the outset of the story we see Macomber "dressed in the same sort of safari clothes that Wilson wore except that his were new," a thirty-five year old man who keeps "himself very fit," is "good at court games," and has "a number of big-game fishing records"; but like many Americans of Hemingway's other work he is a romantic, concerned with the meaning of life rather than with life itself, dominated by a wife who needs to keep him a coward. Macomber's short happy life is the life of a hero capable of acting specifically, purely, ideally, for a moment. "You're both talking rot," Margot Macomber tells the men after their successful shooting of the lion. "Just because you've chased some helpless animals in a motor car you talk like heroes." But the transformation has occurred and the three of them know it; Macomber has renounced a life of attitudes in which heroism is only an abstraction, and experienced an ineffable, almost mystical joy which his wife can neither share nor tolerate.

"The Snows of Kilimanjaro" dramatizes the theme of renunciation at its most exquisite moment, the moment before death. Harry has failed to develop the self-discipline necessary to renounce those aspects of America—money and luxury—that have destroyed him; only at death does he torture himself by measuring what he has become and what he has never accomplished. Unable to climb the mountain, like the leopard, he has sacrificed the idealism he once possessed; and he has sacrificed the necessary concomitant of idealism—hard work—to the authority of a rich, seductive America.

Few authors have been so obsessed by the need to work as Hemingway. His persistent resolution to the absurdity of life, after he has renounced traditional values, is formed not only by the various characteristics of his famous code but by diligence and hard work, too. In the midst of interviews he complains that he is being taken from his desk. At the moment of hedonistic exhilaration he celebrates work, as if, after having sacrificed all the theological trappings of his Puritan past, made saccharine and insipid by the sentimental idealism of his mother and her kind of religion, he still finds the virtue of work the only remaining virtue; he still finds himself able to extol this aspect of Puritanism. As we shall see, the tendency to worship work, or the memory of work, grows increasingly obsessive as Hemingway grows older.

This is surely the euphoric vision of Harry in "The Snows of Kilimanjaro": he would never do his work, Hemingway records bitterly, "because each day of not writing, of comfort, of being that which he despised, dulled his ability and softened his will to work so that, finally, he did no work at all. The people he knew now were all much more comfortable when he did not work." He and his American wife have "made this safari with the minimum of comfort. There was no hardship; but there was no luxury and he had thought he could get back into training that way. That in some way he could work the fat off his soul the way a fighter went into the mountains to work and train in order to burn it out of his body."

Work is a kind of earthly salvation for Hemingway. Work purifies when all else loses meaning; it represents his idealism in a world where nothing else can be trusted. "What I had to do was work," he writes in *The Green Hills of Africa*. "I did not care, particularly, how it all came out. I did not take my own life seriously any more, any one else's life, yes, but not mine. They all wanted something that I did not want and I would get it without wanting it, if I worked. To work was the only thing, it was the one thing that always made you feel good, and in the meantime it was my own damned life and I would lead it where and how I pleased." He has minimized the significance of all other things in his life because they have no permanence: *The Green Hills of Africa* is in part a record of what he has put aside and has sacrificed, of what now gives him pure pleasure. "If you serve time for society, democracy, and the other things quite young, and declining any further enlistment make yourself responsible only to yourself, you exchange the pleasant, comforting stench of comrades for something you can never feel in any other way than by yourself. That something I cannot yet define completely but the feeling comes when you write well and truly of something. . . ." Work provides the kind of pleasure that love affords and the striking analogy that he uses later in his life epitomizes his self-conscious conclusion: "When you stop [writing for the day] you are as empty, and at the same time never empty but filling, as when you have made love to someone you love." These two elements are isolated from the rest of life so that they are intensely, preternaturally real, and they come to dominate and distort all of Hemingway's later writing: the hero has still renounced abstractions, particularly as they are associated with America, but he now brings an idealistic, almost a childlike attitude toward love and work that serves as his protection against the absurdity of the world.

Work naturally becomes more significant and necessary for survival the less Hemingway writes. But considered together with the renunciation of American values it assumes a special importance, for it comments ironically upon what Americans have debased in their own culture. When Hemingway calls the roll of American authors in *The Green Hills of Africa* and dismisses Emerson, Poe, Thoreau, Hawthorne, Melville, and Whittier, he is speaking largely in terms of language; but, inevitably, he is also rejecting an American heritage grounded, so he feels, on an idealism not viable in his life, an idealism created out of "nice, dry, clean minds." At the end of this travel book, which is a paean to Africa and the naturalness it represents, Hemingway renounces America in absolute terms: "I would come back to Africa but not to make a living from it," he asserts in language that is curiously similar to that of Thoreau, a writer whom he claims he cannot read at this point in his career.

> I would come back to where it pleased me to live; to really live. Not just let my life pass. Our people went to America because that was the place to go then. It had been a good country and we had made a bloody mess of it and I would go, now, somewhere else as we had always had the right to go somewhere else and as we had always gone. You could always come back. Let the others come to America who did not know that they had come too late. Our people had seen it at its best and fought for it when it was well worth fighting for. Now I would go somewhere else. We always went in the old days and there were still places to go.

This lament for the betrayal of America, recorded also in the important work of Fitzgerald and Faulkner, is even more pronounced in *To Have and Have Not*. The snapshots of vapid Americans that close the novel are in contrast to the bitter death of Harry Morgan and suited to a period when capitalism is viewed as only predatory. But Hemingway's artistic control is gone and those scenes in which Richard and Helen Gordon, the Laughtons and Professor MacWalsey practice adultery, or remember abortion, or destroy each other are confessions of hatred, embarrassing, propagandistic overstatements, and little more. Hemingway may be accurate in his picture of the American rich who are asleep on their yacht and who have made their money "from selling something everybody used by the millions of bottles, which costs three cents a quart to make, for a dollar a bottle in the large (pint) size, fifty cents in the medium, and a quarter in the small"; but there is a vulgarity and naïveté of conception, a mere rejection in *To Have and Have Not* that must be attributed to the simplicity of thought which characterizes so much American fiction of the 1930's.

The shift in Hemingway's moral position throughout this period of his work develops, as Lionel Trilling perceived years ago, in the surrender of the artist to the man: the pronouncements against America that punctuate *The Green Hills of Africa* and that mar the concluding sections of *To Have and Have Not* clearly reflect the need of the artist to respond to contemporary politics, to be liberal and *engagé,* as if the bitter and genuine and private renunciation of the 1920's had found a larger meaning in the public renunciation of capitalistic America in the 1930's. But the failure of *To Have and Have Not,* which is basically a failure of point of view, is not so significant as that of *For Whom the Bell Tolls,* a failure of essentials and of the artistic discipline that Hemingway had struggled so hard to achieve. The first forty-eight stories are convincing because they are charged with the tension of silence—renunciation of outworn myths is also renunciation of the loose words used to express the myths. *For Whom the Bell Tolls* is turgid and overwritten, a mockery of the earlier style. The denial of the mind that seems so valid in the stories is now abandoned for the self-conscious intellectual posturings of Robert Jordan. Few critics have ever claimed that Hemingway could think—his power lies fundamentally in his capacity to feel—and the long passages of introspection in *For Whom the Bell Tolls* are dull and ordinary, rendered particularly offensive by the pseudo-biblical language, the pomposity of the diction, the pretense of contemplation that informs them. More disappointing, however, is the realization that there is almost no genuine feeling in this novel—not even in the absurd, factitious love scenes with Maria—for Hemingway feels the compulsion to discuss each emotion until, as he knew so clearly in his early work, the original emotion is dissipated and meaningless.

The technical failures of *For Whom the Bell Tolls* are too patent to belabor, but they inevitably grow out of conceptual changes, and these perhaps are less obvious. Hemingway's early work is informed by renunciation; even in *A Farewell to Arms,* the "arms" of Catherine Barkley are renounced as well as the arms of war, and the unreality of the love affair is viewed in terms of the very real, growing infant, bringing with it death—death at the moment of birth. But in his novel of the Spanish Civil War, Hemingway places Robert Jordan's private code of heroism and his love affair in a context of purposeful political action—this war makes sense and, as the hero repeats to himself, he believes in the abstractions of democracy and knows that "If this war is lost all of those things [Liberty, Equality, Fraternity, Life, Liberty, and the Pursuit of Happiness] are lost." No one disputes the nobility of these sentiments, which seem so strange and even embarrassing in the light of Hemingway's previous pronouncements, but clearly they destroyed the artist in the man. Furthermore they suggest the increasing need that Hemingway felt for a private solution to the world he had renounced in the 1920's: the celebration of bullfighting in *Death in the Afternoon,* of hunting in *The Green Hills of Africa,* of fishing in *To Have and Have Not* was not enough to support personal meaning, even when considered as reactions against a denial of inherited moral values, and in *For Whom the Bell Tolls* he returned to the two aspects of his life that now held meaning for him—love and work.

When one scrapes away the encrusted rhetoric, the pretentious observations on Life, and the stilted, unnatural dialogue, one finds *For Whom the Bell Tolls* concerned with the validity of love and work. Gone are the humor and cynicism that once leavened the tragic lives of Hemingway's characters—Robert Jordan is serious about his love and especially about his work. "Don't ever kid yourself about loving someone," he reminds himself. "It is just that most people are not lucky ever to have it. You never had it before and now you have it. What you have with Maria, whether it last just through to-day and a part of tomorrow, or whether it last for a long life is the most important thing that can happen to a human being. There will always be people who say it does not exist because they cannot have it. But I tell you it is true and that you have it and that you are lucky even if you die tomorrow." Statements like these recall similar, previous sentiments of Hemingway and they are convincing as statements—as platitudes, to be more exact. But the love affair with Maria is less than childish, it is unreal, as unreal as the fantasy love affair of the mass media that Hemingway deplores; once again it is "the abstraction of a lyric emotion."

More convincing is Hemingway's attitude toward work. Work preserves the man and gives his life a sense of dignity and purpose in a world where other values can no longer be trusted because they have been debased; and Robert Jordan's need to work becomes almost obsessive as the novel progresses. When Pilar tells him that "in the head you are very cold" he answers, "It is that I am very preoccupied with my work." She persists, "But you do not like the things of life?" and Robert Jordan defends himself, "Yes. Very much. But not to interfere with my work." Pilar knows that he likes to drink and he agrees, but, as always, "not to interfere with my work." Later, after he has had intercourse with Maria—"Did the earth move for thee before?" she asks him mystically and "truly" he answers, "Never"—she knows that he is thinking "of something else now" and of course it is his work. The snow that the two of them later witness is "very beautiful," as Robert Jordan comments, "but it is bad for the work"; his brooding about the various men he has killed is "very bad for [him] and for [his] work"; he does not want Maria, who "would like to be intelligent about [his] work," to talk about his mission of blowing up the bridge.

Work is the most significant aspect of life and in the novel it is given a purpose that the hero does not completely understand. Robert Jordan has received orders to blow up a bridge and he knows that "You will blow it one day or you will blow it another. Or if it is not this bridge it will be some other bridge. It is not you who decides what shall be done. You follow orders. Follow them and do not try to think beyond them." As in life, the only meaning that the hero can extract from his immediate circumstances is the specific work that he must do. He remembers his grandfather who "fought four years in our Civil War," and he realizes that he has "a long time to go yet and [he is] very well fitted for the work"; he also realizes, as he measures his own heritage in preparation for his specific task, that "if there [is] any such thing as ever meeting [in a hereafter], both he and his grandfather would be acutely embarrassed by the presence of his father"—the father, by committing suicide with the same pistol that the grandfather had used so well, was not able to sustain himself through work or self-discipline of any sort. Later, Robert Jordan offers his confession of faith to Maria, and fuses the elements of love and work that have informed his short, happy life: "I love thee as I love liberty and dignity and the rights of all men to work and not be hungry."

Once Hemingway ceases to make pronouncements about the significance of work—this moment comes when Pablo has returned to the cave after having betrayed the guerillas—and traces the movements of Robert Jordan as he blows up the bridge, we are compelled by the truth of the book, we are reminded of Hemingway's remarkable ability to capture "the real thing, the sequence of motion and fact which [makes] the emotion. . . ." But three-fourths of *For Whom the Bell Tolls* is burdened by the static quality of Robert Jordan's mind, his need to expatiate upon his various beliefs. And this tendency characterizes all of Hemingway's later writing.

Heroism is remembered in *Across the River and Into the Trees,* it is given the counterweight of fragility in the present; and what is remembered as the distinctive characteristic of Colonel Cantwell's heroism is the accomplishment of work. "I'm not lonely when I'm working," Colonel Cantwell tells Renata. "I have to think too hard to ever be lonely." He spends most of his last moments talking with the girl about his *"sale* metier"—indeed, love and work are so polarized in *Across the River and Into the Trees,* so heightened by the Colonel's threatening death that the novel is about little else. At first glance, Hemingway's book of the Second World War, which reads like a last will and testament, is absurdly mannered, a mockery of his former accomplishment that justly deserved to be parodied. But the mannerisms—jerky, awkward, always off-center—are compatible with the subject, the manner in which a man meets his death, and properly slow, ritualistic, and intense. Love in the present is a sentimentalized work of art, a portrait of an Italian girl, and it is contrasted with the memory of American girls who have corrupted love and whom the Colonel can remember only with disgust. "With us," he tells the portrait of Renata, "if a girl is really beautiful, she comes from Texas and maybe, with luck, she can tell you what month it is. . . . They teach them how to count, and keep their legs together, and how to put their hair up in pin curls. Some time, portrait, for your sins, if you have any, you ought to have to sleep in a bed with a girl who has put her hair up in pin curls to be beautiful tomorrow. Not tonight. They'd never be beautiful tonight. For tomorrow, when we make the competition. . . . I see her [Renata] in the street with the lovely long-legged stride and the wind doing anything it wants to her hair, and her true breasts under the sweater, and then I see the nights in Texas with the pin curls; tight and subjected by metallic instruments." The deterioration of love in America is very clear but the form of lyrical love, as embodied by Renata, is of course the fantasy of a dying man; and this limitation should not be dismissed as a typical and traditional Hemingway weakness, for his inability in this novel to create the complex and credible emotions of a love affair undermines all that he says of war. Since both aspects of life are given serious weight by Colonel Cantwell, the reader naturally suspects the extravagance of statement when it applies to war as much as when it applies to love.

As the Colonel prepares himself for death, love surrenders to the memory of his work, his *"sale metier."* He talks on endlessly about war, fearful always that he will bore the girl; and though he bores us, if not the girl, we realize that work is all the man can remember with any dignity. "It is not a dirty trade," Renata corrects him, echoing his own real sentiment: "It is the oldest and the best, although most people who practice it are unworthy." But it is only remembered in *Across the River and Into the Trees,* either abstractly or in terms of military maneuvers the reader can not reconstruct in his own imagination.

The Old Man and the Sea dramatizes, indeed deifies work, and is convincing as *Across the River and Into the Trees* is not because action and thought are juxtaposed at the same moment of time; and the union of work and love is at last organic and credible. Other fishermen spoke of the sea "as a contestant or a place or even an enemy. But the old man always thought of her as feminine and as something that gave or withheld great favours, and if she did wild or wicked things it was because she could not help them. The moon affects her as it does a woman. . . ." The love that the old man feels for the sea suggests the love that he feels for life: his affirmation is made with full awareness of his personal loss of luck, of the evil that exists in the world and that is represented by the sharks, and of his own senescence and fragility. Santiago is destroyed but not defeated, heroic in his willingness "to dive"—to borrow Melville's phrase—, in his choice "to stay in the deep water far beyond all snares and traps and treacheries . . . to go there beyond all people. Beyond all people in the world." He is not defeated because of the "tricks" he has learned over a lifetime. Alone with the marlin, alone so that no one can "help either one of" them, the old man depends for his dignity and survival upon the skill that he has achieved as a fisherman—"the thing that [he] was born for." He knows that he has been beaten because he "went out too far," but in his boldness lies his heroism, his pursuit of an ideal that lies beyond the authority of his human limitations; and though he wins nothing but the skeleton—for that is the condition of life, the winner takes nothing as Hemingway pointed out years before—he has exhibited a nobility which stems directly from all that he has learned about fishing, about his work.

"Work could cure almost anything, I believed then [in the early 1920's], and I believe now [in 1960]." So Hemingway wrote in *A Moveable Feast,* whose subtitle could be the "romance of work"; so Hemingway tried to believe in the last years of his life.

Ultimately, of course, he could not work at all, the cure was ended, and suicide the only possibility. But that is a private matter—or, if the stature of the writer must make the pathetic story public, then an informed biographer like Carlos Baker must record it. For all of us who know the writing, who see and speak and feel differently because of the writing, one or two final judgments are appropriate after all the smaller reservations have been made.

The theme of renunciation, as expressed in the best of Hemingway's early work, has become the dominant theme of most serious American literature in our time. Clearly Hemingway sets the standards, not only because of his banishment of certain words and certain modes of flatulent thought, but because of the obvious truth of man's condition which he presents; modern man is, after all, wounded, and the wound does stem to a great extent from ceaseless war and violence. Whether we accept Hemingway's personal solutions to survival—the therapeutic value of work that will not go stale, the need of a rather rigid code of behavior to meet an irrational and threatening universe, the profound significance of love— is finally personal; but as conveyed in Hemingway's best work—in the short stories, *The Sun Also Rises, A Farewell to Arms,* and *The Old Man and the Sea*—they are solutions that derive organically from the tragic condition of man which he describes so credibly. Hemingway has not only modified our attitudes toward language, although that would surely be accomplishment enough; he has recorded permanently the conditions under which twentieth-century man has lived in the western world. Contemporary authors like Bellow, Salinger, Ellison, Baldwin, and Mailer have been unwilling to accept the finality of Hemingway's view, but his absolutely lucid vision makes their unwillingness possible. Between the Emersonian hero and the Quixotic hero broods Hemingway's disenchantment with the authority of moral abstractions in America: his disenchantment is the point of departure for the present writers, who can think affirmatively largely because Hemingway expressed renunciation with so impressive a finality.

Hemingway's artistic authority had its effect on his contemporaries as well; and when one thinks of that contemporary, concerned also with the decline of the heroic ideal, upon whom he had the greatest effect, one naturally thinks of F. Scott Fitzgerald.

3

F. SCOTT *The*

FITZGERALD *Hero*

in

Retrospect

"I talk
with the authority of failure," runs the famous comparison, "and
Ernest with the authority of success. We could never sit across the
same table again." Although Fitzgerald is measuring the relative
achievement of Hemingway and himself as authors—although he
is yielding to his melancholia, his pervasive tendency toward self-
abasement—he is also making a shrewd distinction between the
very nature of his artistic vision as compared to Hemingway's, as
compared to that of any writer who tries to tell us how to live.

Fitzgerald's fiction is retrospective; in Hemingway's the past
does not exist with anything like the vitality of the present. Fitzgerald sends us back to an innocence that is not even a memory,
and the Fitzgerald revival seems to develop from his concentration
on lost idealism, on the death of uniqueness, as much as from an
admiration of his art, accomplished as we now know that art to be.
Hemingway offers answers; he writes for the present and the
future, and his work is the artistic and ideological criterion against
which authors of our generation measure their own achievement. 221

Fitzgerald has the archaic virtues of being a classic—of being old-fashioned. We read him at a distance, safely, measuring the frivolities and irresponsibilities, the youth, of another era. We admire the chiseled prose of his later period, his fine perceptions, his wit, his developing sense of tragedy; but we know that we are reading of something—a "romantic readiness" to believe in the possibilities of life, of idealism and hope, of simplicity, of the awkward, youthful gesture—that has left our lives and that Fitzgerald knew was leaving the lives of the people in his generation. He concludes his "Echoes of the Jazz Age" (1931):

> Now once more the belt is tight, and we summon the proper expression of horror as we look back at our wasted youth. Sometimes, though, there is a ghostly rumble among the drums, an asthmatic whisper in the trombones that swings us back into the early twenties when we drank wood alcohol and every day in every way grew better and better, and there was a first abortive shortening of the skirts, and girls all looked alike in sweater dresses, and people you didn't want to know said, 'Yes, we have no bananas,' and it seemed only a question of a few years before the older people would step aside and let the world be run by those who saw things as they were—and it all seemed rosy and romantic to us who were young then, because we will never feel quite so intensely about our surroundings any more."

The decline of passion not only develops from the recognition that youth is gone but also from the realization that there has died a certain heroic attitude toward life, a certain hope and belief in the future. Fitzgerald wrote with authority about failure, and he wrote at a critical moment in the history of our literature. He predicated so much of his early life and work on the realization of fantasies, of "winter dreams"—the beautiful girl, the diamond as big as the Ritz, the intensity of youth, the heroism on the battlefield or the gridiron, the creation of a great, illustrious career—and he concentrated, in a later life which begins at the decadent age of twenty-nine when he completed *The Great Gatsby,* upon "the orgiastic future that year by year recedes before us," upon a Babylon revisited or the broken careers of Abe North and Dick Diver in *Tender is the Night,* or upon his own crack-up, or upon the phosphorescent ambition of Monroe Stahr in *The Last Tycoon,* dying from burned-out passions at the age of thirty-four. Both phases of Fitzgerald's life and work are important, for if his art is indeed retrospective, and if the early loss of idealism causes it to be retrospective, then the nature of that idealism assumes more than ordinary significance. The May day riots in 1919 and the stock market crash in 1929 not only mark Fitzgerald's arbitrary dates for the Jazz age, but they also mark a profound shift in American literature—and a measurement of Fitzgerald's achievement is one way of estimating the nature of that changing perspective.

It would be wrong to assume that Fitzgerald's early work is characterized by an innocence and idealism that are only in sharp contrast to his later work; for the tone of *This Side of Paradise,* as Fitzgerald assured Edmund Wilson before the book was published, is neither "sensational nor trashy," its romantic qualities are controlled by a wit and satire that Fitzgerald would later make less pretentious and more organic to his general intentions; moreover, in spite of the fact that Amory Blaine is so young, Fitzgerald already expresses, through his hero's undeveloped sensibility, his own disillusionment in the possibilities of heroism. The war, Amory complains to a literary friend, Tom D'Invilliers, "certainly ruined the old backgrounds, sort of killed individualism out of our generation. . . . Oh, Lord, what a pleasure it used to be to dream I might be a really great dictator or writer or religious or political leader—and now even a Leonardo da Vinci or Lorenzo de Medici couldn't be a real old-fashioned bolt in the world. Life is too huge and complex. The world is so overgrown that it can't lift its own fingers, and I was planning to be such an important finger—" And when D'Invilliers asks him if he thinks "there will be any more permanent world heroes," Amory Blaine asserts, "Yes—in history— not in life. Carlyle would have difficulty getting material for a new chapter on 'The Hero as a Big Man.'"

Now, Amory's loss of faith suffers from the most trivial kind of attitudinizing, and is burdened by a sentimentality and false intellectualism that Edmund Wilson, among dozens of later critics, justly condemned; but Fitzgerald's central idea is already present —the hero sees himself in the midst of his own decline, he witnesses the death of his idealism—and though Fitzgerald has neither the language nor the narrative with which to develop his idea, one can sense, in *This Side of Paradise* and in *The Beautiful and the Damned* as well, the validity of his perception: one can understand Gertrude Stein's approval of the young Fitzgerald as the man who "really created for the public the new generation."

Amory Blaine describes himself accurately as a "cynical idealist." The early parts of his adventures are like experiences that fill, in his own words, the "quest book," and he is little more than a boy who dreams of becoming heroic in love, in athletics, in college activities—of "becoming" but never of "being"; and all of his idealistic attitudes and pretensions, hardly more than catalogued for us, vanish into memories before they are experiences. One always has the feeling that the Fitzgerald hero is watching life as he lives —storing up the experience for later use as a memory when it will seem more vital because it is remembered and refracted, indeed altered and intensified, by his imagination.

Few American writers have been so self-consciously literary as Fitzgerald, and it is the early Fitzgerald who is most self-conscious, most intent upon displaying his intellectual wares: Amory Blaine becomes a writer because he seems equipped to become nothing else; Anthony Patch emulates his friend, Richard Carmel, but is unsuccessful as an author. In the latter part of his career, Fitzgerald strengthened his work by creating heroes who were non-literary, at times even antiliterary: Nick Carraway, it is true, has written "a series of solemn and obvious editorials for the *Yale News*," but his interests are confessedly mercantile—when he alludes to El Greco at the end of the novel the persona is gone and Fitzgerald himself is speaking; Gatsby's interests have nothing whatever to do with culture—he has not yet cut the pages of the book he owns; Dick Diver seems to have no real concern about books, and the artistic people who surround him are essentially vulgar, precursors of his own inevitable decline; and Monroe Stahr, though he works in a medium that partially depends upon literature and though he respects the cultured person, never reads himself— he depends upon other people for his knowledge. As these later heroes grow less intellectually pretentious, Fitzgerald's own style becomes less flaccid and more virile, less dependent upon itself for effects, less intent upon merely dazzling.

Still, in Fitzgerald's beginning—however awkward and mannered that beginning may be—is his central meaning. Through all the meretricious prose of *This Side of Paradise,* through all the fraudulent sophistication, remain those last lines that intimate the real significance of Fitzgerald's work:

As an endless dream it went on; the spirit of the past brooding over a new generation, the chosen youth from the muddled, unchastened world, still fed romantically on the mistakes and half-forgotten dreams of dead statesmen and poets. Here was a new generation, shouting the old cries, learning the old creeds, through a revery of long days and nights; destined finally to go out into that dirty gray turmoil to follow love and pride; a new generation dedicated more than the last to the fear of poverty and the worship of success; grown up to find all Gods dead, all wars fought, all faiths in man shaken. . . .

In *The Beautiful and the Damned,* Fitzgerald sends his new generation, only slightly grown up, into the world, to suffer a premature disillusionment, to watch with fascination over its own decline. Anthony Patch and Gloria Gilbert fear poverty and worship success, and their faith has surely been shaken—although one hardly knows why. At the outset of the novel, when Anthony meets Gloria, a girl who knows that she can dominate life so long as she is young and beautiful, he wants to appear "to her in novel and heroic colors"; but he has no heroic qualities—no real ability to dominate life—and he appears as a passive, self-pitying, pathetic victim. "Show me a hero and I will write you a tragedy," Fitzgerald notes in his ledger years later. But in *The Beautiful and the Damned* there is no hero and consequently no tragedy—only deterioration. Both of Fitzgerald's early novels grope towards tragedy, they fumble in their attempt to mourn the death of Gods, the loss of faiths—they want so eagerly to be tragedies; but they are really suggestions rather than statements, and they suffer from an uncertain perspective towards the tragedy that Fitzgerald feels but cannot dramatize effectively. The most convincing portions of these novels trace the decline of the central figures—then Fitzgerald seems certain, then he writes with authority for he writes of failure; the early sections that present the characters in their impulsive naiveté are too obviously written for and serve as a prelude to the elegiac commentaries at the end of each novel. And these commentaries seem hollow and artificial because they rest upon ideographs rather than characters, upon the idea of a story rather than the story itself; where there should be story, there is gesture, and, as Edmund Wilson suggests, we are left with striking beginnings and "with a burst of ideas toward the close," but with no narrative center.

Fitzgerald solved this problem of perspective by presenting the tragedies of his major novels retrospectively: the irrevocable fate that awaits Gatsby and Daisy, Dick and Nicole, Stahr and Kathleen, is grounded in experiences that have occurred before the present action; and the suggestive qualities that give a great density to these characters grow out of their past, a past that bears them ceaselessly back to a moment of greater strength which now is irrevocably lost. Furthermore, the point of view, which Fitzgerald first successfully controls in *The Great Gatsby,* colors the past events with a certain morbidity that intensifies the former heroism of the central figure: we learn from Nick Carraway that "it is what preyed on Gatsby, what foul dust floated in the wake of his dreams" that has caused his own disillusionment; we discover, with the healthy and normal Rosemary Hoyt, that Nicole is sick and we sense that Dick, her analyst-husband, will soon appear dissipated and morbid himself; we feel the pervasive illness of Monroe Stahr, surrounded by corruption of various kinds, as he is remembered by the tubercular Cecilia. The morbidity that attaches itself to the past inevitably affects the present and permits Fitzgerald to exaggerate those extraordinary characteristics of his heroes: for if Gatsby is preyed upon by the meanness of his society then we can accept more readily his literally absurd behavior; if Nicole suffers from relapses of her illness then we can understand Dick's inability to pursue his own career, we can believe in his erratic behavior; if Stahr is constantly threatened by death, then his eagerness to live his last moments intensely almost resurrect in him his earlier heroism. By connecting his tragedies to a past that broods over the present action and by informing the present with the unhealthy atmosphere of uncertainty, Fitzgerald is able to describe the decline of the heroic and idealistic posture in his generation.

No one was more conscious of his dependence on the past than Fitzgerald himself. The "worst fault" in *The Great Gatsby,* he knew, "is a BIG FAULT: I give no account (and had no feeling about or knowledge of) the emotional relations between Gatsby and Daisy from the time of their reunion to the catastrophe. However the lack is so astutely concealed by the retrospect of Gatsby's past and by blankets of excellent prose that no one has noticed it—though everyone has felt the lack and called it by another name." Fitzgerald could not describe Gatsby's affair with Daisy, for the mythical element in Gatsby's character would be lost; Gatsby would seem too human and the implications of his tragedy would appear too ordinary. By forcing us to consider Gatsby in terms of his past, Fitzgerald established the tragic tone of his tale. In that "retrospect of Gatsby's past" we learn of his vision and of his connections with Dan Cody "who during one phase of American life brought back to the Eastern seaboard the savage violence of the frontier brothel and saloon" and who brings us back to a time in American history when individualism was still possible, even though it was perhaps ruthlessly achieved. Later in the novel Gatsby describes his former love affair with Daisy, which is in sharp contrast to the sordid affairs and jaded attitudes of the people in the present action. Still later, after his death, we are reminded of Gatsby's boyhood by the famous schedule and resolutions in which he is to develop his body, "study electricity," and "practice elocution, poise and how to attain it," in which he reminds himself not to waste time or smoke, to bathe every other day, and to read one improving book or magazine per week, and "to save $5.00 [crossed out] $3.00 per week."

This passage, which appears in the latter part of the final chapter, is juxtaposed with Nick Carraway's memories of his own childhood, his own realization that "this has been a story of the West, after all"—that is, a story of innocence, after all—and that the characters "possessed some deficiency in common which made [them] subtly unadaptable to Eastern life"—that is, unadaptable to the authority of evil that envelops Tom and Daisy, that destoys Gasby, and that disillusions Nick. And the passage is also in our mind when we read the last poignant page in which Nick Carraway connects Gatsby's death with the tragic death of individualism in America—the "vanished trees" of America had, after all, made way for Gatsby's house, they "had once pandered in whispers to the last and greatest of all human dreams," and Gatsby, like the Dutch sailors, has failed, although he does not know that his dream is "already behind him, somewhere back in that vast obscurity beyond the city, where the dark fields of the republic [roll] on under the night."

The boy who emulates Benjamin Franklin and Horatio Alger, who thinks of himself calvinistically as elected for heroism, is very clear, even though he is briefly evoked; the host who bids his guests farewell, who meets Daisy at tea after five years' separation, and who sits in the suite of the Hotel Plaza, unable to realize his dream, is equally clear. But the Gatsby of the intervening years is less than a blur, less than a man whom Fitzgerald "never at any one time" saw clearly; he truly has no existence. Gatsby is real only in his innocence (his state of romantic possibility) or his defeat (his state of helpless grandeur). There is no tragic dimension for Gatsby; the girl for whom he has sacrificed his life has always been limited. At the beginning she was a child, at the end she is really still a child, still unable to act—"What'll we do with ourselves this afternoon," she cries, "and the day after that, and the next thirty years?"—and Gatsby seems never to have realized the smallness of her character, the fundamental cruelty of her character; the dream of self-fullfillment has always been behind him, as Fitzgerald states explicitly in the last paragraphs, although Gatsby seems to have lost any quality of self-perception he once may have possessed.

Gatsby is indeed much closer to a clown than to a tragic hero; in the title itself we feel that we will privy to a circus show in which the Great Gatsby will perform. Gatsby betrays no awareness of the tragic dimensions of his story, and whenever Fitzgerald tries to raise his character to the level of the tragic he always tells us, never shows us, and he tells us through, of course, the mind of Nick Carroway, a distinctly unheroic man. Any critical attempt to make the novel into a tragedy is doomed to an inevitable discussion of Gatsby as a "mythical" character, described by Nick Carraway rather than convincingly demonstrated by Gatsby himself; for Gatsby is the objective correlative to Nick Carraway, and he becomes richer in his meaning only as Nick Carraway develops and gives him meaning. There is no argument that Gatsby gains in mystery and perhaps in intensity by not being closely defined; and it is undoubtedly true that in this vague sense Gatsby appears to have a quality of the tragic because of the tragedy which engulfs him. But the reservations of Edith Wharton and Edmund Wilson about the lack of fullness in Gatsby's character still are very much to the point: Fitzgerald has created a tragic conception of America but not a tragic character; his prose, his setting, his point of view, his idea or donné, as James would have put it, all contribute to the sense of tragic loss, but the character is never really noble, except as his gestures are interpreted and refined and given greater symbolic dimension by Nick Carraway. When we see Gatsby he is much more absurd—and at times more vulgar—than any tragedian would have his hero be: he is impotent before Daisy at Nick's little tea party; or he lies outrageously to Nick as they drive to Manhattan in his fantastic Rolls Royce; or he boasts awkwardly and childishly by tossing his colored shirts onto the bed of his incredible home.

The myth and the man never really merge, no matter how impassioned the language becomes—and the language usually becomes impassioned when Fitzgerald elaborates upon the idea that informs the book, when he writes on the abstract level. He keeps Gatsby at a distance so that even the few remarks he does make—"her voice sounds like money"; "In any case it was just personal"—sound mystical. Gatesby never holds us on the human level; whenever observed closely, he appears childlike, vulnerable, pathetic, or meretricious, and we are reminded of the great disparity between the man and the myth, between the man as we see him and the myth as Nick Carraway evokes it. There is a tragedy in *The Great Gatsby*, but it is not Gatsby's, it is that of the country—the dark republic—as understood and conveyed by Carraway. That tragedy is, of course, the death of romantic possibility, of hope, of all that America once offered the ambitious, self-reliant man; and it assumes compelling proportions so long as it is described abstractly, or, so long as its incarnation, Gatsby, is seen in terms of his innocence and his defeat—before and after life, as it were.

Tender is the Night is more novelistic than *The Great Gatsby* and more explicit in its description of character; but it too depends upon the tragic vision. Here the death of idealism occurs when life seems to be at its ripest: in the hot Riviera sun, or at night among parties where charming, talented people scarcely conceal their crippled natures, where illness and health seem almost indistinguishable from one another. It does not matter which version of the novel we use; this sense of sickness or death—not unlike that which Keats speaks of in "The Ode to a Nightingale"—lurks just beneath everyone's cultivated gesture. And we know that Fitzgerald intends us to feel that Dick Diver himself is "socially the most charming and inwardly corrupt" when he meets Rosemary, that "the difficulty of taking care of" Nicole "is more than he has imagined and that he has gone more and more to pieces, always keeping up a wonderful face."

In *Tender is the Night*, Fitzgerald has far more of a sense of the "emotional relations" between Dick and Nicole than he has between Gatsby and Daisy, and, once again, he describes them mainly in terms of their breakdown. When he came to revise the novel, he interpolated a four-page hurried account of Dick and Nicole's marriage and early life together, which, as Arthur Mizener points out, is necessary and which Fitzgerald did not use often enough; still, as effective as this synoptic, impressionistic record is, we know that it is mainly a device, a technique, a *tour de force*. Fitzgerald brings us to the point of Rosemary's arrival and at once we feel his real interest and success in describing Dick Diver and his world—externally and superficially so fascinating to Rosemary.

Because of his original intentions the first version of the novel is more than merely the most effective dramatic arrangement of Fitzgerald's material but the proper one thematically, too. Fitzgerald conceived of the novel in terms of the deterioration of Dick Diver and the first intimations of decline occur when he stands with Rosemary at one-thirty on a hot afternoon on the French Riviera, in the year 1919, and tells her that "it is not one of the worst times of the day." The early portion of the novel, told from Rosemary's point of view, and the last sections, which examine the attrition of Dick Diver and his world, are surely the most compelling in the book because they are written with the authority that Fitzgerald usually brings to his description of failure. The intervening chapters, which quickly trace Dick and Nicole's love affair and his decision to marry her are equivalent to the retrospective passages that evoke Gatsby's love for Daisy, and do not belong at the beginning of the novel: *Tender is the Night* is not a *Bildungsroman* nor a defeat à deux but rather the personal tragedy of Dick Diver, and Fitzgerald's instinct of first dramatizing Dick at his most charming —both publicly and personally—was sound.

No twentieth-century novel suffers more than *Tender is the Night* from our knowledge of the author's difficulties in creating it. Everyone seems to be in agreement with Edmund Wilson that Fitzgerald's "conception of his subject in *Tender is the Night* had shifted in the course of his writing it so that the parts of that fascinating novel do not always hang together"; and there are probably few modern readers who encounter the book without being oriented by Malcolm Cowley, a sympathetic editor who reluctantly concludes that "Fitzgerald could never have revised *Tender* into the perfect novel that existed as an ideal in his mind. He had worked too long over it and his plans for it had changed too often . . ."

But these observations—accurate, so far as they go—indicate

our obsession with form, as Cowley himself implies when he adds that "a novel has to be judged for what it gives us, not for its defects in execution, and *Tender* gives us an honesty of feeling, a complexity of life, that we miss in many books admired for being nearly perfect in form." One is not essentially distracted by the structure of the novel. The Divers' past, appearing at the center of the book, illuminates their present difficulties and brings us into an intimate relationship with them that is impossible from Rosemary's point of view; moreover, technical questions of this sort seem superficial when one considers Fitzgerald's achievement: the convincing description of this vast group of expatriates, each suggestive of some inner decay, each drawn with a concision and subtlety that imply the novelist's knowledge of his characters' entire lives; the sense of place, permanently and naturally beautiful in contrast to the ephemeral and artificial beauty, charm, and—in Nicole's case—the human illness of the people themselves; and, finally, the highly polished prose, fixed on the page like words on granite, Keatsian in its heavy, somber, sensuous luxuriance, firmly controlled in contrast to the insecurities of the people it describes.

Of course, Fitzgerald himself is greatly responsible for conditioning our attitudes toward *Tender is the Night*. "I did not manage, I think in retrospect, to give Dick the cohesion I aimed at," he later confessed to an admirer of the novel; and his famous letter to Maxwell Perkins is in our mind whenever we think of the book:

> It has become increasingly plain to me that the very excellent organization of a long book or the finest perceptions and judgment in time of revision do not go well with liquor. A short story can be written on a bottle, but for a novel you need the mental speed that enables you to keep the whole pattern in your head and ruthlessly sacrifice the side-shows as Ernest did in 'A Farewell to Arms.' If a mind is slowed up ever so little it lives in the individual part of a book rather than in a book as a whole; memory is dulled. I would give anything if I hadn't had to write part III of 'Tender is the Night' entirely on stimulant. If I had one more crack at it cold sober I believe it might have made a great difference.

But his self-criticism is similar to Fitzgerald's feeling in 1938 that the novel should have been revised—one tends to agree with Dan Piper that this decision grew out of a natural desire to be read again, to achieve the popularity that Fitzgerald thought the novel had deserved when it first appeared in 1934. Fitzgerald's reservations about his novel are simply the idealistic expression of the conscientious author; in retrospect, *Tender is the Night* seems to be not only a far more ambitious novel than *A Farewell to Arms* but one that is artistically more satisfying—more satisfying, indeed, and richer in its total achievement than any other novel in twentieth-century American literature, with the exception of Faulkner's early work—*The Sound and the Fury, Light in August,* and *Absalom, Absalom!*

The great advance in *Tender is the Night* lies in Fitzgerald's conception of Dick Diver. Like Gatsby he is an idealist; and like Gatsby he has great self-confidence, he thinks of himself heroically. "He is a superman in possibilities," Fitzgerald reminded himself in his notes for the novel; "however he lacks the tensile strength— none of the ruggedness of Brancusi, Léger, Picasso." Unlike Gatsby, Dick is by training and by temperament self-conscious, morbidly aware of his developing tragedy, although he can do nothing to prevent it; unlike Gatsby, his tragedy is not only symbolic in its significance but personal as well—we always feel the human consequences in *Tender is the Night.* "Wanting above all to be brave and kind, he had wanted even more than that, to be loved. So it had been. So it would ever be, he saw. . . ." This reflection, which occurs directly before the Divers' decision to separate, is merely one of Dick's final perceptions about himself; indeed, the haunting aspect of his deterioration is that he can diagnose it so accurately, he can bring to bear the sensibility of the psychiatrist and yet remain impotent.

He can measure the deteriorating American society around him, too, and his judgments give greater scope to his personal tragedy; for Fitzgerald wants to feel that *Tender is the Night* is not only the decline of an idealistic American in Europe but the death of American idealism itself. Morbidity gives the book its tone and contributes to the public as well as to the personal deterioration of the various characters. The incestuous father; the schizophrenic Nicole; the frigid Baby Warren; the alcoholic Abe North; the homosexuals Campion and Dumphry; the lover Tommy Barban, who suggests the absence of civilized sensitivity; the faded novelist McKisco, who, according to his vapid wife, has chosen as a plot "a decayed old French aristocrat" and put "him in contrast with the mechanical age"—all these expatriates are viewed by Rosemary Hoyt, who is innocent and apparently healthy, although dominated by her mother and by Hollywood to the degree that she has not yet lived according to adult standards.

At the center of this group of people—surrounded by their weaknesses and problems—is Dick Diver, who has inherited "good instincts, 'honor, courtesy, and courage'" from his father and who appears stable and robust to Rosemary at the outset of the novel— "You were the first man," her mother tells Dick. "You're an ideal to her"—but who has already begun to deteriorate. Fitzgerald meant Dick to be "an approximation of the *hero* seen in overcivilized terms—taste is no substitute for vitality but in the book it has to do duty for it. It is one of the points on which he must never show weakness as Siegfried could never show physical fear." Dick has inherited from his father the "somewhat conscious good manners of the young Southerner coming north after the Civil War" and he does maintain them; but he shows overt weakness towards the end of the novel, even his charm becomes ineffectual, as Fitzgerald explicitly defines the nature of his tragedy—"The change came a long way back," Dick confesses to Rosemary, "but at first it didn't show. The manner remains intact for some time after the morale cracks."

The last pages of the novel confirm Fitzgerald's intention to associate Dick's tragedy with that of idealism in general. After Nicole and Tommy Barban sleep together—in an act of lust more than of love—they hear Americans sing "Oh, way down South in the land of cotton hotel bums and business rotten"; a moment later Nicole insists that Tommy kiss her on the lips and Tommy responds, "That's so American. . . . When I was in America last year there were girls who would tear you apart with their lips, tear themselves too, until their faces were scarlet with the blood around the lips all brought out in a patch—but nothing further"; and, at the end of the scene, as prostitutes wave to their departing sailors, Fitzgerald comments ironically, "'Oh, say can you see the tender color of remembered flesh?'—while at the stern of the battleship rose in rivalry the Star Spangled Banner." Several pages later we read of Mary North and her English friend, Lady Caroline Sibley-Biers, "pretending to be sailors on leave" and picking up "two silly girls"—an amusing prank but nevertheless lesbianic and sordid and, inevitably, involving Dick, who is always ready to be used. Then, in the next scene, as Tommy Barban forces Dick and Nicole's separation into the open—"You don't understand Nicole," he tells Dick. "You treat her always like a patient because she was once sick"—Fitzgerald interrupts the tense conversation with "an insistent American, of sinister aspect, vending copies of the *Herald* and of the *Times* fresh from New York"; significantly the boy insinuates himself upon the group by calling all of them "Buddies." The combination of Nicole's remembered illness and of Dick's lost profession together with the success of the barbaric impulse toward lust and greed as represented by Tommy Barban and by "the millions of Americans," who are cartooned in the newspapers as "pouring from liners with bags of gold," suggests the personal and public tragedy that Fitzgerald wants us to remember.

Each gesture, each incident serves as an ironic commentary upon the death of hope: Tommy Barban's speaking French, as if to avoid his identification with America, although of course he is at one with the newspaper vendor intent upon sharing the American wealth; the racing boys on bicycles, led by "a lone cyclist in a red jersey," who reminds us of Dick as we first saw him, doubly so because Baby Warren tells Nicole in the next chapter that "we should have let him confine himself to his bicycle excursion"; the Divers themselves, Dick "with his face half-shaved matching [Nicole's] hair half-washed"; Nicole's white eyes, which in the penultimate chapter fuse with "a white sun, chivied of outline by a white sky"—all in bitter contrast to the corruption that has occurred. The early idealism of Dick Diver, first sacrificed to the Warren money, is now scarcely a memory, and is crushed beyond possible resurrection by the greed of Americans in general—by the Americans who turn "upwards from several umbrellas" to watch the fallen hero bless the beach, as if to suggest the religion that they have adopted, the religion for which Dick has crucified himself.

The decline of moral heroism is also the central issue in *The Last Tycoon*. "There is no world so but it has its hero and Stahr was the hero," Cecilia remarks at the end of the second chapter. "Most of these men [the working men at the Hollywood studios] had been here a long time—through the beginnings and the great upset, when sound came, and the three years of depression, he had seen that no harm came to them. The old loyalties were trembling now, there were clay feet everywhere; but still he was their man, the last of the princes. And their greeting was a sort of low cheer as they went by."

Stahr has elicited the affection of these employees because he represents the man who has risen through his own initiative and energy, and yet not forgotten or forsaken his past. Like Gatsby and Dick Diver he has an heroic conception of himself, he too has followed schedules and resolutions, he too has pursued his dreams; but unlike either of Fitzgerald's earlier heroes he is more rooted in the reality of his world, he does not assume the corruption of those people close to him, and—unlike Dick Diver—he protects himself by his great ambition, his capacity for work. "Like many brilliant men, he had grown up dead cold. Beginning at about twelve, probably, with the total rejection common to those of extraordinary mental powers, the 'See here: this is all wrong—a mess—all a lie— and a sham,' he swept it all away, everything, as men of his type do; and then instead of being a son-of-a-bitch as most of them are, he looked around at the barrenness that was left and said to himself, '*This* will never do.' And he had learned tolerance, kindness, for-bearance, and even affection like lessons."

In many other ways Stahr is different from Fitzgerald's other heroes. Whereas they are seen only in their moments of leisure, Stahr is viewed almost exclusively as a working man—work offers the only meaning to a life that has lost all personal significance. Stahr is a Jewish boy from the Bronx who has risen through his own cunning and diligence, whereas both Gatsby and Dick Diver— not to mention Fitzgerald's earlier heroes, Amory Blaine and An-thony Patch—are financially if not morally aided by others. Stahr seems provincial when compared to Gatsby and especially Dick Diver; but in his provinciality lies his special strength, he is narrow but profound, distinctly American in the high order of his special-ized knowledge. Fitzgerald's other heroes are intricately involved with the very rich, and the consequences of their lives depend upon how they differ from them; Stahr never seems deeply concerned with wealth, he assumes it as part of the "grandeur" that he "de-mands of life." He has gone beyond financial considerations, except insofar as these considerations assume the aspects of power—he is the last tycoon, but ironically he is not a businessman; as Boxley, the English script writer recognizes, he is, first and last, an artist.

The concept of heroism, especially in terms of its relationship to past American culture, is constantly before us as we read the novel. In the first chapter, Cecilia goes with Manny Schwartz, a defeated producer, and Wylie White, a cynical script writer, to the "Hermitage, Home of Andrew Jackson." It is dawn and Wylie comments, "I was born here—the son of impoverished southern paupers. The family mansion is now an outhouse." The sense of decay is emphasized more significantly when Wylie and Cecilia leave Schwartz, who will soon commit suicide, at Jackson's home and Cecilia observes: "He had come a long way from some Ghetto to present himself at that raw shrine. Manny Schwartz and Andrew Jackson—it was hard to say them in the same sentence. It was doubtful if he knew who Andrew Jackson was as he wandered about, but perhaps he figured that if people had preserved his house Andrew Jackson must have been someone who was large and merciful, able to understand. At both ends of life man needed nourishment: a breast—a shrine." Thus we hold in juxtaposition the vitality of Jackson and the impotence of Manny Schwartz, who like Stahr has clawed his way to a position of significance and who prefigures Stahr in his ultimate defeat; "once," Schwartz reminds himself and the others, "I used to be a regular man of decision—you'd be surprised."

The contrast between an American past of rugged individualism and a present that is filled with destructive commercialism—with repressive forms of authority—is of course dramatized by Stahr, who as the last hero seems already rather old-fashioned: like "Edison and Lumiere, Griffith, and Chaplin—a marker in industry"; his achievements are in the past, he has no future. Fitzgerald does not permit us to forget the heritage that has been desecrated. In a later scene, after Stahr has told "the money men" of Hollywood that they should sponsor a picture that will lose money because it is a "quality picture," he walks into the commisary with his guest, Prince Agge of Denmark, who sees an actor dressed like Abraham Lincoln, "his kindly face fixed on a forty-cent dinner, including dessert, his shawl wrapped around him as if to protect himself from the erratic air-cooling—now Prince Agge, who was in America at last, stared as a tourist at the mummy of Lenin in the Kremlin. This, then, was Lincoln. Stahr had walked on far ahead of him, turned waiting for him—but still Agge stared. This, then, he thought, was what they all meant to be. Lincoln suddenly raised a triangle of pie and jammed it in his mouth, and, a little frightened, Prince Agge hurried to join Stahr." Finally, Fitzgerald makes the explicit connection between Stahr and Lincoln: "Stahr like Lincoln was a leader carrying on a long war on many fronts; almost single-handed he had moved pictures sharply forward through a decade, to a point where the content of the 'A productions' was wider and richer than that of the stage. Stahr was an artist only, as Mr. Lincoln was a general, perforce and as a layman." It is clear by this point in the novel that Fitzgerald's central intention is to examine the loss of idealism in America, that Stahr is the last of such heroes as Jackson, Lincoln, Edison, Lumière, Griffith, and Chaplin. "Don't start trusting Americans too implicitly," Stahr tells Kathleen, his English girl friend, "they may be out in the open, but they change very fast . . . very fast and all at once, . . . and nothing ever changes them back." And she responds: "You frighten me. I always had a great sense of security with Americans." In the last chapter of this unfinished novel, Fitzgerald has the American individualist, Stahr, confront the communist Brimmer. Stahr is at his weakest, defeated in love and soon to be defeated in his work, no longer the "technological virtuoso" of his youth; when he grows helplessly drunk, Brimmer looks with contempt upon him and thinks: "Is *this* all? This frail half-sick person holding up the whole thing?"

We have only the skeleton of the novel, of course, but there is no question that Fitzgerald would have fleshed out these incidents and given them greater strength and subtlety. In the summary of the plot, as Fitzgerald foresaw it, Edmund Wilson notes that "Stahr for the first time visits Washington with the intention of seeing the city; and it is to be presumed that the author meant to return here to the motif introduced in the first chapter with the visit of the Hollywood people to the home of Andrew Jackson and their failure to gain admittance or even to see the place clearly: the relation of the moving-picture industry to the American ideals and tradition."

In *The Last Tycoon* Fitzgerald found the proper setting for his tragedy of American idealism—the illusory texture of Hollywood as contrasted with the reality it seeks to represent—and the historical perspective necessary for the death of heroism: Manny Schwartz juxtaposed with Andrew Jackson, an effete actor masquerading as Abraham Lincoln, Stahr trying unsucccessfully to maintain the old virtues—tolerance, kindness, forbearance, affection —against the mechanized world of modern America that is contributing to his own wish for death. "I have set it safely in a period of five years ago to obtain detachment," Fitzgerald wrote the editor of a magazine in which he hoped to serialize *The Last Tycoon,* "but now," in 1939, "that Europe is tumbling about our ears this also seems to be for the best. It is an escape into a lavish, romantic past that perhaps will not come again into our time."

And as we measure Fitzgerald's achievement we realize that his special significance lies in his dramatic awareness of those elements that "will not come again into our time;" of idealism and hope, of the singular individual fashioning his future as if a future can be fashioned, of the "romantic readiness" that informs his central figures but that inevitably is crushed by the hardness of the very rich, as in *The Great Gatsby,* or by the atrophying will of the idealist himself, as in *Tender is the Night,* or by the forces of history, grown monopolistic and predatory and increasingly centralized, as in *The Last Tycoon.* "I talk with the authority of failure"—a failure that in retrospect is historically true and dramatically valid, and fixed in our imagination as we look back upon the few genuine artists in our literature. Fitzgerald points to the tragedy of the heroic ideal at the moment of its decline, and the authority with which he writes of failure is the authority of an author who has embodied the complexities of his time and recorded them in works of art that give permanent meaning and beauty to the burden of being an American in the twentieth century—of being a man unable to find grandeur except in memories.

In the early work of writers like Bellow, Salinger, and Mailer there is the brutal authority of mechanized America against which frail victims can scarcely rebel. None of the heroes of these authors —the dangling man, Holden Caulfield, or Lieutenant Hearn—can challenge authority with the "romantic readiness" of Gatsby or Dick Diver or Monroe Stahr; Fitzgerald's figures may only remember the heroic ideal that informed their boyhood, but at least they remember it within themselves, within their own lifetime. For contemporary authors heroism is America's vestigial organ, buried somewhere in the body of the country—some lost, useless organ whose nerve was never felt in the writers' own lifetime. The new figure of American literature seems hardly a hero—Ihab Hassan's term, the rebel-victim, is an apposite description of him. But he becomes in time—in our time—more than rebellious, more than a victim; for all his eccentricities and excesses, he becomes a genuine hero, one who refuses to accept the absolute decline of idealism despite the fact that "the controls of this vast society" make his idealistic posture seem at times oddly convoluted (this is Salinger's Seymour) or strained by self-pity (Bellow's Herzog) or excessively egocentric (the Norman Mailer of *Advertisements for Myself*). The hero emerges, his face a little blurred by the shadow of a question mark but nevertheless struggling to distinguish itself from that of the organization man, from the corporate, bland, industrial image of modern America. The hero seeks to resurrect the concept of heroism from his knowledge of America's history— from America's past if not from the present of his own lifetime.

FIVE

The Quixotic Hero

1

SAUL   *The*
BELLOW *Victim*
        and
        the
        Hero

"But let us
look at one of the dominant ideas of the century, accepted by many
modern artists," Saul Bellow suggests in a recent interview, "—the
idea that humankind has reached a terminal point. We find this
terminal assumption in writers like Joyce, Celine, Thomas Mann.
In Doktor Faustus politics and art are joined in the destruction of
civilization. Now here is an idea, found in some of the greatest
novelists of the twentieth century. How good is this idea? Frightful
things have happened, but is the apocalyptic interpretation true?
The termination did not fully terminate. Civilization is still here.
The prophecies have not been borne out. Novelists are wrong to put
an interpretation of history at the base of artistic creation—to speak
'the last word.' It is better that the novelist should trust his own
sense of life. Less ambitious. More likely to tell the truth."

In trusting his own sense of life, in being less ambitious but no
less serious than some of his contemporaries, Saul Bellow has at- 243

tempted an answer to a major question of our time: "How can we resist the controls of this vast society without turning into a nihilist, avoiding the absurdity of empty rebellion?" He has sought to go beyond Hemingway's bitter rejection of idealism, Fitzgerald's regret for a lost idealism, and the unwarranted pessimism of some of his contemporary nay-sayers. And, "like most Americans," he has "involuntarily favored the more comforting or melioristic side of the question"; he has insisted that "there may be some truths which are, after all, our friends in the universe." Bellow's idealism, which grows more insistent with each succeeding novel, stems from the hero's self-conscious choice to suffer and to discover his humanity through suffering. Bellow avoids a hollow negation, a political or literary radicalism that he feels is finally "contentless," and seeks instead to express "a genuine radicalism, which truly challenges authority" and which makes idealism humanly credible.

In Bellow's work the hero has become an Americanized fusion of Dostoevsky's Underground man and Kafka's Joseph K, not so much a victim of external authority as of his own weaknesses, not so much a man forced out of American society as someone who has forced himself out of that society. The condition of Bellow's victims, from *The Dangling Man* to *Herzog,* is suffering, and the thematic direction of that suffering is toward love, salvation, and self-perception. Bellow's figures are often misanthropic (like Joseph of *The Dangling Man*) or irresponsible (like Tommy Wilhelm of *Seize the Day*) or sentimental and self-pitying (like Herzog), but they have not sacrificed an incorrigible idealism at the center of their character. More than any important American writer since the Second World War, Bellow has made affirmation the self-conscious mark of his writing. He has rejected the concept of heroism that earlier authors naturally adopted so that his characters have few of the formal strengths we associate with the hero: Joseph, Leventhal, Augie, Henderson, Wilhelm, and Herzog are, for the most part, quixotic, vacillating, grotesque figures who tremble before the particular choice they must make, who wish to act idealistically and transcend the constrictions of their lives but who find themselves crippled by their own frailty—losers almost, victims of their frailty.

These characters share many common qualities, but the attitude toward the world's authority which each of them exhibits is different. The Dangling Man and Leventhal complain whereas, in Bellow's words, "Herzog makes comic use of complaint. . . . Obliged to choose between complaint and comedy, I choose comedy, as more energetic, wiser, and manlier." The heroes of Bellow's later fiction do not lose in this ultimate sense: mocked, maimed, often miserable, they emerge at the end of their journey as quixotic, quasi-triumphant figures who affirm life. We may not like the kind of hero Bellow claims is representative of this moment in American history; like Norman Mailer, we may think of the hero in traditional terms, as a man who not only embodies his period but is superior to it. But the hero of Bellow's later work—as opposed to the victims of his earlier novels—is a hero for our time: exceptional and even courageous in his capacity to suffer, a man who, like Herzog, may imprison himself "in a shameful and impotent privacy" but who eventually acts and enters into social intercourse with the human race. He may not be the largest man, but he is no anti-hero—not in his final perception of the suffering that has informed his life, not in his intransigent idealism, not in his comic affirmation.

Traditional heroism is explicitly rejected at the outset of Bellow's career. This is "an era of hardboildom," the narrator of *The Dangling Man*, writes. "Today, the code of the athlete, of the tough boy . . . is stronger than ever. Do you have feelings? There are correct and incorrect ways of indicating them. Do you have an inner life? It is nobody's business but your own. Do you have emotions? Strangle them. To a degree, everyone obeys this code . . . The hardboiled are compensated for their silence; they fly planes or fight bulls or catch tarpon, whereas I rarely leave my room."

The dangling man may not often leave his room, but when he does he chooses action in a compulsive, even frenetic manner because fundamentally he does not wish to choose at all. When an ex-comrade of the Communist Party meets him, Joseph insists that he has the "right to be spoken to" because the man by obeying an order not to communicate with a defector is "helping to abolish freedom and begin tyranny"; when Joseph finds himself confronted by his wealthy, willful niece, he acts willfully himself; when his wife nags him, he drifts into an adulterous affair; when Spring fails to bring warmer weather, he defies the elements and walks in the park in his Spring coat and, as Bellow emphasizes, suffers for it; when a banker refuses to cash his wife's city check

he threatens the man and then admits that "It was a foolish incident. A year ago I would have accepted his explanation politely
and have moved away"; when he refuses to become his wife's
errand boy because she takes it "for granted that [he has] nothing
to do," his wife accuses him with some justification: "You think
everybody's trying to take advantage of you. Even I. . . ."

The dangling man is inevitably frustrated in his attempt to
express his freedom, but free choice does not lead to an altogether
purposeless suffering. Joseph has learned, as he says, the need "of
trying to preserve oneself" and one's mind, of preserving the self
by learning to govern it. "Chance must not govern it, incident
must not govern it. It is our humanity that we are responsible for
it, our dignity, our freedom." Although he is relieved finally that
he is "no longer to be held accountable for" himself, his relief is
only physical, only superficial. He is tired of being a dangling man
and grateful that a decisive choice has been made for him in the
form of his induction into the Army; but in a more permanent
life, Bellow suggests, the self will have to be governed, and suffering will lead to an affirmation of the mind. In rejecting the "hardboiled" school of fiction, which "has an inhibitory effect" on "the
truest candor" and which is "unpracticed in introspection," Bellow
affirms the "inner life" and claims that whatever suffering may fill
a man's life, his choice must be for the preservation of human
dignity. *The Dangling Man* is a timid novel, and Joseph is more
victim than hero, a passive rather than an active man who can
conceptualize an heroic ideal but cannot embody it. As Bellow has
remarked, there is a "solemnity of complaint" about this and his
other early work, a "plaintive, sometimes querulous" tone. The
dangling man knows the significance of choice, but he himself
cannot choose in a meaningful manner; his frustration, his inability to become a hero rather than remain a victim, causes him
to be querulous and misanthropic.

When one speaks of choice—as one must in discussing Saul
Bellow's fiction—one thinks of Kierkegaard and his perceptive,
influential remarks about the fear and trembling we suffer when
confronted by choice—and especially about the choice that the
extraordinary man must make, as he is challenged by a moral
crisis, of becoming either a saint or a demon. In Bellow's fiction
the word "extraordinary" assumes comic proportions—the hero is
more Don Quixote than Lancelot—but choice is no less significant

and it often takes the direction of either saintliness or demonism. The dangling man, in his youth, is accused of being Mephistopheles, and "for a long time [he] believed there was a diabolic part" to him; ultimately he frees himself "from this morbidity" and realizes that he is seeking the simple affirmation of his human dignity. The "devil" present in *The Victim*, Bellow's second and far more intricate novel, is a man named Allbee who pursues the protagonist Leventhal and accuses him of various sins: Leventhal has caused Allbee's unemployment, his wife's death, almost Allbee's own suicide. And it is through the demonic character of Allbee that the point of the book is made: "We don't choose much," he tells Leventhal. "We don't choose to be born, for example, and unless we commit suicide we don't choose to die, either. But having a few choices in between makes you seem less of an accident to yourself. It makes you feel your life is necessary."

Allbee claims that "when it came to the important things in my life [his wife's death, the loss of his job] I never had the chance to choose"; but finally he is able to make the crucial decision of his life. "I've been at one end and I can get to the other," he assures Leventhal. "It makes sense to me that a man can be born again.—I'll take a raincheck on the Kingdom of Heaven, but if I'm tired of being this way I can become a new man." Allbee does become a new man, he is reborn, although not until he has sunk to depravity and to a suicidal attempt; and, of course, his rebirth is modified and rendered credible by his inner corruption— it can never be total. At the end of the novel, Allbee may be escorting a movie star, faded a little and dissolute herself, but "his color," as Levanthal observed, "was an unhealthy one. Levanthal had the feeling that it was the decay of something that had gone into his appearance of well-being, something intimate." Rebirth is relative, and Allbee admits that he has "made [his] peace with things as they are. . . . I'm not the type that runs things. I never could be. I realized that long ago. I'm the type that comes to terms with whoever runs things." For him this modified rebirth is a moral achievement of some consequence: his shabby dignity at the end of the novel is the most affirmative posture that he can assume.

Rebirth is achieved by the other characters, too. Leventhal's brother, Max, who has been absent at the time of his child's death, returns for the funeral and tells Leventhal that he is "going south with the idea of a new start"; he doesn't "expect much," he feels "half burned out already," but he will nevertheless make the attempt. Leventhal himself has not been able to save his brother's baby, but he has saved Allbee's life and he himself will soon become a father. "Congratulations," Allbee says to him, making his last ironic and anti-semitic remark. "I see you're following orders. 'Increase and multiply.' "

One of Bellow's points, in a novel that is first of all about anti-semitism, is that something has died in Christian America. Allbee, a New England protestant, most obviously marks the detritus of a tradition that was once morally vigorous; one of his "ancestors was Governor Winthrop," he boasts to Leventhal.

> I'm a fine one to be talking about tradition, you must be saying. But still I was born into it. And try to imagine how New York affects me. Isn't it preposterous? It's really as if the children of Caliban were running everything. You go down in the subway and Caliban gives you two nickels for your dime. You go home and he has a candy store in the street where you were born. The old breeds are out. The streets are named after them. But what are they themselves? Just remnants. . . . I go into the library once in a while, to look around, and last week I saw a book about Thoreau and Emerson by a man named Lipschitz. . . .

This anti-semite attempts to victimize Leventhal, although he imagines himself victimized by the Jew, who symbolizes for him all of these immigrants who have helped to corrupt the heritage of individual enterprise: *The Victim* recalls those many novels at the turn of the century—one remembers Howells' *A Hazard of New Fortunes* (1889), Albion W. Tourgée's *Murvale Eastman* (1890), Harold Frederic's *The Damnation of Theron Ware* (1896), Thomas Nelson Page's *John March, Southerner* (1909), and scores of others—in which fundamentally conservative and traditional American types have great difficulty adjusting to the democratization of America, to the hordes of strange faces that populate New York. "The day of succeeding by your own efforts is past," Allbee complains to Leventhal. "Now it's all blind movement, vast movement, and the individual is shuttled back and forth. He only thinks he's the works. But that isn't the way it is. Groups, organizations succeed or fail, but not individuals any longer." The generalization, Bellow's novel implies, is true, dangerously true; but the protestant ethic has not been destroyed by immigrant Jews alone. It has been debased more insidiously, more organically, by Christians like All-bee—in the figure of Allbee the persecuted and the persecutor have become one.

The breakdown of Christian values is suggested from another point of view by the family of Leventhal's brother. Max Leventhal's marriage to an Italian Catholic has produced two children: one dies—Max's hostile mother-in-law blames the mixed marriage for the tragedy—and the other, an adolescent boy, looks like a Leventhal. At the funeral, Asa Leventhal reflects that "the chapel displeased him. Elena [Max's wife] had undoubtedly insisted on a Catholic funeral. That was her right. But from the Leventhals' side, and the boy was one of them, too, it was peculiar, after so many generations, to have this." Later Leventhal falls "to thinking that to his father what had happened in Staten Island today would be incomprehensible. . . . How strange if he could know that his own grandson was one of these, buried in a Catholic cemetery. . . . He would not have understood it." Not only are the health and survival of Philip, the older boy, contrasted with his dead brother—"Philip was going to turn out like Max and me," the protagonist remarks with some satisfaction. "A Leventhal"—but the imminent birth of Leventhal's own baby and the quiet security of Leventhal's own wife at the end of the novel are in striking contrast to the sickness and hysteria of his sister-in-law's house which set the tone at the beginning of the book.

To isolate these religious themes is to distort their dramatic importance—in fact, Bellow weaves them subtly into the larger pattern of freedom (or choice), suffering (or, in this novel, victimization) and affirmation (or dignity). Both Allbee and Leventhal suffer—Leventhal's perception is that they both suffer and through an understanding of their suffering achieve a small measure of dignity. "Someday science will conquer death," a fatuous character remarks at one point in the book, but the present truth that Bellow wants us to remember is still reflected in Allbee's statement that the few choices between life and death succeed in making a man feel that his "life is necessary." And the crucial choice is for human dignity. "It's bad to be less than human and it's bad to be more than human," a Jewish journalist remarks, underscoring the meaning of the novel. "What is all the shouting about? A man is nothing, his life is nothing. Or it is even lousy and cheap. . . . If a human life is a great thing to me, it *is* a great thing. Do you know better? I'm entitled as much as you. And why be measly? Do you have to be? Is somebody holding you by the neck? Have dignity, you understand me? Choose dignity. Nobody knows enough to turn it down."

Choose dignity. Bellow's major figures turn their limited freedom into a burden of suffering before they make the affirmative choice—the direction of their lives, sooner or later, is toward the choice of dignity. The theme is consistent, but the human manifestation of the theme changes. "I think that when I wrote those early books I was timid," Bellow has remarked. "I still felt the incredible effrontery of announcing myself to the world (in part I mean the WASP world) as a writer and as an artist. I had to touch a great many bases, demonstrate my abilities, pay my respects to formal requirements. In short I was afraid to let myself go." Asked "when do you find a significant change occurring?" Bellow answered, "When I began to write *Augie March*. I took off these restraints. I think I took off too many and went too far, but I was feeling the excitement of discovery. I had just increased my freedom, and like any emancipated plebeian I abused it at once." In releasing himself aesthetically, Bellow also took a bolder view of his central theme—the choice of dignity—and created heroes who acted rather than victims who spoke of acting or merely dreamed of acting. The shift in Bellow's attitude begins with *Augie March,* although it is still not conclusive; it is still not a complete affirmation of the heroic ideal. Augie attempts to resolve his ambiguities by imagining an idealistic life for himself:

> What I'd like most is to get married and set up a kind of home and teach school. . . . I'd get my mother out of the blind-home and my [mentally retarded] brother George from the South. Oh, I don't expect to set up the Happy Isles. I don't consider myself any Prospero. I haven't got the build. I have no daughter, I never was a King, for instance. . . . I thought maybe I could get accredited with the state or county or whoever does it, as a foster-parent, and get kids from institutions. This way the board and keep would be taken care of, and we'd have these kids.

Augie's vision, for it really amounts to that, comes after a lifetime in which he has carefully guarded his ostensible freedom and has repeatedly rejected the temptations of others—his brother's ways of acquiring wealth, his mistresses' eccentricities. He has chosen not to act and has acted only when brought to some decision by other people: until the moment of his decision, he is acted upon, an amiably weak figure whose adventures are imposed upon him, a man who has not been "able to give an account" of himself, as he says, and who has always been "manipulated," although not manipulated in any profound ethical sense. Augie moves from one person to the next in what seems to be freedom, but the freedom brings no joy—it brings continual dissatisfaction as Augie rejects the offers of the Einhorns and Renlings, of Charlotte Magnus and Thea Fenchel, of Simon and all the others who tempt him, a dissatisfaction that does not cease until Augie accepts his character, his fate as a limited man—not a Prospero, not a king—who is committed to "the axial lines" of his life—"Truth, love, peace, bounty, usefulness, harmony!"—before which "all noise and grates, distortion, chatter, distraction, effort, superfluity, [pass] off like something unreal." Augie agrees with Heraclitus: "A man's character is his fate"; and his adventures demonstrate that fact. In the end he realizes his limitations, his human vulnerability, his inability to seize hold of his experiences and give any vital expression to his idealism—he is no traditional hero, he hasn't "the build," and he fails, perhaps, as an idealist; but he reminds us that his failure does not mean that the heroic ideal is therefore illusory or even impossible. Committed to "truth, peace, bounty, usefulness, harmony!" he intends to affirm life and aspire to something beyond himself. Augie is no Prospero, but neither is he Nick Carraway, lamenting "the dark republic that year by year recedes before us"; he is, more fittingly, the quixotic figure of our time. Bellow affirms this comic vision at the conclusion of the book: "Look at me, going everywhere! Why, I am a sort of Columbus of those near-at-hand and believe you can come to them in this immediate *terra incognita* that spreads out in every gaze. I may as well be a flop at this line of endeavor. Columbus too thought he was a flop, probably, when they sent him back in chains. Which didn't prove there was no America."

When compared with Fitzgerald's conclusions to *The Great Gatsby* or *Tender is the Night,* when juxtaposed with Hemingway's many bitter remarks about the death of idealism in America, Bellow's affirmation in *Augie March* and in his other works may appear tentative and dissatisfying. But Hannah Arendt's comments upon the charisma of disintegration, as expressed in *The Origins of Totalitarianism,* and Lionel Trilling's gloss upon those comments in his essay, "William Dean Howells: The Roots of Modern Taste," should place in perspective the two generations of writers and their ideological differences. There is an attraction toward disintegration, Hannah Arendt suggests, that can be as sentimental as a thoughtless optimism—sentimental and equally prone to distortion. Hemingway kept his nihilistic vision in check by the joy he derived from an affirmation of the senses and by his idealization of work; Fitzgerald controlled his sentimental despair (so evident in *This Side of Paradise* and *The Beautiful and the Damned*) by his wit and his capacity for self-caricature. But both authors, in their less effective moments, and many other writers of the 1920's, romanticize decadence just as Bellow and many of his contemporaries are at times guilty of a kind of abstract affirmation. There is an assertion of idealism in the work of Salinger, Ellison, Baldwin, and Mailer that is not always warranted by the experiences described—a kind of hope grafted onto despair that is measurably different from the bleak—and perhaps equally gratuitous—conclusions one finds in the influential literature of the twenties. In a fundamental, personal way Hemingway and Fitzgerald are far more pessimistic than our present generation of writers, even though their pessimism seems, in retrospect, less justified by the facts of the external world than any despair that contemporary authors might record. Certainly they are more pessimistic than Saul Bellow, who has found " 'pessimism' to be in most of its forms as empty as 'optimism,' " who refuses to "speak the last word," to adopt the notion of his predecessors and of his contemporaries that "humankind has reached a terminal point." Bellow puts the contrast between the previous generation and himself in clear terms:

> But modern literature was dominated by a tone of elegy from the twenties to the fifties, the atmosphere of Eliot in "The Waste Land" and that of Joyce in *A Portrait of the Artist as a Young Man.* Sensibility absorbed this sadness, this view of the artist as the only contemporary link with an age of gold, forced to watch the sewage flowing in the Thames, every aspect of modern civilization doing violence to his (artist-patrician) feelings. This went much farther than it should have been allowed to go. It descended to absurdities, of which I think we have had enough.

Some of these absurdities suggest the differences between Bellow and the writers, the nay-sayers, of his own time.

> No wonder the really powerful men in our society, whether politicians or scientists, hold writers and poets in contempt. They do it because they get no evidence from modern literature that anybody is thinking about any significant question. What does the radicalism of radical writers nowadays amount to? Most of it is hand-me-down bohemianism, sentimental populism, D. H. Lawrence-and-water, or imitation Sartre. For American writers radicalism is a question of honor. They must be radicals for the sake of their dignity. They see it as their function, and a noble function, to say Nay, and to bite not only the hand that feeds them (and feeds them with comic abundance, I might add) but almost any other hand held out to them. Their radicalism, however, is contentless. A genuine radicalism, which truly challenges authority, we need desperately.

These statements—and the one that introduces this chapter—ought to be juxtaposed with Melville's famous tribute to Hawthorne: "There is the grand truth about Nathaniel Hawthorne. He says No! in thunder; but the Devil himself cannot make him say yes. For all men who say yes, lie." Melville's outburst has been generally saluted by modern critics; * it is, to use Bellow's words, a form of genuine radicalism. But it is not the only form of radicalism. Saul Bellow does not say no in thunder and he does not lie. Ralph Ellison says no, but the major direction of his fiction and essays is toward affirmation. J. D. Salinger writes a literature of negation at the outset of his career, but he later asserts himself affirmatively. It is too facile to see Melville's statement as central to that of our greatest writers—too facile and too much of a distortion.

Choose dignity—the dignity of selflessness. The tentative affir-

---

* Ihab Hassan, for example, concludes *Radical Innocence* by quoting Melville's statement and by complimenting Leslie Fiedler "who understands that fiction must be negative in order to fulfill its essential moral obligation." This kind of easy apocalyptic formulation distorts the work of Emerson, Whitman, James, Bellow, Salinger, Ellison, and Mailer, who do not share completely Hawthorne's thunderous no. To say that in Melville's tribute "No more succinct statement on the aspiration of the American self could be found" is to render the American literary experience gratuitously simple. Ours is a complex fate, and all of it is not negative.

mation of Augie March is blurred by the prolixity of the novel; but it is given clearer and more energetic definition in *Seize the Day,* a central work in which complaint is controlled by comedy and ultimately becomes comedy, in which the victim emerges as a hero because quite simply he no longer feels sorry for himself. Tommy Wilhelm, that suffering hero-manqué, is presented as a victim of his own self-pity, a loser, a man whose freedom has been limited by the financial burdens of his separated wife and their children. Once he sought to change his life by becoming a movie actor, and even though he was "the type that loses the girl to the George Raft type," even though he was cast as "a loser," he felt then that he would "be freed from the anxious and narrow life of the average," and could possibly shine like a hero. He cast off his father's name of Adler and was reborn as Tommy Wilhelm, but he was never really able to achieve a new identity: "Wilhelm had always had a great longing to be Tommy. He had never, however, succeeded in feeling like Tommy, and in his soul had always remained Wilky [which was his childhood name]."

In middle age Tommy Wilhelm has concluded that "there's very little that a man can change at will. He can't change his lungs, or nerves, or constitution or temperament. They're not under his control. When he's young and strong and impulsive and dissatisfied with the way things are he wants to rearrange them to assert his freedom. He can't overthrow the government or be differently born; he only has a little scope and maybe a foreboding, too, that essentially you can't change. . . . In middle age you no longer thought such thoughts about free choice." Feeling that he has lost his freedom through a series of mistaken choices— the wrong wife, the wrong investments—Tommy Wilhelm suffers and seeks deliverance from his suffering. "Let me out of trouble," he prays. "Let me out of my thoughts, and let me do something better with myself. For all the time I have wasted I am very sorry. Let me out of this clutch and into a different life." His crucial error is to depend on two older men: his father, who will provide him with permanent security, and Tamkin, who will make him instantly rich. "Don't talk to me about being free," he complains to his father, Dr. Adler. "A rich man may be free on an income of a million net. A poor man may be free because nobody cares what he does. But a fellow in my position has to sweat it out until he drops dead." His father, however, is severe, and tells him, "Wilky, it's entirely your own fault." The old man, an unattractive patri-arch, stubbornly and consistently refuses to help his son but in spite of his own selfishness, Dr. Adler offers the basic lesson of Wilhelm's life: Wilhelm must deliver himself from his troubles and gain dignity alone, through genuine self-reliance.

Wilhelm also depends on Tamkin, the confidence man, who promises to make his middle-aged protégé rich on the stock market and who preaches the doctrine of self-reliance. "You don't know what you've got within you," he suggests to Wilhelm. Although Tamkin is in his own way as reprehensible as Dr. Adler, he also teaches Wilhelm a fundamental lesson, one that Wilhelm's father himself has never learned. "With me, I am at my most efficient when I don't need the fee. When I only love. Without a financial reward. I remove myself from the social influence. Especially money. The spiritual compensation is what I look for. Bringing people into the here-and-now. The real universe. That's the present moment. The past is no good to us. The future is full of anxiety. Only the present is real—the here-and-now. Seize the day."

Tamkin, for all his faults, possesses the joy of living; at the moment he is duping Wilhelm, he expresses the truth, he tries to persuade Wilhelm not to "marry suffering. Some people do. They get married to it, and sleep and eat together, just as husband and wife. If they go with joy they think it's adultery . . . there's a small percentage of those who want to live. That's the only sig-nificant thing in the whole world of today. Those are the only two classes of people there are. Some want to live, but the great majority don't." Tamkin leaves Wilhelm financially bankrupt, but spiritually his advice is sound.

It is a special irony of Bellow's work that the most persuasive counsel often comes from the least attractive people—Allbee in *The Victim* and Dr. Adler and Tamkin in *Seize the Day*. Dr. Adler lacks compassion and refuses to suffer—"You want to make yourself into my cross," he warns Wilhelm. "But I am not going to pick up a cross"—and his willful indifference to his son's prob-lems makes him morally offensive; but the trait of self-responsibil-ity that he insists upon is precisely what his son most needs to acquire. As Wilhelm himself finally realizes, he must forgo his role as dependent son, as middle-aged boy, and become a man. Dr. Tamkin has compassion but no responsibility; yet through his own joy of life he teaches Wilhelm the futility of self-pity and suffering that has no purpose. By learning from the partial lessons of these two men—and from his wife, also, who tells him that he must "stop thinking like a youngster," his wife who expects him "to pay the price of his freedom" from her—Wilhelm reaches "that point where he may do something better with himself," where he may be able to express the idealism that is so fundamental to his nature. By recognizing his common humanity, and by realizing that the dead man whom he inadvertently sees at the end of the novel has suffered too, Wilhelm is able to shed tears for someone else and thus attain a dignity he has not yet possessed: he approaches as close to the heroic as someone like him can. Tommy Wilhelm's greatest moment of affirmation comes when he denies himself, his financial and domestic troubles, and seizes the meaning of his day—then he can shed tears for "another human creature," and go past "words, past reason, coherence."

Although the settings of two novels could scarcely be more dissimilar than those in *Seize the Day* and *Henderson the Rain King,* the same ideological pattern persists in both novels: freedom leads to suffering and an ultimate affirmation. The voice within Henderson that painfully repeats, "I want," yearns for freedom. At fifty-five, Henderson is so wealthy he would seem to have unlimited freedom, but he feels himself stifled by domestic life in Connecticut—he "wants" despite the fact that he has no material reason to want. Although his wife tells him, "Gene, when you suffer you suffer harder than any person I ever saw," Henderson knows that it is a suffering that has no satisfying release for him. By changing the setting, the language and the customs, by altering his life entirely, Henderson achieves a new freedom and a meaningful suffering that finally has purpose.

When Henderson first comes to Africa he seeks to relieve the suffering of others. "Do you know why the Jews were defeated by the Romans?" he asks Itelo, the leader of the Arnewi tribe. "Because they wouldn't fight back on Saturday. And that's how it is with your water situation. Should you preserve yourself, or the cows, or preserve the custom? I would say, yourself. Live . . . to make another custom. Why should you be ruined by frogs?" Just as Henderson has broken from the custom of his own life and seized the day, so he urges the native prince to act in a similar fashion and not suffer meaninglessly. He knows that "suffering is about the only reliable burster of the spirit's sleep," and he has always wished to be a medical missionary or a doctor so as to understand and heal suffering. His attempt to purify the water for the Arnewi tribe fails, and his failure is mock-heroic; but he has nevertheless witnessed and, to a degree, shared the suffering of others—he is a larger person for having had the experience. In his role as rain king for the tribe of King Dahfu, he has also come to understand other people and he senses that "there must be some distinction in this." King Dahfu himself underscores Henderson's lesson: "the soul will die if it can't make somebody else suffer what it suffers"—at the time of suffering it "feels peace and joy." Henderson discovers a life of affirmation after his experiences in Africa, for he knows that he wants "to get [his hands] on the sick. [He] want[s] to cure them. Healers are sacred"; and he has learned that his limitation has been his egocentricity, his selfishness, his need to complain. "I had a voice that said, 'I want! *I* want? It should have told me *she* wants, *he* wants, *they* want. And moreover, it's love that makes reality reality. The opposite makes the opposite."

Rebirth and metamorphosis can come in strange guises and in strange places under strange conditions. "Yes," Henderson concludes, "I believed I could change; I was willing to overcome my old self; yes, to do that a man had to adopt some new standard; he must even force himself into a new part; maybe he must deceive himself a while, until it begins to take; his own hand paints again on that much-painted veil." Henderson cannot become precisely the kind of man that King Dahfu wished—a king himself, a hero, and Dahfu's successor—but he can become more selfless. The voice that repeated "I want . . . wanted reality. How much unreality could it stand?" And reality for Henderson is "kindness and love," some form of idealism that can give coherence to a life that has lost its moral center. The reassertion of idealism gives Henderson the heroic posture necessary for his life in America.

In *Herzog* these ideas are given their most self-conscious and deliberate treatment, for as an intellectual and writer, Herzog is articulate enough to express his various views of freedom, suffering, and affirmation; as a hero-manqué, he has suffered so greatly—in his marriage and in his career—that the novel considers almost nothing but his suffering and his attempt to understand it. "I go after reality with language," Herzog admits. "I must be trying to keep tight the tensions without which human beings can no longer be called human. If they don't suffer, they've gotten away from me." Enough people do get away from him—especially his ex-wife and her lover, who Herzog claims do not "have a *Conscience,*" do not have the capacity to suffer—but he succeeds finally in understanding himself, he manages to free himself from his condition of "suffering without proper dignity."

All of Bellow's work leads thematically to *Herzog,* his most emphatic attempt to write a literature of comedy rather than of complaint, to indicate how the victim can become the quixotic hero. The intensity with which Bellow examines the ideas of freedom and suffering, the confessional tone of the writing, the many external similarities between Herzog and his author, invite the conclusion that the attitudes of Herzog are a kind of mature and final statement—a loose commentary on how life ought to be lived in mid-century America. Unlike Bellow's other central figures, whose physical movements dramatize the point that Bellow wishes to make, Herzog's real movement is mental—he moves from one state of mind to another and the many notes and letters he writes "frantically" are records of his mental progress.

Since the mind is of particular significance in *Herzog,* the ambitious book that the hero has failed to finish is a clear and suggestive index to his attitudes: "his study was supposed to have ended with a new angle on the modern condition, showing how life could be lived by renewing universal connections; overturning the last of the Romantic errors about the uniqueness of the Self; revising the old Western, Faustian ideology; investigating the social meaning of Nothingness . . . people can be free now but the freedom doesn't have any content." Later in the novel, as he waits to make love to his mistress, he broods upon the illusory nature of freedom and idealism in the contemporary world, the various ways in which they have been suppressed by the authority of a mass society, the loss of human dignity; and he wonders

what it means to be a man. In a city. In a century. In transition. In a mass. Transformed by science. Under organized power. Subject to tremendous controls. In a condition caused by mechanization. After the later failure of radical hopes. In a society that was no community and devalued the person. Owing to the multiplied power of numbers which made the self negligible. Which spent military billions against foreign enemies but would not pay for order at home. Which permitted savagery and barbarism in its own great cities. At the same time, the pressure of human millions who have discovered what concerted efforts and thoughts can do. As megatons of water shape organisms on the ocean floor. As tides polish stones. As winds hollow cliffs. The beautiful supermachinery opening a new life for innumerable mankind. Would you deny them the right to exist? Would you ask them to labor and go hungry while you enjoyed delicious old-fashioned Values? You—you yourself are a child of this mass and a brother to all the rest. Or else an ingrate, dilettante, idiot. There, Herzog, thought Herzog, since you ask for the instance, is the way it runs.

And so runs the development of Herzog. The attempt to make a life for himself in spite of the devaluation of the human personality in this American century; the desire to free himself of a meaningless suffering in which he is trapped by his own self-interest and self-pity; the need to renew human if not "universal connections"—these become the obsessive concerns of this wayward idealist who tries vainly to hold in check the authority of his civilization. It is the only kind of hero he can be.

Herzog himself is nominally free after two unsuccessful marriages, but his freedom has no "content" because he suffers meaninglessly. He continues to torment himself by dwelling upon the character of his ex-wife Madeleine; he pities himself until he is even driven to a murder as abortive and unsuccessful as his other public actions. Herzog is Dostoevsky's underground figure projected in a twentieth-century American form; he broods alone, "hidden in the country," communicating through the written word. When he emerges from his solitude—to go to Martha's Vineyard for a brief vacation or to murder his wife and her lover—he acts explosively, placing himself near those people who wish to humiliate him. He has lost the self-reliance that once had made him distinctive: far enough back he was the man "who gave the class oration—who spoke on Emerson"; more recently he "made a brilliant start in his Ph. D. thesis" and wrote an important book, *Romanticism and Christianity,* "but the rest of his ambitious projects [have] dried up, one after another." Like his work, his private life has lost "its focus" and it is "painful to think of it." But by the end of the novel, after he has come to realize the fruitless suffering that all his thoughts about Madeleine bring him, he has at least ordered the scattered parts of his life: "For perhaps the first time he felt what it was to be free from Madeleine. Joy! His servitude was ended, and his heart released from its grisly heaviness and encrustation." With the sense of genuine freedom, he is able to affirm the meaning of his life, to offer as his final testament a statement of affirmation. A man must suffer with proper dignity, he concludes; he must learn to accept himself, however limited and inadequate he may be.

> Anyway, can I pretend I have much a choice? I look at myself and see chest, thighs, feet—a head. This strange organization, I know it will die. And inside—something, something, happiness. . . . "Thou movest me." That leaves no choice. Something produces intensity, a holy feeling, as oranges orange, as grass green, as birds heat. Some hearts put out more love and some less of it, presumably. Does it signify anything? There are those who say this product of hearts is knowledge. . . . But this intensity, doesn't it mean anything? Is it an idiot joy that makes this animal, the most peculiar animal of all, exclaim something? And he thinks this reaction a sign, a proof, of eternity? And he has it in his breast?

The response that Herzog makes to these questions is typically inadequate and indirect: "But I have no arguments to make about it. . . . I am pretty well satisfied to be, to be just as it is willed, and for as long as I may remain in occupancy."

We may well say that so elaborate and painful a self-examination deserves a more persuasive conclusion rather than one that is so frustratingly tentative and passive; but the ending is organic to Bellow's conception, for as a suffering middle-aged man, Herzog is too scarred to believe in traditional, romantic heroism—"the uniqueness of the Self" which he set out to deny in that book he was writing but could never finish—too introspective to champion idealism, too self-conscious and doubting to offer any more than a muted affirmation. "Thou movest me"—the heart insists on producing "intensity, a holy feeling." That is all we know, that is all we need to know. Like the figures of Bellow's other novels, Herzog has moved from external suffering to internal torment; he has taken his modicum of freedom and used it to acquire self-understanding and human dignity. Like the figures in Bellow's other works, Herzog is never far from the absurd—which is another way of saying that he is always reminding us of his humanity. The complaint about the human condition and one's own private life now has taken a comic turn, which for Bellow is "more energetic, wiser and manlier." It is his way of expressing a "genuine radicalism, which challenges" the authority of the world around us.

That radicalism—which takes full account of the few significant choices open to man, which records the private suffering that can result in human dignity, and which issues ultimately in moderate idealism, in muted comic affirmation—is the burden of Saul Bellow's fiction. Tommy Wilhelm, Henderson, and Herzog are not the heroes of our literary imagination—no Emersonian heroes, no Southern gentlemen, no violent protesters out of the world of Negro literature, no hardboiled stoic Hemingway figures who deny abstractions, not even the lost idealists of Fitzgerald's work. Across the lives of Bellow's quixotic heroes falls the authority of the realistic world—that world inevitably makes them less than romantic.

> Pit any ordinary individual—and realistic literature concerns itself with ordinary individuals—against the external world, and the external world will conquer him, of course. Everything that people believed in the nineteenth century about determinism, about man's place in nature, about the power of productive forces in society, made it inevitable that the hero of the realistic novel should not be a hero but a sufferer who is eventually overcome. So I was doing nothing very original by writing another realistic novel about a common man and calling it *The Victim*. I suppose I was discovering independently the essence of much of modern realism.

But *The Victim* represents that literature of complaint which Bellow has rejected. He does not create "any really good men. . . . Realism has restrained [him] too much for that." But by putting Tommy Wilhelm, Henderson, and Herzog in a comic framework, Bellow presents them as men who believe that "existence is worthful," who wish "very much to have effective virtues," who seek to realize ideals and wish desperately to become the Romantic heroes of their own imagination. They cannot become Romantic heroes —Wilhelm can never become Tommy the movie idol; Herzog can never finish his book on Romanticism and Christianity. But they can become, indeed they do become, quixotic heroes who affirm idealism in an increasingly powerful, authoritative contemporary America.

2

J. D. SALINGER

Suicide and Survival in the Modern World

"*Salinger* was the most gifted minor writer in America," Norman Mailer tells us in his recent requiem on Salinger's career, "the finest writer *The New Yorker* ever produced, but profoundly minor. . . . The Glass stories are not literature, but television. And Salinger's work since *The Catcher in the Rye* is part of his long retreat from what is substantial, agonizing, uproarious, or close to awe and terror. *The Catcher in the Rye* was able to change people's lives. The new books aren't even likely to improve the conversation in college dormitories."

We have heard the lament before, in a variety of voices, until it has become a cliché of contemporary criticism. But Mailer, like so many others, has not really explored those reasons for Salinger's popularity that lie beyond the superficial charms and at times irritations of his craft. It is easy enough to catalogue Salinger's faults —few important writers are more vulnerable than he; but the more relevant task would seem to be a consideration of why he has interested and often obsessed more readers than any other serious American author since the Second World War, why he has been, as Mailer himself admits, "everybody's favorite."

We might begin by citing Salinger's compassion for the victims and fallen figures of an urban America; his self-conscious, chastening wit; or his remarkable ability to illuminate character through the finest detail. But the deeper, more permanent attraction of Salinger's work must have something to do with his treatment of suicide and survival, his attempt to suggest a mode of survival in this world that is not without meaning and a little dignity. Suicide, we realize, as we trace the development of Salinger's fiction from "A Perfect Day for Banana Fish" to *Seymour, an Introduction* and *Hapworth 16, 1924* haunts his characters; and it becomes more self-conscious, more present, as he draws increasingly closer to Seymour Glass, signifying, in the case of the Glass family, not only the tragic death of an ideal man but the suicide of the poet and the consequent failure of art to survive in the modern world. The act of suicide—at times it seems the *only act* in all of Salinger's fiction—occurs in 1948, when Salinger first begins to write with a clarity of focus and with real efficacy; the rest is a painstaking and elaborate account of how individuals seek to forsake madness by understanding death and suicide, how they manage to survive in the world without yielding to an ultimate act of despair and yet, as Buddy Glass puts it, without "going astray in any cheap way."

Whatever else we may say of him, Seymour Glass is a hero tenaciously commited to the ideal of art—he is the artist as hero. Apparently he could not modify his idealism when the authority of the real world encroached; suicide tore him away from the unbearable. But Seymour's suicide has allowed the other Glass children— particularly Buddy Glass—to survive; and in that sense it has not been without purpose.

In Salinger's fiction one feels a persistent idealism despite the profound distrust of all those forms of authority that contribute to conformity of mind and spirit. Indeed the struggle between idealism and authority causes the special tension of Salinger's work; it is a struggle that drives the hero to the point of madness and suicide. These concerns are evident in Salinger's early work as the idealist searches for a form of compassion that is all but impossible to realize, as his sanity is threatened by the trivial vanities of other people. *The Catcher in the Rye,* as Holden Caulfield tells us, is "about this madman stuff that happened to me around last Christmas just before I got pretty run-down and had to come out here [to a sanitarium] and take it easy." Holden discovers compassion only through his sister—for her he commits his one act of heroism, for her alone is he able to express his idealism by erasing an obscene word from her innocent eyes. The boy can not adjust, as we say, to the deceit of his society—all of his action, or inaction as it were, is modified by his self-abasement, his tendency toward morbidity, even his potential madness; he creates an ideal world in his mind, filled with children whose innocence he will protect, that expresses his fear of experience. There is no resolution in *The Catcher in the Rye;* the entire book is the depiction of a morbid state of mind, one that reveals Holden in a hostile relationship towards all authority—"This is a people-shooting hat," he remarks about his hunting cap," I shoot people in this hat"—and only his self-honesty, the knowledge that he is weak and irresponsible, romantic and craven, prevents him from absolute despair.

In the tales that Salinger reprinted in *Nine Stories,* the victimized figures are at times filled with an anxiety that approaches madness, or, at other times, are driven to suicide itself. "A Perfect Day for Banana Fish" sets the mood of the collection and introduces Seymour Glass, the central character of Salinger's fiction, committing the central act of that fiction. His suicide in the story stems from a conflict with his vapid wife that comes at the climax, as we see in his later appearances, of an ideological conflict with a world in which his extraordinary, poetic, and ideal character can find no suitable place. In "A Perfect Day for Banana Fish," poetry assumes only a suggestive form in the myth of the banana fish that Seymour tells to the girl on the beach; the power of the story, nevertheless, resides in the implied collision of the poet and the actual world. Seymour's suicide initiates the morbid tone of *Nine Stories:* "Uncle Wiggily in Connecticut," "For Ésme With Love and Squalor," and "Teddy" share its mood of anxiety and terror, its sense of proximate madness; other stories—"Just Before the War With the Eskimos" and "Pretty Mouth and Green My Eyes"—

also treat of aberration and neurosis. But it is not really until the publication of *Franny and Zooey* that Salinger's central ideas assume a clear pattern and that Salinger begins an elaborate, painstaking examination of the conflict between art and life, between the poetic vision and the vanity of existence, a conflict which Seymour himself could not resolve but which the other creative members of the Glass family—writers, actors, entertainers—grow to understand as they explore the meaning of Seymour's ideas and, ultimately, of Seymour's suicide.

The tension in *Franny and Zooey* is between the idealism of Franny, expressed through the book of mysticism that she is reading, and the vulgarity of the outside world, represented in the first story by Lane Coutell and in *Zooey* by the Fat Lady. Franny rejects the reality of her particular world, those small-minded academicians who have forgotten that "knowledge *should* lead to *wisdom*" and who breed small-minded students in the form of Franny's lover, Lane Coutell. "You don't face any facts," Zooey criticizes her, and the degree to which she cannot accept the actual world, filled with people who want "to *get* somewhere, do something distinguished and all, be somebody interesting" is the degree to which she is losing her mind. Like Salinger's other characters she shuns the real world for the ideal one in her mind, represented in Franny's case by the memory of her eldest brother, Seymour.

Ultimately Franny retains her balance and achieves transcendence by referring her problem to Seymour. When Zooey despairs of helping his sister, he suggests that they try to speak to Buddy, but Franny tells him that she wants "to talk to Seymour," who of course has been dead for almost a decade and who in any case was eighteen years her senior and can now be only a dim, distorted image to her. Unable to receive direct advice from the one man who has seemed wise to her, she is nevertheless saved by Seymour through Zooey's parable of the Fat Lady. Seymour's former insistence that Zooey shine his shoes and that Franny smile for the Fat Lady—Salinger's gross symbol of humanity, suffering from boredom and cancer of the flesh and spirit—is his metaphoric way of saying that Zooey and Franny must obey the ideal in their own minds; for if the Fat Lady is Christ himself, suffering in her coarse and helpless way, and if Franny and Zooey must bring her their own finest selves, bound to the concept she embodies in whatever tenuous way, they are finally obeying the ironic name of their radio program—"It Takes a Wise Child"—by exhibiting wisdom, by coming to understand the suffering audience that they entertain. Wisdom is what Franny wishes, not "knowledge for knowledge's sake," and wisdom she attains, even though it appears years after she has abandoned her small role as "a wise child" and after her saintly brother has died.

Buddy Glass, who is the narrator of *Zooey,* claims that his current offering isn't a mystical story, at all. *"I* say it's a compound, or multiple, love story, pure and complicated." Which is not wholly true. *Zooey,* as well as *Franny,* is first of all a love story—a story of love that Franny discovers for human nature; but it is also a mystical, if not a religiously mystifying story, for it speaks of the Real as opposed to the Understanding (in Emersonian terms), Wisdom as opposed to Knowledge, Love as opposed to Lust. In these two stories, the transcendental has been grafted onto the realistic in a rather dissatisfying way, but our dissatisfaction stems perhaps from the embarrassment of making an affirmative statement in the contemporary world: what seemed natural in Emerson seems factitious in Salinger.

But in *Franny and Zooey*—and the same may be said of *Raise High The Roof Beam, Carpenters* (1955), published in the same year as *Franny*—our dissatisfaction is not fundamental: it is more annoyance at the crotchety mannerisms that stem from Salinger's awkward, straining, self-conscious affirmation. The difficult juxtaposition of the real and the ideal becomes a greater literary problem, however, in Salinger's last two stories—*Seymour, an Introduction* and *Hapworth 16, 1924*—as he concentrates exclusively on Seymour Glass, as he struggles to make the idealist a man with distinct human features. So long as Seymour serves as a moral frame of reference for Franny, Zooey, and Buddy, he can effectively illuminate their lives; but as Salinger avoids any account of the terrifying authority of the outside world and writes only of an inward idealism and affirmation, he loses the implied tension in all of his best work.

Seymour, an Introduction is difficult to read because it functions exclusively through indirection, as if Salinger does not see his hero clearly—the parts of Seymour's personality never quite mesh coherently. Still, as a narrative, *Seymour, an Introduction* is more significant thematically than any of Salinger's other works and it is, after all, only an introduction to Seymour. However much

Salinger has sacrificed the actual world in *Seymour, an Introduction* (or in its successor, *Hapworth 16, 1924*); however much he has conceived of Seymour as joyful and saintly, precocious and prophetic, we know that this man will finally take his own life—his suicide is a response to the outside world, and though we do not know the full terms of that response, it nevertheless conditions Seymour's former affirmation and makes that affirmation macabre and less conclusive, less authoritative. Rarely have a writer's works been so dependent on one another as Salinger's: "A Perfect Day for Banana Fish"; *Raise High the Roof Beam, Carpenters; Seymour, an Introduction;* and *Hapworth 16, 1924* are frustrating because they are incomplete, fragments of a mosaic that can not really be persuasive until Salinger moves toward the eye of the tragedy itself —Seymour's suicide.

Evil, so vivid a force in Salinger's early work, is almost wholly absent from the formal texture of *Seymour, an Introduction* and *Hapworth 16, 1924,* although Salinger provides us with hints, as in Seymour's uncanny ability to suspend pain and suffering by a trick of the mind, a trick that the boy has learned by the age of seven but one that obviously will not work for all his later experiences. These torpid narratives strike us, for the most part, as clumsy temporizing before the central problem that Salinger has set for himself: the failure of the poet to survive in the modern world. As Buddy Glass warns us, in *Raise High the Roof Beam, Carpenters,* "not one goddamn person, of all the patronizing, fourth-rate critics and column writers, had ever seen him [Seymour] for what he really was. A poet for God's sake. And I mean a *poet."* And in *Seymour, an Introduction,* Salinger begins to explore the place of the poet in a world comprised of

> middle-aged hot-rodders who insist on zooming us to the moon, the Dharma Bums, the makers of cigarette filters for thinking men, the Beat and the Sloppy and the Petulant, the chosen cultists, all the lofty experts who know so well what we should or shouldn't do with our poor little sex organs, all the bearded, proud, unlettered young men and unskilled guitarists and Zen-killers and incorporated Teddy boys who look down their thoroughly unenlightened noses at this splendid planet where (please don't shut me up) Kilroy, Christ, and Shakespeare all stopped.

Seymour is, as Buddy Glass confesses, also a sick man—one of Buddy's more traumatic moments occurred when he "was eleven years old and watched the artist and Sick Man I've loved most in this world, then still in knee pants, being examined by a reputable group of professional Freudians for six hours and forty-five minutes." Buddy admits that "by every logical definition, he *was* an unhealthy specimen, he *did* on his worst nights and late afternoons give out not only cries of pain but cries for help, and when nominal help arrived, he *did* decline to say in perfectly intelligible language where it hurt." But Seymour was also a poet and therefore, in Salinger's terms, a seer; unlike the critics and scholars who "don't listen properly to cries of pain when they come," Buddy knows that "the bulk . . . of pain really come[s] from the heart. However contradictory the coroner's report—whether he pronounces Consumption or Loneliness or Suicide to be the cause of death—isn't it plain how the artist-seer actually dies? I say . . . that the true artist-seer, the heavenly fool who can and does produce beauty, is mainly dazzled to death by his own scruples, the blinding shapes and colors of his own sacred human conscience."

Seymour, an Introduction is as unsatisfactory to Buddy Glass as it is to the reader, for if Seymour is the hero and poet—a "full Dichter," an artist-seer—then we must know the particular qualities that will induce our admiration; Buddy knows this, but he claims that Seymour is "the one person who was always much, much too large to fit on ordinary typewriter paper—any typewriter paper of mine anyway." Seymour's poems are of little help, moreover, for "the more personal Seymour's poems appear to be, or *are,* the less revealing the content is of any known details of his actual daily life in this Western World"; and the physical descriptions only frustrate Buddy and the reader—"Hurrah," he confides after attempting to describe Seymour's nose, "the nose is over. I'm going to bed"—because they do not illuminate the man. Although the intention of the Glass stories is ultimately to explain the meaning of Seymour's suicide—the details of which, as Buddy Glass remarks, the narrator doesn't expect to examine "for several more years"—, Buddy can scarcely introduce his brother, no less write about him in detail, because he exists as an ideal in his mind. "I'm writing about the only person," he tells us, "I've ever known whom, on my own terms, I considered really large, and the only person of *any* considerable dimensions I've ever known who never gave me a moment's suspicion that he kept, on the sly, a whole closetful of naughty, tiresome, little vanities."

If Seymour represents the ideal that haunts each member of the Glass family, it is because the essence of his character is selflessness, the denial of personal pride. As the ideal poet he has transcended the real world—therein lies Buddy's difficulty in fixing him on the printed page; and, as the poet who finally rejects what the *real* world offers, he moves inexorably toward suicide. As Seymour himself writes, in *Hapworth 16, 1924,* surely the most precocious letter ever written by a seven year old child, "Unfortunately, here [in *Hapworth*], as elsewhere on this touching planet, imitation is the watchword and prestige the highest ambition. . . . Close on the heels of kindness, originality is one of the most thrilling things in the world, also the most rare." Seymour is painfully conscious of his precocity, and the burden of his youth, as revealed in *Hapworth 16, 1924,* is his attempt to find a *modus vivendi,* a "course of action" that is "both humane and acceptable." He cannot, of course, and the significance of his suicide is the inability of the extraordinary person to exist in contemporary America. "You are in a much stabler position to dislike heroes and heroism utterly," Seymour writes his parents, "if you yourself are quite equipped to do something heroic." Seymour does not have the heroism necessary to survive; the other Glasses are not heroic, either, although they manage to survive through the lesson of Seymour's life: "If you are not equipped to do anything heroic," Seymour continues, "you may still enter the discussion honorably, but with terrible caution and reasonableness, very deliberately and painstakingly turning on every single light in your body, also perhaps re-doubling your fervent prayers to God not to go astray in any cheap way." This is precisely the way of Buddy Glass, the family chronicler, who has now become fused indistinguishably with Salinger himself, and the suggested way of the Glass family in general.

"Seymour once said that all we do our whole lives is go from one little piece of Holy Ground to the next. Is he *never* wrong?" So Buddy Glass concludes *Seymour, an Introduction,* and thus suggests how he will escape the suicide of his brother. By accepting his students, by confessing that "There's no place I'd rather really go right now than into Room 307 [his college classroom]," Buddy Glass has made his separate peace with the world. There is an element of factitious emotion when he claims that "there isn't one girl in there, including the Terrible Miss Zabel, who is not as much my sister as Boo Boo or Franny," just as there is a false note of acceptance when Zooey reveals the meaning of Seymour's Fat Lady to Franny: these gestures represent Salinger's attempt to transcend the self-love of the Glass family and to express compassion for all people, to love the world even if he cannot completely understand it. And in his attempt, which becomes increasingly didactic with each new story, is a lesson for our time. So much in our America forces us to question if not satirize the idealistic statement, as everything within Salinger must contradict and doubt and suspect idealism (for how could he write the tortured prose that burdens *Seymour, an Introduction,* if he were not scarred by self-doubt), but his affirmation seems as far as a responsible person and an artist can take himself today—not the pretentious affirmation of Zooey, who substitutes a parable of idealism for genuine suffering, but the quiet acceptance of Buddy Glass, Salinger's true fictional self, who knows—"not always," as he says, "but he knows"— "There is no single thing I do that is more important than going into that awful Room 307." That perception, which stems from his life as a member of the Glass family and his role as Seymour's disciple, is the perception of an ordinary man who has witnessed the heroism of the artist. Acceptance of oneself, of one's occupation is finally the acceptance of dull students—and the heroic brilliance of one's brother; of survival—and the madness of one's brother; of life—and the suicide of one's extraordinary brother; of all that lies outside oneself and one's family.

Finally, of course, it is not the affirmative statement that compels us to recognize Salinger as one of the few genuine American writers since the Second World War; it is the struggle toward the statement that is filled with the awe and terror of significant fiction. If Salinger is everybody's favorite, as Norman Mailer has claimed, he is for reasons other than craft or ingeniousness—although let us not minimize the achievement of our "most gifted minor writer," he has written the finest short stories of contemporary American literature. Salinger touches upon our collective desire and need to salvage whatever idealism we can in a country increasingly dominated by authority. As each member of the Glass family seeks to avoid Seymour's suicide, which is the fate of the exceptional man, of the artist-seer, so Salinger's readers seek a survival that is not altogether one that compromises ideals, one that does not "go astray in any cheap way." And Buddy Glass's resolution to accept his dual role as teacher and writer, learned from his ideal elder brother, who was in his turn a teacher and a poet, and—unlike Buddy—a hero, seems a convincing resolution, after all. The relationship between the artist and the world is always a precarious one, at best; in Salinger's fiction it leads to a suicide that serves as edification. Seymour withdraws completely— the hero martyrs himself in the name of his ideals; but Buddy's withdrawal is never quite absolute, for he still maintains his telephone in New York and he has, more significantly, all those "twenty-four young ladies" waiting for him in Room 307. He has them as nourishment, bland as that nourishment may sometimes be, to feed his own frail idealism.

NORMAN *The*

MAILER *Quest*

for

Heroism

More than
any other novelist of his generation, Norman Mailer has been specifically concerned with the authority of institutionalized life in
America, with what he characterizes as the totalitarianism of
America. Mailer has urged a reaffirmation of that "dynamic myth
of the Renaissance" which once lived in our history and which, if
reborn, can challenge and defeat the variety of forms that authority
has assumed; and he has searched for a rebirth of heroism everywhere—in the American Negro, in President Kennedy, in the
younger generation, in the American writer, in the Hollywood
director, in the architect and athlete and artist and lover, in finally
himself. Scarcely an aspect of American life has escaped Mailer's
scrutiny in his self-appointed role as analyst of the nation, and because he himself has sought to incarnate the myth of the Renaissance—our novelist, our social critic, our ad man, our murderer
manqué, our war hero, our intellectual eccentric (and even clown),
our TV debater and journalist and teacher, our politician manqué,
272 our lover—he has scattered his talents shamelessly, demanding

heroic effort of himself, although it has become increasingly clear that he is not, in any of his aspects, a hero of our time.

Mailer refuses, nevertheless, to relinquish the heroic ideal, and his fiction is the clearest mirror of the problems that have troubled America since the Second World War. He is, if not our hero, our representative writer—as Emerson and Simms, Twain and Howells, Eliot and Hemingway were representative of other Americas; if he has not become the hero he always wanted to be, he has written most perceptively about the concept of heroism, precisely because of his own limitations: his vision is greater than his accomplishment. Indeed, in another age, when the conflict between idealism and authority seemed less urgent, when the crises of the moment appeared not to shift so quickly, he might have sat still to create solid, substantial novels like *The Naked and the Dead*. Instead he has run with the times, growing into far more than a seismograph of contemporary letters, yet not quite becoming the hero he once thought he could be.

Mailer has laid waste his gifts as a novelist and an essayist by using them diffusively—"squandered them," he has said of himself, "wasted them"; but he has had the courage if not the genius of the great writer—this alone is a rare enough quality today—and he has explored with candor, to use his own language, "that subterranean river of untapped, ferocious, lonely and romantic desires, that concentration of ecstasy and violence which is the dream life of the nation." Few writers tell us more about the America in which we live, its impulse toward indiscriminate power, its need for idealism and personal courage. And after all, after the mist of Mailer's own rhetoric and self-indulgent bombast clears, the works do bear close attention: *The Naked and the Dead* and *The Deer Park* are among the finest novels since the Second World War; essays like "The White Negro," "Superman Comes to the Supermarket," and the commentary on *The Deer Park* in *Advertisements for Myself* are composed with great care and perception; "The Man Who Studied Yoga" and "A Time of Her Time" are successful accounts of the conflict between the will and the idea, remarkable pieces whatever Mailer's larger ambitions may have been; and his recent political journalism, *Armies of the Night* and the report of the political conventions, illuminate the terror of authority in contemporary America with an immediacy and eloquence not felt in other writers —he makes so many of his contemporaries seem simply dull. Mailer has had "an unprecedented kind of honesty"—this has always been his private form of idealism—and the ability, in Richard Gilman's words, to "place our public acts and lives in a human context." No, he is not quite our hero—no one really is; but he is more sensitive to the need for heroism than any other writer of our time.

Although *The Naked and the Dead* is derivative in form and style, a "safe" novel as it were, it is still the most impressive treatment of the Second World War; and it introduces us to Mailer's concern—one is tempted to use the word "obsession"—with power, his attraction to authority (as embodied in General Cummings and Sergeant Croft) and his suspicion that humanism (as reflected in Lieutenant Hearn and Red Valsen) is too often pathetic and ineffectual. One must be cautious in formulating facile distinctions between Cummings and Hearn or between Croft and Valsen, however, for in effect all four men are idealists, and Mailer's purpose is to trace the various directions their idealism assumes: the intensity with which these characters embody their vision—the courage that they bring to the enactment of their vision—is the degree to which they elicit Mailer's fascination, even his awe. In Mailer's first novel the tension between idealism and authority that informs all of his later work is clearly focused upon these potential and at moments actual heroes.

"You can look at it," General Cummings remarks, in one of his many observations to Lieutenant Hearn, "that we're in the middle ages of a new era, waiting for the renaissance of real power. Right now, I'm serving a rather sequestered function; I really am no more than the chief monk, the lord of my little abbey, so to speak." As the idealist who has become the totalitarian leader, Cummings embodies the authority of the army—and by extension of society itself—which succeeds in frustrating the weak idealism and independence of those men who serve him, specifically of Lieutenant Hearn: in the face of Cummings' authority the humanistic instinct appears fragile, unclear, almost feminine. But the most commanding figure in the book, as Mailer himself later acknowledged, is Sergeant Croft, and it is Croft's unexpressed idealism that draws one's attention. "There was a crude unformed vision in his soul," Mailer suggests early in the book, "but he was rarely conscious of it"; and the inability to realize this idealistic vision in the twisted pattern of his life has caused Croft to be ceaselessly frustrated and belligerent, to release his anger only in sporadic, violent outbursts. Unlike his ancestors, who "pushed and labored and strained, drove their oxen, sweated their women, and moved a thousand miles," Croft has turned his frustrations and need to excel into love of self and hatred of the external, love of power and violence for their own sake and hatred of anything which threatens that morbid love. This conflict between Croft's idealism and his hostility toward any authority that is not of his own creation lends strength to the most effective section of the book—the ascent of Mount Anaka. In the formal context of the novel, the mountain serves as the fitting symbol of ultimate, unconquerable authority, and Croft's attempt to triumph, his mounting passion, is man's desire to transcend his human limitations, his reason, and to achieve the miraculous. Croft himself "could not have given the reason, but the mountain tormented him, beckoned him, held an answer to something he wanted. It was so pure, so austere." In the last third of the novel, Croft's courage and tenacity, his final deranged idealism, compel Mailer's and thus the reader's admiration, despite the obvious repugnance of Croft's character: one can feel and respect the way in which Mailer has obeyed the organic structure of his book and permitted Croft to become its natural hero, although he never becomes a fully realized hero. There is little more than tenacity in Croft, passion without purpose or complete perception. Unlike Camus's version of Sisyphus, who is most happy at the height of the mountain because finally he understands his fate, Croft never gives his struggle a larger meaning; it always remains a vague yearning, buried deep within the underground of his mind.

Yet, Croft would not be convincing if he were not incomplete as a character, if there were not a blunted edge to the surface of his sensibility; in his extreme bitterness, in his irrational idealism, we discover those elements that suggest tragedy. The violent emotions stirred within us throughout the book find their relief if not their purgation in the failure of Croft to turn his idealistic vision into any concrete, ennobling act. Dimly Croft recognizes that he, that man, needs the unattainable as an element in his life and he admits that he is "relieved that he is not able to climb the mountain . . . rested by the unadmittable knowledge that he had found a limit to his hunger." Mailer's sympathy for Croft becomes so manifest toward the end of the novel that one concludes that Croft's perverted idealism, his desire for transcendence, is more vital than the flaccid humanism of Hearn and Valsen, for it has been born of private suffering and courage: Croft's failure humanizes him as much as is possible, given the constrictions of his character, the twisted emotions at the center of him, and it is the sense of his human limitations that we are left with at the end of the novel:

> He had failed, and hurt him vitally. His frustration was loose again. He would never have another opportunity to climb it [Mount Anaka]. And yet he was feeling the anxiety and terror the mountain had roused on the rock stairway. If he had gone alone, the fatigue of the other men would not have slowed him but he would not have had their company, and he realized suddenly that he could not have gone without them. The empty hills would have eroded any man's courage. . . .
>
> Croft kept looking at the mountain. He had lost it, had missed some tantalizing revelation of himself.
>
> Of himself and much more. Of life.
>
> Everything.

The failure of idealism to function before overwhelming authority, the inability of human nature to form a complete and satisfying design for its courage is the subject of *Barbary Shore* too, although here Mailer has conceived a novel of ideas in which authority is wholly external to the characters and to the action of the novel, assuming the image of an American bureaucracy which has succeeded in stifling the human personality. All hope for the individual, the narrator Lovett tells us, perished with the failure of the Russian Revolution: "Look, that revolution was the greatest event in man's history, and if it had not been confined to the one country, if it had spread. . . . It didn't. . . . and so it died, and ever since, the crisis of the world has deepened, until now it's only your bureaucrat who can raise man as you put it, and it's a measure of the disaster that everywhere the bureaucrat has the magic power."

Surrounding Lovett is a circle of people who serve as variations on the theme of lost faith: Lannie, a girl driven nearly insane in her futile search for purity among the jaded people of the novel; McLeod, an idealist who still believes in a time when there "will be the opportunity to discover of what we are capable and what we shall never achieve" and who leaves Lovett "the remnants of [his] socialist culture [i. e. his social idealism]," although Lovett knows that he is a "poor hope" for this heritage; Guinever and Hollings-worth, representatives of the actual America in all its grossness and vulgarity. Idealism has been crushed by mechanistic society and, as Lovett concludes, "the blind will lead the blind and the deaf shout warnings to one another until their voices are lost"; but in *Barbary Shore* Mailer has achieved little else than the sense of Lovett's philosophical and social dislocation—its actuality is not really grounded in any dramatic action. The abstract discussions between Cummings and Hearn in *The Naked and the Dead* are given relevance by the immediate events around them, the characters are never merely spokesmen; but *Barbary Shore* is completely a novel of ideas and the ideas are not sufficiently interesting to sustain a book in which action and the intricacies of human character are almost wholly absent. Idealism is a memory in *Barbary Shore* and the narrator does little more than dream about it.

One is reluctant to judge Mailer's second novel too harshly, for *Barbary Shore* is clearly a transitional work, in which form and theme have not cohered, in which Mailer is breaking with old techniques and old ideologies and searching for a distinctive style and point of view, a personal creative posture flexible enough for his developing ideas about the loss of self-reliance and idealism in our time. The work which explores this theme more successively and which was Mailer's preoccupation for at least eighteen years is *The Deer Park*. There seems little question that it is the central work in his middle career: most of the absorbing portions of *Advertisements for Myself* (1959) are preparations for the novel to be written (as in "Advertisements for Myself on the Way Out") or epilogues to the finished novel (as in "The Time of Her Time") or authorial reflections on how the book was improved from draft to draft (as in the creative history of *The Deer Park* itself). Mailer has been so engaged by the characters and their reactions to idealism and authority that he has re-introduced them, scarcely changed, into dramatic form more than ten years later. Everything between the publication of *Barbary Shore* and *An American Dream* seems a gloss to *The Dear Park*.

The most impressive gloss is "The Man Who Studied Yoga," which was to be the prologue to "an eight part novel" and which describes "the day of a small frustrated man, a minor artist manqué." Whatever it was meant to be, it is Mailer's richest story, and its treatment of frustrated love and the loss of personal courage points to the basic argument of *The Deer Park* and to all of Mailer's later work.

The power of "The Man Who Studied Yoga" lies in the straightforward, almost Tolstoyan analysis of Sam Slovoda's marriage by an anonymous narrator who defines the meaning of the Slovodas' life and who stands in opposition to Sam's psychoanalyst Sergius. Although Sam Slovoda refers his every action to Sergius, anxious over the interpretations that the analyst might soon place on his behavior, he clearly doesn't need Sergius: the analyst is an accoutrement to his life, like his furniture, his movie projector, his friends, even his wife—part of the existence of a middle-class American who has been married ten years and is thoroughly bored. The true analyst is the narrator, for he has not compromised himself to society and to a host of sociological and psychoanalytical clichés, and the true analysis comes in the form of the narrator's confession: "I suppose I am a romantic. I always feel that this [the time of a pre-marital affair] is the best time in people's lives. There is, after all, so little we accomplish, and that short period when we are beloved and triumph as lovers is sweet with power. . . . even worse than being unattractive to the world is to be unattractive to one's mate . . ."

In love then is power, and for Sam Slovoda that power existed for a short time in his romance with his wife before their marriage. Now the ideal of love has failed him: love is momentary lust, enacted while a pornograhpic film serves its erotic function; love is a kind of impotence, a simulation of the passion that Sam and his wife can no longer create within themselves. But for Sam impotence also assumes the form of his misspent career. He is unable to divorce love and work: when his work held meaning for him, his love thrived; now that he cannot respect his work as a continuity writer of cartoons, his loved has turned insipid.

> He has wasted the day, he tells himself, he has wasted the day as he has wasted so many days of his life, and tomorrow in the office he will be no more than his ten fingers typing plot and words for Bramba the Venusian and Lee-Lee Deeds, Hollywood Star, while that huge work with which he has cheated himself, holding it before him as a covenant of his worth, that enormous novel which would lift him at a bound from the impasse in which he stifles, whose dozens of characters would develop a vision of life in bountiful complexity, lies foundered, rotting on a beach

of purposeless effort. Notes here, pages there, it sprawls through a formless wreck of incidental ideas and half-episodes, utterly without shape. He is not even a hero for it.

One could not have a hero today, Sam thinks, a man of action and contemplation, capable of sin, large enough for good, a man immense. There is only a modern hero damned by no more than the ugliness of wishes whose satisfaction he will never know. One needs a man who could walk the stage, someone who—no matter who, not himself. Someone, Sam thinks, who reasonably could not exist.

The novelist, thinks Sam, perspiring beneath blankets, must live in paranoia and seek to be one with the world; he must be terrified of experience and hungry for it; he must think himself nothing and believe he is superior to all. The feminine in his nature cries for proof he is a man; he dreams of power and is without capacity to gain it; he loves himself above all and therefore despises all that he is.

In love then is lasting power and courage: this is the leitmotif that runs through all of Mailer's later work, through *The Deer Park* and *An American Dream,* through all the elaborate rhetoric in his many essays and interviews. He is indeed a romantic who reasserts his self-reliance, his self-importance against the authority of America and the threat of totalitarianism in the many aspects of America. At times he is more than half-in-love with that authority, whether it take the form of General Cummings or Sergeant Croft in *The Naked and the Dead,* of John Kennedy in *The Presidential Papers,* or of Barney Oswald Kelly in *An American Dream.* Like Sam Slovoda "he dreams of power and is without capacity to gain it"; like Sam Slovoda, the persistent question is, "however could he organize his novel? What form to give it?" For he has come to believe that "It is complex. Too loose . . . too scattered."

The interplay of love and power pervades *The Deer Park* itself, especially as reflected in the character of Eitel. "The artist was always divided between his desire for power in the world and his desire for power over his work," Sergius O'Shaugnessy, the narrator, observes in his consideration of Eitel's idealism. "With this girl [Elena, his mistress] it was impossible to thrive in the world except by his [Eitel's] art, and for these weeks, these domestic weeks when all went well and the act of sitting beside her in the sun could give him a sense of strength and the confidence of liking himself, he would feel indifference to that world he had found so hard to leave. To quit it by the bottom—that was nice, it gave a feeling there was fruit to life."

Eitel's public and private lives—his need for power and his quest for love—form the chief interest of the novel, and they educate Sergius O'Shaugnessy into a knowledge of his own life; as Marion Faye tells Elena, Eitel is "a frustrated teacher. Can you begin to understand that type? Deep-down, a John like Eitel is always obsessed with wanting people to trust him." O'Shaugnessy and the other characters in the novel do trust him—"you're good for everybody," Eitel's last mistress, Lulu, assures him—and the basic lesson of this didactic novel is learned from him.

That lesson concerns Eitel's idealism, a peculiarly pure nineteenth-century idealism as opposed to that of Sergius, who is, as Eitel tells him, "a twentieth-century gentleman." Eitel refuses to inform on those people in the movie industry from no sense of affection for the people themselves—for them "he felt nothing"; his own pride prevents him—"one did not go crawling in public." This personal courage commands the respect of all those who know him, especially of Sergius and Marion Faye, and it gives him a moral authority that no one else in the book possesses. But Eitel's courage is inextricably and precariously linked to his personal work: so long as he feels that he has "power over his work" he does not feel that need to satisfy "his desire for power in the world." What we witness in the novel is the corrosion of his idealism and private authority, the brief resurgence of self-reliance through his love affair with Elena, and the final compromise with "his desire for power in the world."

Eitel's compromise—his decision to speak to the Subversive Committee, his decision to turn out commercially appealing movies —stems from his inability to adapt the old nineteenth-century virtues of courage and honor to the twentieth-century world that is mirrored by the movie industry and by the town of Desert D'Or, "a town built of no other obvious motive than commercial profit, where no trees bear leaves" and where the only "bright green foliage" is "its love and its money." The Desert D'Or, populated by vapid movie people and wealthy entrepreneurs lures Eitel away from himself—it promises "the power in the world" and destroys through a kind of moral attrition the "desire for power over his own work." Eitel's movie, that potentially significant work which "can justify so much bad work," is "the tale of a modern saint," an heroic tale, but when Eitel repeats the outline to Collie Munshin, son-in-law of the movie mogul Teppis, the practical Munshin can only satirize it. "Charley, it's too hip [i. e., too idealistic]. It's a whorehouse. Your hero is a creep. A character who's making thousands of dollars a week on TV, and he decides to give it up. For what? To go out and help people? To end suffering? They'll laugh your picture off the screen. You think an audience wants to pay money to be told this character is better than they are?" Munshin's "solution is simple. You need a prologue to the picture. Let your hero start as a priest. . . . You build him up as a heel, and then you give the switch. Something happens to give him humility. I don't know what we can find, but I wouldn't even worry about it. Something with a crucifix or a cross. Show a Christ motif on the screen and who cares about motivation? The audience will buy it."

What seems so repugnant to Eitel at the moment of conception is accepted, however reluctantly, by the time of creation; and years later, when Sergius O'Shaugnessy sees the film, he offers final judgment of it: "It was not a bad picture as pictures go, and it was well made, and it did not have too many scenes which were embarrassing but it was nothing magnificent either, at least not for me . . . I hate to admit it, but there was a part of the picture I did admire. For although Eitel had claimed that he knew nothing about the Church, he had a very neat sense of the Church in a small way, a neater sense than I did of the kind of picture to make if Catholics were to enjoy it."

This is precisely the judgment that Eitel himself might make of the movie. If his courage has become a form of dignified cowardice—publicly and privately—, he has discovered a measure of truth about himself, he has at least not sacrificed that self-honesty which gives him a kind of final grace. After Eitel loses Sergius' respect through his political confession to the committee, he tells the younger man, "you're old enough to do without heroes," and in effect tells himself that he is too old for heroism, for courage, for the sort of self-reliance he once was able to demonstrate. He has sacrificed his idealism and courage for what his last mistress, Lulu Meyers, the Hollywood beauty, tells him is "real dignity"; and Eitel realizes that "dignity, real dignity" is simply "the knowledge written on one's face of the cost of every human desire." Though he has failed, though he has slipped into the easy life of domesticity with Elena and adultery with Lulu and commercial success in Hollywood, though he has witnessed "that unhappy time which marked . . . the end of his overextended youth," he has retained enough self-dignity to engage Sergius' trust and to permit him still, in the last pages of the book, to be the teacher of his surrogate son, his protégé and his twentieth-century heir. He passes on the lesson he has learned but did not himself have the courage to live; he remembers "the knowledge he wanted to give to Sergius, "suffering the sad frustration of his new middle age, since experience when it is not told to another must wither within and be worse than lost."

> "For you see, . . . I have lost the final desire of the artist, the desire which tells us that when all else is lost, when love is lost and adventure, pride of self, and pity, there still remains that world we may create, more real to us, more real to others, than the mummery of what happens, passes, and is gone. So, do try Sergius . . . try for that other world, the real world, where orphans burn orphans and nothing is more difficult to discover than a simple fact. And with the pride of the artist, you must blow against the walls of every power that exists, the small trumpet of your defiance."

Sergius has discovered something of what Eitel means. Searching for a form to the art he wishes to create, he has hit upon bull-fighting; but he soon realizes that he is "too old to learn to be really good" and, like Eitel, he takes on the role of teacher—he opens "a school for bullfighters" in, absurdly enough, New York City. Like Eitel, he seeks creative expression and begins a bullfighting novel, enjoying momentarily "the comfort that" he is "beginning to belong to that privileged world of orphans where art is found." But his real work of art is *The Deer Park* itself, in which the lives of the characters have become more real to him than anything of his own.

When one reads *The Deer Park* one is always aware of the artist writing the novel, struggling for natural effects but never quite achieving them. One carries in his mind a variety of literary echoes: the terror of the law as viewed by Kafka; the intricacies of the feminine mind (especially in Elena's letter to Eitel) as measured by Joyce; the form and discipline of bullfighting (and used in *The Deer Park* as a thematic coda to the novel itself) as defined by

Hemingway. One hesitates to make any more extensive comparisons, for Mailer is a writer of the second rank and he fails to achieve the effects of those authors who have influenced him—his work will not bear comparison. But one inevitable and illuminating reference in any judgment of *The Deer Park* does seem pertinent, and that is the reference to Fitzgerald—not so much to *The Great Gatsby,* although the point of view and a number of the scenes, particularly the parties, are reflected in *The Deer Park* and lack Fitzgerald's sharp, evocative style, but to that other novel of Hollywood, *The Last Tycoon.*

Fitzgerald knew Hollywood, as Edmund Wilson reminds us, from the inside. The long sequence in which Monroe Stahr meets a variety of Hollywood types whose entire lives are adumbrated in a few telling remarks is an achievement of which Mailer is simply incapable. More important is the richness of Stahr's character, the degree to which Fitzgerald understood his moral heroism and his absurdity, his courage and his human frailty before death: as fragmentary as *The Last Tycoon* is, Stahr has a reality that Eitel never achieves. Eitel talks and talks, but the conversation is centered on the abstractions of courage and honesty, heroism and idealism— we never really see the man in action, as we see Stahr move through different situations, each reflecting a particular dimension of his character. We can perhaps forgive the superficial treatment of the less significant figures in *The Deer Park,* all of them the familiar types we carry in our mind from all the Hollywood novels we have read, but neither Eitel nor O'Shaugnessy is ever fully revealed to us—their complexity is scarcely more than a statement or a series of statements so that ultimately they too are types. It is easy to see how, given Mailer's desire to write a play, *The Deer Park* was converted into drama; for the characters of the novel seem forever still, in a frozen setting, confronting each other in a group of staged dialogues, talking about the life we never see them live. For the novelist character is action, as Fitzgerald reminded himself in his notes for *The Last Tycoon,* but in *The Deer Park* character is too often conversation.

Conversation. That is the word one invariably associates with Norman Mailer in the middle years of his career, the years dominated by *The Deer Park.* After two substantial novels, a few fine stories, and one or two essays of real interest, too much of the rest is conversation—published conversation. In the italicized portions of *Advertisements for Myself, The Presidential Papers,* and *Cannibals and Christians,* Mailer carries a one-way conversation with the reader; in the essays of these same books he addresses John F. Kennedy or Lyndon Johnson as a social critic, sometimes as an imaginary friend; or he scolds contemporary writers as though he is their moral instructor more than their critic—at times their friend, at times their enemy, but always their adversary; or he reproduces a debate, perhaps even a book of poems that are no more than fragments from the surface of his mind; or he has endless interviews—one-third of *Christians and Cannibals* is made up of his loose talk with various interviewers, too much of it reprinted *in toto* from former volumes. The books are burdened increasingly by the author's personality, by advertisements for himself—as the novels become increasingly, tediously autobiographic—and the more Mailer talks the less effective he is, for every sentence must be alarming and very sentence, of course, must be published. After the air has cleared, Mailer emerges from his self-imposed corner of the ring, scarred by self-love, reminding us too often of Hemingway's caricature of New York writers: "All angleworms in a bottle, trying to derive knowledge from their own contact and from the bottle." All of these gestures scarcely conceal the insecurity of the novelist who is not writing fiction which is its own advertisement, its own final statement. And yet—and yet, one can never speak the last word on Mailer, as one can on so many other authors: his end is unknown. No sooner than one bemoans the narcissim of so much of his autobiographical writing, one discovers *Armies of the Night,* which uses autobiography and egocentricity objectively and suggests the proper limits of the self-involved man; one reads the book—and then one reads Mailer's other superb journalism—and knows that a period cannot be put to his work.

The two novels in the past thirteen years which represent Mailer's attempt to make a significant advance beyond *The Deer Park* are *An American Dream* and *Why Are We In Vietnam?* Although both books are formal failures they are worth examining, for they suggest how clear his perception can be at the moment his form is "too loose, too scattered," how he draws us to his ideas precisely when we lament his technical blunders.

In its clumsy way, *An American Dream* explores the public and private lives of a gifted man, a hero manqué. The public life of Stephen Rojack includes his role as a war hero, a Congressman, a TV star, a "professor of existential psychology," a murderer, indeed a very authoritative man; his private life is that of an idealist, an innocent man, even a coward. He quits politics, as he confesses, to purge himself of his public deceit: "I wanted to depart from politics before I was separated from myself forever by the distance between my public appearance which had become vital on television, indeed nearly robust, and my secret frightened phases of the moon." He seeks to free himself of his burdensome past life—"I had come to decide I was finally a failure," he states at the outset—and discover, through whatever violence or murder may be necessary, a new idealism, a new innocence, a new courage.

Like *The Deer Park, An American Dream* recalls the work of Fitzgerald. Deborah Kelly, the girl whom Rojack seduces and marries and kills, is "a girl who would have been bored by a diamond as big as the Ritz," beautiful, hard in spite of her attractiveness, evil, and ultimately unattainable—an updated, sensual Daisy Buchanan whose voice is seductive, whose smell (to use Mailer's own image) is like a bank. "I'm evil," Deborah Kelly tells Rojack. "But I despise it, truly I do. It's just that evil has power." Unable to dominate Deborah, Rojack must murder her. But he finally meets his proper adversary in the form of her millionaire father, a mythical man like Gatsby who also recalls his rise to fortune, his marriage to a corrupt European, his escapades on the Riviera (reminiscent of those in *Tender is the Night*), even his incestuous desire for his daughter Deborah. This section is impressive because Kelly is seen through the jaded eyes of Rojack—for a moment the hero manqué is not mired in his own self-pity; but the point of view, which is similar to that of *The Great Gatsby,* is only briefly sustained, and for most of the novel we are given the narrative in the turgid and imprecise rhetoric of Rojack, we are not witness to a character of tragic dimensions but rather to one who is at all times pathetic—a little man, after all; a "whimperer," as Deborah calls him; a coward.

"I met Jack Kennedy in November, 1946. We were both war heroes, and both of us had been elected to Congress." * From this

* The key figures in Mailer's novels are wounded war heroes—Philip Young's reading of Hemingway's fiction is almost as pertinent to Mailer's work. Nothing after Mailer's war experiences was ever quite so intense; and his brief adventure as a soldier is always there, like an affidavit, to buttress his various considerations of courage and cow-

recollection of heroism, which Rojack describes with affection, we are taken through a series of events in which the promising figure is seen at his frailest, a victim of his own weaknesses. He cannot resurrect his life on the ashes of his dead wife, though "Deborah's dying had given [him] a new life," though he has discovered the girl who would be willing to be with him—a girl with "one of those perfect American faces," bearing the incredible name of Cherry. He prays: " 'let me love that girl, and become a father, and try to be a good man, and do some decent work. Yes God,' I was close to begging, 'do not make me go back and back again to the charnel house of the moon.' " He makes a love pact: " 'I think we have to be good,' by which I mean we have to be brave." But he hasn't the inner conviction to be brave—when he meets Barney Oswald Kelly, his regenerated heroism crumbles from lack of inner authority, and the putative hero is destroyed by the American figure of power.

In the epilogue, Mailer defines his meaning clearly: Rojack has been defeated by American materialism and conformity. "Nobody knew that the deserts of the West [to which Rojack has fled], the arid empty wild blind deserts, were producing again a new breed of man . . . I was part of the new breed." The barrenness of Las Vegas and its surrounding desert mirrors the empty purpose of American life, where day is night, night day, a saturnalian mockery of all that was once vital and natural in our culture. For Rojack the jungle of another country and another time is preferable to this sterile life: "There was a jungle somewhere in Guatemala which had a friend, an old friend, I thought to go there. And on to Yucatan." The last lines of the novel recall those of *Gatsby;* like Carroway's requiem on the death of the idealistic vision of America, Rojack's lament is couched in terms of what has perished from American life:

> The night before I left Las Vegas I walked out in the desert to look at the moon. There was a jeweled city on the horizon, spires rising in the night, but the jewels were diadems of electric and the spires were the neon of signs ten stories high. I was not good enough to climb up and pull them down. So wandered farther

---

ardice. In his recent book, significantly called the *Armies of the Night,* Mailer sees himself as a leader in the march on Washington and makes constant references to the Civil War and to his own military experiences.

out to the desert where the mad before me had come, and thought of walking into ambush.

Through all of Mailer's bombast, his awkward structure, his careless diction, the absurd sexual experiences and pseudo-intellectualism of his hero, the incredible dialogue, the sentimentality—through all of these limitations, which finally reduce *An American Dream* to an interesting attempt rather than any kind of real accomplishment, lies the idea; it is the idea that makes the imbroglio even tolerable. The image of society destroying America's natural beauty and dwarfing the individual—in the form of Natty Bumppo or Huckleberry Finn or Ike McCaslin or Nick Adams—finds one of its minor modern statements in *An American Dream*. Like Huck Finn, Rojack lights out for the territory, although the territory is foreign, more of a wish than a reality, away from America rather than toward anything definite.

"Well, Huckleberry Finn is here to set you straight," warns the narrator of *Why Are We In Vietnam?*, and through him and his obscene wit, Mailer expresses his great disenchantment with America. This *tour de force* is surely Mailer's most pessimistic book, the dark work of his creative soul, and his most overt indictment of heroism in contemporary America. The book is an anal vision of our country, a discharge of the bowels, releasing and revealing the stench that America has made of itself. Formal criticism seems almost beside the point, an academic exercise when put beside the urgency of the book: the entire novel is a scatalogical and hilarious howl, pitched on a high, wild, and almost unendurable note, and Mailer's point that we kill for the sake of killing, that our violence no longer has even a rationale, and that we have substituted ruthless power for our heroic ideal is projected in a form that is insidiously organic. Yet we know that the book can be this bitter only because its author is so drawn to the very concept he satirizes: we read about the death of heroism as if Mailer is describing the death of a monster who once was strong, handsome, a hero once who now has lost control of his physical functions because he has lost his soul. The words on the printed page stick in our throat; they read like a death rattle.

The bitterness and obscenity of *Why Are We In Vietnam?* is linked, as we discover in *Armies of the Night*, to Mailer's love of America.

There was no villainy in obscenity for him, just—paradoxically, characteristically—his love for America: he had first come to love America when he served in the U. S. Army, not the America of course of the flag, the patriotic unendurable fix of the television programs and the newspapers, no, long before he was ever aware of the institutional oleo of the most suffocating American ideas he had come to love what editorial writers were fond of calling the democratic principle with its faith in the common man. He found that principle and that man in the Army, but what none of the editorial writers ever mentioned was that the noble common man was obscene as an old goat, and his obscenity was what saved him. The sanity of said common democratic man was in his humor, his humor was in his obscenity. . . . The common discovery of America was probably that Americans were the first people on earth to live for their humor; nothing was so important to Americans as humor. In Brooklyn, he had taken this for granted, at Harvard he had thought it was a by-product of being at Harvard, but in the Army he discovered that the humor was probably in the veins and the roots of the local history of every state and country in America—the truth of the way it really felt over the years passed on a river of obscenity from small-town storyteller to storyteller there down below the bankers and the books and the educators and the legislators—so Mailer never felt more like an American than when he was naturally obscene—all the gifts of the American language came out in the happy play of obscenity upon concept, which enable one to go back to concept again.[1]

Mailer identifies himself with the rich tradition of humor in American culture—his work does indeed become increasingly comedic as it develops—and we begin to realize that not only in his work but in that of so many important contemporary writers, wit is a shield against the humorless authority of America. Like Bellow, Salinger, Albee, Ellison, Heller, and others, Mailer finds humor the human factor which permits him to measure, understand and tolerate the abuses of the country that he loves and hates and returns to love once again. Indeed in *Armies of the Night* he names himself the comic hero—he decides to "make our comic hero the narrative vehicle for the March on the Pentagon"—although he is always the ambivalent, ambitious comic hero: "is he finally comic, a ludicrous figure with mock-heroic associations; or is he not un-heroic, and therefore embedded somewhat tragically in the comic?"

The comic tone of *Armies of the Night,* Mailer's ability finally to see himself in human and historical perspective as the comic hero—not quite Don Quixote, not quite Falstaff, but bearing vestiges of both these figures—permits him to speak most seriously about his lover's quarrel with America. The struggle in *Armies of the Night* is between idealism and authority, between the divergent idealistic forces that march to the Pentagon and the unheeding authority of the government: the two are locked together, and in the middle of that struggle, as actor and observer, is Norman Mailer. In lyric passages of intense feeling and beauty, Mailer is able to analyze the Manichean conflict that threatens every American:

> A generation of the American young had come along different from five previous generations of the middle class. The new generation believed in technology more than any before it, but the generation also believed in LSD, in witches, in tribal knowledge, in orgy, and revolution. It had no respect whatsoever for the unassailable logic of the next step: belief was reserved for the revelatory mystery of the happening where you did not know what was going to happen next; that was what was good about it. Their radicalism was in their hate for the authority—the authority was the manifest of evil to this generation. It was the authority who had covered the land with those suburbs where they stifled as children while watching the adventures of the West in the movies, while looking at the guardians of dull genial celebrity on television; they had had their minds jabbed and poked and twitched and probed and finally galvanized into surrealistic modes of response by commercials cutting into dramatic narratives, and parents flipping from network to network —they were forced willy-nilly to build their idea of the space-time continuum (and therefore their nervous system) on the jumps and cracks and leaps and breaks which every phenomenon from the media seemed to contain within it.
>
> The authority had operated on their brain with commercials, and washed their brain with packaged education, packaged politics. The authority had presented itself as honorable, and it was corrupt, corrupt as payola on television, and scandals concerning the safety of automobiles, and scandals concerning the leasing of aviation contracts—the real scandals as everyone was beginning to sense were more intimate and could be found in all the products in all the surburban homes which did not work so well as they should have worked, and broke down too soon for mysterious

reasons. The shoddiness was buried in the package, buried somewhere in the undiscoverable root of all those modern factories
with their sanitized aisles and automated machines; perhaps one
place the shoddiness was buried was in the hangovers of a working class finally alienated from any remote interest or attention
in the process of work itself. Work was shoddy everywhere. Even
in the Warren Commission.

Finally, this new generation of the Left hated the authority,
because the authority lied. It lied through the teeth of corporation
executives and Cabinet officials and police enforcement officers
and newspaper editors and advertising agencies, and in its mass
magazines. . . .

The aesthetic of the New Left now therefore began with
the notion that the authority could not comprehend nor contain
nor finally manage to control any political action whose end was
unknown. They could attack it, beat it, jail it, misrepresent it,
and finally abuse it, but they could not feel a sense of victory because they could not understand a movement which inspired
thousands and hundreds of thousands to march without a co-
ordinated plan. The bureaucrats of the Old Left had not been
alone in their adoration of the solid-as-brickwork-logic-of-the-
next-step; no, the bureaucrats of the American Center, now liked
it as much, and were aghast at any political activity which ignored
it.

This acute analysis of young idealists confronting the authority
of the state is rendered particularly powerful because it is not altogether objective. At the outset Mailer agreed to join the March to
Washington with the greatest reluctance—he "hated to put in time
with losers"—and his early experiences at an academic party and
at a political rally indicate his detached, cynical, and at times
contemptuous view. But because of his association with the march-
ers, he loses the obsession with himself and discovers the roots of
his own idealism. He can be critical of the "villains who were
hippies" because they have "fractured their sense of past and
present," but his "final allegiance" is to them and their dissent. The
conflict of idealism and authority is ultimately trapped within the
skull of the comic hero:

. . . the sense of America divided on this day now liberated some
undiscovered patriotism in Mailer so that he felt a sharp searing
love for his country in this moment and on this day, crossing some

divide in his own mind wider than the Potomac, a love so lacerated he felt as if a marriage were being torn and children lost—never does one love so much as then, obviously, then—and an odor of wood smoke, from where you knew not, was also in the air, a smoke of dignity and some calm heroism, not unlike the sense of freedom which also comes when a marriage is burst —Mailer knew for the first time why men in the front line of a battle are almost always ready to die: there is a promise of some swift transit—one's soul feels clean; . . . walking with Lowell and MacDonald, he felt as if he stepped through some crossing the reaches of space between this moment, the French Revolution, and the Civil War, as if the ghosts of the Union Dead accompanied them now to the Bastille, . . . they were going to face the symbol, the embodiment, no, call it the true and high church of the military-industrial complex, the Pentagon, blind five-sided eye of a subtle oppression which had come to America out of the very air of the century (this evil twentieth century with its curse on the species, its oppressive Faustian lusts, its technological excrement all over the conduits of nature, its entrapment of the innocence of the best—for which young American soldiers hot out of high school and in love with a hot rod and his Marine buddies in his platoon in Vietnam could begin to know the devil of the oppression which would steal his soul before he knew he had one) yes, Mailer felt a confirmation of the contests of his own life on this March to the eye of the oppressor, greedy stingy dumb valve of the worst of the Wasp heart, chalice and anus of corporation land, smug, enclosed, mortally blind Pentagon, destroying the future of its own nation with each day it augmented in strength, and the Novelist induced on the consequence some dim unawakened knowledge of the mysteries of America buried in these liberties to dissent—What a mysterious country it was. The older he became, the more interesting he found her.

The human, historical, and specifically American context of this conflict is always before us in the book, in incidental references to William Ellery Channing and Matthew Brady; in comparisons between the Civil War and this present March—once again ignorant armies clash in the night, brother against brother; and finally, most significantly, in comparisons between himself and Robert Lowell, between the comic hero in whose personality there was "a last remaining speck of the one personality he found absolutely insupportable—the nice Jewish boy from Brooklyn"—and the Protestant,

New England poet who "gave off at times the unwilling haunted saintliness of a man who was repaying the moral debts of ten generations of ancestors." Lowell takes us back to the world of Emerson and Thoreau and indeed James Russell Lowell—poor poet that he was, his politics were in the rebellious, idealistic tradition of his contemporary ancestor. Robert Lowell reminds us of that protestant tradition which had been debased in modern America but which flowers for the moment in this March on Washington. Mailer has traveled the different route of the self-conscious literary parvenu—the immigrant—who has fought imaginary battles with Papa Hemingway and Fitzgerald and with all of his contemporaries, who must display his talent the way the *nouveau riche* flash their money, and who represents the broad tradition of liberalism that was so compelling from the thirties to the sixties. "It was only natural that he should have a love affair with America—how much worse if the grandsons of the immigrants did not." So Lowell and Mailer linked arms and marched together in the name of idealism.*

They marched, although temperamentally they were not altogether suited to this kind of political demonstration—Lowell even less than Mailer. What finally gives *Armies of the Night* its peculiar strength is a quality that goes beyond brilliant reportage and analysis, beyond the record of a national crisis, beyond all of Mailer's rich artistic gifts; the book is a confession—in its way a prose analogue to Lowell's "confessional" poetry—of the artist's responsibility in human affairs. Mailer remembers Fitzgerald's haunting line—"That long dark night of the soul when it is always three o'clock in the morning"—and he blesses

> Fitzgerald for his clear line—and why that long dark night, yes, why, when all was said? and Wolfe dead too early and Heming-

---

* It is aesthetically as well as historically fitting that these two writers should link arms on such an occasion. Lowell's own career has moved from harsh rebellion in *Land of Unlikeness* (1944) to one of modified affirmation in *Life Studies* (1959), *For the Union Dead* (1964), and *Near the Ocean* (1967). Like Mailer he has been absorbed by the abuses of authority, although Lowell has written more of the innocent victims of authority—the distance between idealism and authority is greater in his work than in Mailer's. Like Mailer and so many current authors, his later writing is more tentative than definite. "When I finished *Life Studies*," he has said, "I was left hanging on a question mark. I am still hanging there. I don't know whether it is a death-rope or a lifeline."

way a suicide—how much guilt lay on the back of a good writer—it grew worse and worse. As the power of communication grew larger, so the responsibility to educate a nation lapped at the feet, new tide of a new responsibility, and one had become a writer after all to find a warm place where one was safe—responsibility was for the pompous, and the public servants; writers were born to discover wine. It was an old argument and he was worn with it—he had written a good essay once about the failure of any major American novelist to write a major novel which would reach out past the best-seller lists to a major part of that American audience brain-washed by Hollywood, TV, and *Time*. Yes, how much of Fitzgerald's long dark night may have come from that fine winnowing sense in the very fine hair of his nose that the two halves of America were not coming together, and when they failed to touch, all of history might be lost in the divide. Yes, there was a dark night if you had the illusion you could do something about it, and the conviction that not enough had been done. Or was it simply impossible—had the two worlds of America drifted irretrievably apart?

. . . Brood on that country who expresses our will. She is America, once a beauty of magnificence unparalleled, now a beauty with leprous skin. She is heavy with child—no one knows if legitimate—and languishes in a dungeon whose walls are never seen. Now the first contractions of her fearsome labor begin —it will go on: no doctor exists to tell the hour. It is only known that false labor is not likely in her now, no, she will give birth, and to what?—the most fearsome totalitarianism the world has ever known? or can she, poor giant, tormented lovely girl, deliver a babe of a new world brave and tender, artful and wild? *

We end with a question—a question that casts its light backwards, across the contours of a literature that so often has been concerned with idealism and authority as they fix themselves in the character of American heroes. Emerson and Whitman could educate a nation with the moral strength that stems from a faith in the common man; their conflict was largely external—Americans vis-à-vis Europeans, Americans throwing off their Calvinist heritage —as they encouraged ordinary people to be extraordinary through self-belief and the power of their own inner resources. Southern writers of the nineteenth century—writers like William Gilmore Simms and Thomas Nelson Page—sacrificed the quality of their art, their sense of complexity, before the demands of the Southern cause; they felt their responsibility as Southerners more deeply than the inner demands of their art, and so we do not remember human beings but rather a Gentleman, a Lady, a laughing Negro, figures who haunt us when we think of the racial war in America today. And Negro authors, they too were caught up in this conflict between being a man and being an artist; they had to educate *their* people, express *their* struggle, and not—not until Baldwin, Ellison, and the writers of our own time—attend to the private anguish and joy that come to men of any race at any time in any country. For Hemingway the conflict was ultimately crippling, as he became more of a man than an artist: at first he could renounce the concept of heroism and cling to a private code so that his art became a clean act of renunciation; but his growing commitment to the social scene, to politics and the public life, destroyed the artist in him. For Fitzgerald the two halves of himself—the artist and the man—found expression in those idealists who were destroyed by the authority of wealth and all that wealth implied to Fitzgerald; in his best work he lived with no illusions, he knew that heroism had died in America, that the ideal could not survive the authority of onrushing technology.

Norman Mailer also fears that the two worlds of America have drifted irretrievably apart, but he, as well as Bellow, Salinger, Ellison, Baldwin, and other contemporaries will not "speak the last word"—he ends with a question, not a statement. These writers speak of suffering, suicide, invisibility, impending fire— of cannibalism, in Mailer's case, totalitarianism, authority, of "American heroism corrupted by American know-how." They see all of the ugliness of America with a clarity that derives its power from its ability to threaten our complacency and undermine our every illusion; they are indeed our critics and our teachers, however much they may shun the role, because they—of all the critics and teachers only they—absolutely refuse to lie. And yet—and yet, as critical of authority as these writers are, their idealism is never far behind their criticism. Comic heroes they create—but they are no less earnest than those other American authors who could afford to create more Romantic heroes.

For all his obvious faults, Norman Mailer has fixed his attention on the totalitarian aspects of American life without sacrificing his belief in the heroic ideal; he and the writers of his time struggle to express beliefs in an unbelieving age, to voice idealism when the very term has become a national platitude, to find hope in an age which belongs to the authoritarian. Mailer's excesses are no doubt due to private reasons—let us not be to quick to crucify the author on the cross of totalitarian America, to attribute his failures to wholly external causes—but his frustration has been aggravated by the great difficulty a romantic idealist like himself meets in a country where art is a commodity, when he tries to create a literature that is courageous, honest, and profound—humanly profound; the responsibility "to educate a nation" is indeed great and lures the artist away from his art. Failure is easy enough to score and Mailer's work will not escape a judgment that finds it limited; his is writing *in potentia* more than art fully realized—he has not become the major writer promised by *The Naked and the Dead*. But his small achievement is nevertheless impressive, and in his plea for personal courage, in his scorn of totalitarianism, and his incorrigible belief that a renaissance of idealism is still possible in America—in America if anywhere—Mailer reminds us of our double lives: the visible one of authority and that other one underground, filled with "untapped, ferocious, lonely and romantic desires," that "concentration of ecstasy and violence which is the dream life of the nation."

INDEX